"Sorry. I am what I am."

The life and letters of the South African pianist
and opera coach Gordon Jephtas (1943-92)

Lives
Legacies
Legends

Lives
Legacies
Legends

edited by Hilde Roos, Féroll-Jon Davids, Chris Walton

"Sorry. I am what I am."
The life and letters of the South African pianist and
opera coach Gordon Jephtas (1943-92)

Basler Afrika Bibliographien | 2023

Hochschule der Künste Bern
Haute école des arts de Berne
Bern Academy of the Arts

The open access publication of this book has been published with the support of the Swiss National Science Foundation.

2023
© the authors
© Basler Afrika Bibliographien
Namibia Resource Centre – Southern Africa Library
Klosterberg 23
PO Box
4001 Basel
Switzerland
www.baslerafrika.ch

CARL SCHLETTWEIN
STIFTUNG

The Basler Afrika Bibliographien is part of the Carl Schlettwein Foundation

Cover photograph: Gordon Jephtas, photographed by Coltrain Photo in 1988.

ISBN 978-3-906927-58-9
eISBN (PDF) 978-3-906927-59-6
ISSN 1660-9638
eISSN 2297-641X

https://doi.org/10.53202/BWFA5651

TABLE OF CONTENTS

ACKNOWLEDGEMENTS AND SOURCES

This book is a product of the research project "Cultural relations between Switzerland and South Africa, 1948–1994", funded by the Swiss National Science Foundation (SNSF) at the Bern Academy of the Arts HKB, and conducted in partnership with Africa Open Institute at Stellenbosch University. It has also been made possible by the generosity of several individuals, most of all by the families of Gordon Jephtas and May Abrahamse. They could not have been more helpful, and have given the appropriate permissions for this publication. The letters from Gordon Jephtas to May Abrahamse, documenting 28 years of their lives, were donated in 2015 by May Abrahamse to the Eoan Group Archive (EGA) held at Stellenbosch University's Documentation Centre for Music (DOMUS). Jephtas's surviving brother, Geofferey Jefthas, has generously provided images of Gordon, along with newspaper articles and other related materials, and kindly granted us an interview. We should like to offer especial thanks to Geofferey Jefthas, his wife Maggie Jefthas, May Abrahamse and her daughters Wendy Abrahams and Trudy Rushin.

The editors have endeavoured to obtain all necessary permissions and have also undertaken extensive efforts to contact the family of Gordon Jephtas's wife in America, though without any success. Given that Jephtas admitted entering into marriage for purposes of getting a green card (see his letters from the USA in this book), it remains unclear just how much contact he had with his wife and her family.

The editors would also like to thank the following individuals and institutions: the Bern Academy of the Arts HKB, Africa Open Institute, University of Stellenbosch, Basler Afrika Bibliographien, Stadtarchiv Zürich, Welsh National Opera, Chicago Lyric Opera and the Metropolitan Opera New York; Daniel Allenbach, Kirstin Chapman, Chatradari Devroop, Ian Douglas, Heinz Fischer, Paula Fourie, Thomas Gartmann, Melissa Gerber, Dag Henrichsen, Leavata Johnson, Santie de Jongh, Sabine Jud, Roland Jung, Petra Kerckhoff, Lizabé Lambrechts, Johannes Lüthi, Barbara Mahajan, Mari Moroz, Matthias von Orelli, Dietbert Reich, Barbara Rominski, Aldo Santi, Caroline Senn, Martin Skamletz, Jerome Slamat, Rochelle Slamat, Christian Vandersee, Lisba Vosloo, Jasper Walgrave and Reto Witschi. We are particularly grateful to Stephanus Muller for his help during the editing process.

THE EDITORS

Hilde Roos is the General Manager of Africa Open Institute for Music, Research and Innovation at Stellenbosch University (AOI), and coordinator for AOI's collaboration with the Bern Academy of the Arts on the SNSF-funded research project "Cultural relations between Switzerland and South Africa, 1948-1994". She has published widely about the Eoan Group and is the author of *The La Traviata Affair: Opera in the Age of Apartheid* (University of California Press, 2018) and the joint editor of *EOAN. Our Story* (Fourthwall Books, Johannesburg, 2013).

Féroll-Jon Davids is the principal clarinettist of the Cape Town Philharmonic Orchestra, a part-time clarinet lecturer at Stellenbosch University, and an assistant researcher for the Bern Academy of the Arts on the above-mentioned SNSF research project. He studied at Stellenbosch University and also spent semesters at the Universities of Georgia and Montana State in the USA. His Master's thesis, *Gordon Jephtas (1943-1992): A coloured life in opera* (Stellenbosch University, 2021), was a biographical account of the life of Gordon Jephtas that investigated how apartheid thinking and practices influenced his self-perception as an individual classified as "coloured" during apartheid.

Chris Walton is an honorary professor at Africa Open Institute, Stellenbosch University, a Privatdozent at Bern University, and the head of the abovementioned SNSF research project at the Bern Academy of the Arts. His most recent book is *Richard Wagner's Essays on Conducting* (University of Rochester Press, 2021). Alongside his academic career, he also worked as a freelance vocal coach for several members of the Zurich Opera Studio and Opera House some ten years after Gordon Jephtas was on the payroll there.

EDITORIAL APPROACH AND TERMINOLOGY

Jephtas's letters amount to some 140,000 words in total and include much information that is only of parochial significance. For this reason, and to make the text reader friendly, we have cut these letters down to some 80,000 words. We are aware that any decisions about what to cut, however objective and scholarly our aims might be, are potentially fraught. The editors nevertheless hope that our varied backgrounds, both European and South African, have enabled us to approach these letters from different perspectives and thereby do justice to their author when editing and annotating them. Anyone wishing to consult the complete extant letters can access digital copies of the originals on the Stellenbosch University digital platform, SunDigital.[1] Jephtas and Abrahamse also communicated by taping "letters" and posting them to each other. None of Abrahamse's tapes to Jephtas have survived; at the time of writing, hardly any from Jephtas to Abrahamse are known to be extant. We include a transcription of one such letter here, made on 20 February 1977 in Zurich.

When Abrahamse donated Jephtas's letters to the Eoan Group Archive at Stellenbosch University nearly a decade ago, she had already ordered them carefully. However, the dates of the postmarked envelopes and those of the letters were not always in agreement. For example, one letter dated 8 February 1988 and another of 3 April 1988 are found together in an envelope postmarked 10 August 1988. It seems likely that some letters and envelopes were lost over the years, and extant letters matched on occasion with the wrong envelope. Nevertheless, we have no reason to doubt that the letters reproduced here were sent shortly after Jephtas wrote them.

Small omissions here are designated by an ellipsis; longer omissions (of more than two lines) by an ellipsis in square brackets. Titles of works are given throughout in italics, aria titles in inverted commas. Work titles and names of people and places have also been standardised or corrected in each case without comment, though we have left them in the language used by Jephtas, who sometimes writes (for example) *Barber of Seville*, at others *Barbiere* (it is notable that Jephtas's spelling mistakes in Italian titles become fewer over the years, as his familiarity with the language and the repertoire grows). Minor spelling and grammatical errors and inconsistencies on Jephtas's part have similarly been corrected without comment, such as his frequent use of singular verb forms with plural pronouns (a common mistake among speakers of Afrikaans, a language that does not distinguish between singular and plural verb forms), as have slips of the pen such as in his letter of 27 March 1966 where he writes "puss" when he clearly means "pus". However, slang and idiosyncrasies in his prose style have largely been left untouched unless they obscure the intended meaning, as have his capitalisations and occasional American spellings. His punctuation is at times also idiosyncratic, but since his commas, points and dashes help to convey his voice, we have retained them where they do not obscure the meaning of the text. We have in general retained Jephtas's prepositions, which strictly speaking are often grammatically incorrect, but reflect his frequent engagement with languages other than English – primarily Afrikaans, German and Italian. Underlinings in the letters have been placed here in italics, while musical signs such as flats and sharps have been written out thus, all without comment. Overall, we have endeavoured to keep our visible editorial interventions to a minimum, and to maintain a balance between scholarly correctness and reader friendliness. This has made numerous minor compromises

---

1   SunDigital can be accessed at https://digital.lib.sun.ac.za/ (accessed November 2022).

unavoidable, but we hope that they have also allowed us to let Gordon Jephtas's voice come through clearly.

For reasons of space, we have generally identified the composers of works on their first appearance in the main text of the book. Titles of works are listed in the index under their respective composer. Brief biographical information is given on the people named in the letters at their first mention only. In the case of members of the Eoan Group, even basic details such as dates of birth and death are often lacking. Here, the vagaries of the apartheid system are to blame, as it deemed those not classified as "white" as less worthy of documentation. The absence of such details in our footnotes is thus a consequence of apartheid, not an editorial decision on our part.

The spelling of Gordon Jephtas's surname requires brief comment. He wrote it thus himself, which is the version we use here, though according to his brother Geofferey, the original spelling was apparently Jefthas, which is also how the Zurich authorities spelt the name of his mother in their records ("née Jefthas").[2] Some confusion about the spelling remained, however; in the leaflet produced by his friends for his memorial service in New York, his name is given as "Gordon Jepthas".[3]

We have kept currency designations as in the original letters. Until the end of the Bretton Woods system in the early 1970s, exchange rates were roughly set at US $ 1 = 630 Italian lire = £ 0.4 = CHF 4.4 = 70 Spanish pesetas = ZAR 0.7. Before the introduction of decimal currency in 1971, the United Kingdom used a system of 20 shillings to a pound, 12 pence to a shilling, with a backslash used to divide shillings from pence. Thus when Jephtas writes, for example, in his letter of 28 December 1963 that an opera ticket in Italy cost him 7/6, he means 7 shillings and 6 pence in UK currency (which was equivalent to 37 ½ pence in today's decimal currency). Jephtas occasionally also mentions guineas; a guinea was equivalent to 21 shillings (i.e. one pound and one shilling, today one pound and five pence).

This book is the story of a man who through talent, hard work and willpower succeeded in establishing a career on the international scene despite all the hurdles that a racist, homophobic society placed before him. In engaging with numerous aspects of his homeland, his letters consequently employ terms – often ironically – that are in the 21st century rightly deemed offensive and anything but ironic. Editing these letters thus compels us to confront the racial (and racist) norms of his day. Throughout this book, the term "coloured" is written in the lower case to give it an adjectival function similar to "white" and "black" (which are also here in lower case throughout), thereby depriving the term of the status of an administered racial category that was the norm under apartheid. In his correspondence with Abrahamse, Jephtas uses words such as "negro" and "negress" along with South African terms that are today considered similarly derogatory, such as "boesman" for coloured people and "kaffir" for black South Africans. Their use in letters written in the 1970s and '80s by a South African coloured man with a black American wife naturally places them in a context of their own. To excise them because they are offensive to us would be to deny Gordon Jephtas his voice. If we were to pretend that he had lived in a world in which those terms did not exist, it would implicitly be to deny the lived, racist reality of which those terms were an expression, and with which he was repeatedly confronted, wherever he went in the world. We have thus endeavoured to leave Jephtas's voice as it was.

---

2   Held by the Stadtarchiv Zürich.
3   See Figure 5.10.

ABBREVIATIONS

CAPAB: Cape Performing Arts Board, whose responsibilities included running the Nico Malan Theatre, opened in 1971 (today the "Artscape Theatre") that was home to the Cape Town Opera and Ballet companies.

DOMUS: Documentation Centre for Music, Stellenbosch University.

PACOFS: Performing Arts Council of the Orange Free State.

PACT: Performing Arts Council of the Transvaal, whose responsibilities included running the State Theatre in Pretoria that was inaugurated in 1981, and where Jephtas briefly worked in 1986.

UCT: University of Cape Town.

ILLUSTRATIONS

Cover image: Gordon Jephtas, photographed by Coltrain Photo in 1988.

Chapter 1, Introduction

Figure 1.1 Gordon Jephtas (16) at the piano in 1959, together with Joseph Manca. Source: Eoan Group Archive.

Figure 1.2 Gordon Jephtas in later years in the United States. Source: Eoan Group Archive.

Figure 1.3 May Abrahamse during the recital that she and Jephtas gave at the Nico Malan Theatre in Cape Town in March 1979. Source: May Abrahamse Private Collection.

Figure 1.4 Robert Trussell as Dulcamara during a rehearsal for Eoan's production of Donizetti's *L'elisir d'amore* in 1965. Source: Cloete Breytenbach Collection, DOMUS.

Figure 1.5 The Joseph Stone Auditorium on Klipfontein Road in Athlone in 1969.
Source: Revel Fox and Partners Architects.

Chapter 2, England, South Africa and Wales

Figure 2.1 Gordon Jephtas and Patricia van Graan during a rehearsal in the Cape Town City Hall, surrounded by chorus members of the Eoan Group in 1965. Source: Cloete Breytenbach Collection, DOMUS.

Figure 2.2 Joseph Manca conducting the Eoan Group in rehearsal in the Cape Town City Hall. Source: Cloete Breytenbach Collection, DOMUS.

Figure 2.3 Alessandro Rota, Gordon Jephtas and Joseph Manca in 1965. Source: Cloete Breytenbach Collection, DOMUS.

Chapter 4, Zurich

Figure 4.1 The Zurich Opera House. Source: ETH-Bibliothek Zürich, Bildarchiv/Photographer: Comet Photo AG (Zürich) / Com_BC24-8001-003-008 / CC BY-SA 4.0.

Figure 4.2 The conductor Nello Santi. Photo: Niklaus Stauss, Zurich.

Figure 4.3 Lochergut in Zurich, where Jephtas lived in a flat formerly the home of the writer Max Frisch. Source: Baugeschichtliches Archiv der Stadt Zürich, BAZ_160347.

Figure 4.4 Weinplatz, Zurich, presumably 1970s, with the church of St Peter in the background. Jephtas apparently lived in a small furnished flat in the building marked "Kurt Stäheli & Co". This was his last address in Zurich. Source: Baugeschichtliches Archiv der Stadt Zürich, BAZ_077069.

Figure 4.5 The Lisbon Opera House. Source: Jasper Walgrave.

Figure 4.6 The Hotel Borges, where Jephtas stayed when working in Lisbon. Source: Jasper Walgrave.

Figure 4.7 The first page of Jephtas's letter of 14 September 1973, describing his visit to Renata Tebaldi's home. Source: Jephtas-Abrahamse Correspondence, Eoan Group Archive.

Figure 4.8 Gordon Jephtas and Ismail Sydow in London during the 1975 tour of the Eoan Group. Source: Eoan Group Archive.

Chapter 5, The USA and South Africa

Figure 5.1 May Abrahamse and Gordon Jephtas giving a recital in the Nico Malan Theatre (today Artscape) in Cape Town on 3 March 1979. Source: Amanda Botha Private Collection.

Figure 5.2 The Nico Malan Theatre, which opened in Cape Town in 1971 as a whites-only building. It opened to all races in 1975 and was renamed Artscape in 2001. Source: Wikimedia Commons, Olga Ernst.

Figure 5.3 Gordon Jephtas and Montserrat Caballé in San Francisco in 1981. Source: May Abrahamse Private Collection.

Figure 5.4 Jephtas's passport listing Nellie Barno as his wife. Source: Eoan Group Archive.

1. INTRODUCTION

This book examines the life and career of the South African opera coach Gordon Jephtas (1943-92), primarily through the letters that he wrote home to May Abrahamse from 1963 to 1990. They had become friends through the opera productions organised by the Eoan Group, an institution set up by an English immigrant to South Africa in 1933 for purposes of "cultural upliftment" in the coloured community, as explained in greater detail below. Jephtas left South Africa to make a career for himself abroad; Abrahamse stayed. Her letters to him have not survived; given the peripatetic nature of Jephtas's career, this is as unsurprising as it is naturally regrettable.

We have ordered Jephtas's letters chronologically and in three main sections: his early years in England and in Italy, his career in Zurich (with forays to Lisbon and the USA), then his last decade, spent in the USA with occasional work back in South Africa. Two letters from Jephtas to Abrahamse actually survive from 1962, but they were written before his foreign travels, are cursory in nature, and of only minor interest; for this reason, the letters given here begin with the first he wrote after arriving in Europe in late 1963. Besides the letters from Jephtas to Abrahamse, we also offer essays on Jephtas, Abrahamse, the Eoan Group, coloured identity politics and the different stages of Jephtas's career.

Jephtas offers a fascinating case study of a richly talented artist who struggled to determine his own fate despite all the hurdles facing him in apartheid South Africa, where as a gay, coloured man he was doubly disadvantaged. Yet by any objective measure, his career was astonishingly successful. He performed at the Royal Albert Hall in London, at the Musikverein in Vienna, and after establishing himself at the Zurich Opera House in the 1970s he became widely regarded as one of the finest vocal coaches of his day for Italian opera, working with the leading singers of Europe and the USA from Montserrat Caballé to Luciano Pavarotti and many others. But his letters also reveal in harrowing terms the psychological and physical cost of his success. Besides detailed reports on the opera scene in Europe and America, discussions of vocal technique, copious name-dropping and gossip, we also read of Jephtas's depression, his tendency to self-destruction, his yearning for acceptance – always thwarted – by the white opera scene back home, and his frustration with the identity politics of South Africa – "I've had enough of seeing white people, … I wanna vomit", he told Abrahamse on 20 February 1977. Moving to New York provided him with a more convivial, multiracial, cosmopolitan environment where being gay was widely accepted; but it also led to a drugs habit and ultimately to Aids, ostracism by former friends back home, and a lingering death. Many of those who knew Gordon Jephtas have since died, though we have endeavoured to locate as many of them as possible in order to verify and annotate the information in his letters; their names are listed separately under "Acknowledgements" above.

No other South African pianist of Jephtas's generation – whether white, coloured or black – enjoyed a career such as his; and the editors know of no comparable body of correspondence that offers such a detailed picture of a coloured South African musician abroad. By publishing these letters and bringing them to the attention of a broader public, we hope both to shine a new light on the social, artistic and racial attitudes of South Africa and South Africans in the late apartheid era, and most of all to do justice to the remarkably gifted artist that was Gordon Jephtas.

1.1 GORDON JEPHTAS

Gordon Jephtas was born into a coloured family in Vasco, a suburb in the north of Cape Town, on 8 March 1943. He spent his early years there with his mother, Johanna, a single parent, and two younger siblings, Geofferey and Suzie, who had a different father. They lived on the premises of Jephtas's aunt, Eva Burns. Their meagre finances meant that they never owned or even rented their own house or apartment, but went with Eva and her family whenever they moved.[4] At the age of seven, Jephtas wanted to take up piano lessons because he was intrigued by how the harmonium player at the local church moved his fingers across the keyboard. His mother initially discouraged him, because she believed that there could be no future in music for a coloured boy in apartheid South Africa. However, his aunt Eva gave him the money to take piano lessons in secret from a man in their neighbourhood at 75 cents a month; he practised on his teacher's piano in the afternoons. After a few lessons, Jephtas played to his mother. Impressed by the talent he showed, she subsequently bought him a piano, even though she could not really afford it.[5]

Jephtas grew up in a home in which Western classical music played no role at all, let alone opera. In 1956, when he was 13, Jephtas attended the Eoan Group's rehearsals and performances of Verdi's *La traviata*.[6] Two years later, in 1958, Eoan's music director Joseph Manca attended a private concert where Jephtas accompanied a singer. Afterwards, he invited Jephtas to join the Group as a rehearsal accompanist. A few months later, on 28 February 1959, the *Cape Argus* published a photograph of Jephtas and Manca in a preview of Eoan's third opera and ballet season with the caption: "Pianist Gordon Jephtas listens to conductor Joseph Manca – 'Gordon will one day take my place', says Mr. Manca". Jephtas held the position of principal rehearsal accompanist at Eoan until 1964, and one year later was promoted to the position of répétiteur and "stage conductor", though it is unclear what this actually entailed. From 1960 to 1963 he studied for a Teacher's Licentiate Diploma in Music at the College of Music at the University of Cape Town (UCT), sponsored by the Eoan Group. He received his diploma at the end of 1963 and applied that same year to convert his diploma into a BMus. UCT's Student Records Office reveals that Jephtas was granted a concession to register late for the BMus in 1964, but he never went ahead with it.[7]

The system of apartheid can, from our chronological perspective, appear as a rigid grid of hierarchical categories ordered by arbitrary racial criteria, obscuring the reality of class differences within the designated racial groups recognised by apartheid. But registering class difference is important in reading these letters, because it allows a different reading of Jephtas's self-castigating remarks on colouredness. Both the fact that he was fluent in Afrikaaps,[8] and that he seemingly had his upper front teeth removed some time during his teens (presumably because of peer pressure),[9] suggest a working-class background.[10]

---

4   This and the following information about Jephtas's early years is from an interview conducted with his brother, Geofferey Jefthas (*sic*) on 21 June 2021.
5   Winston (1983).
6   Much of the information offered here is derived from Davids (2021).
7   E-mail correspondence with Cindy Palm of UCT Administration, 21 September 2020.
8   Jephtas conversed in Afrikaaps – a form of Afrikaans spoken among the coloured population in the Cape – with some of his friends in the Eoan Group, such as the tenor Ronald Theys. See the Gordon Jephtas – Ronald Theys correspondence in the Eoan Group Archive in the Documentation Centre for Music (DOMUS), Stellenbosch University.
9   Jephtas later claimed that the removal of upper front teeth was culturally regarded as an affirmation of masculinity. E-mail from Jephtas's former Zurich flatmate Johannes Lüthi to Chris Walton of 21 August 2022; Lüthi had asked Jephtas why he wore dentures.
10 Friedling and Morris (2007): 106.

Figure 1.1 Gordon Jephtas (16) at the piano in 1959, together with Joseph Manca.
Source: Eoan Group Archive.

In his chosen vocation as a pianist and opera répétiteur, Jephtas was therefore not only disadvantaged by his designated race description; he also had to overcome class prejudices. His letters to Abrahamse are not only letters between two South Africans designated by apartheid as
"coloured", but between a gay man who, as far as could be ascertained, came from a working-
class background, and a married woman who led a conventional, domestic, middle-class life.

Jephtas spent three months in Europe from late 1963 to early 1964 (it remains unclear
who paid for this visit). He thereafter returned to South Africa, but in September 1965 he
left for good. He settled initially in London, making a living by working part-time as a music
copyist for the publishing company Boosey & Hawkes. From June to August 1966 Jephtas was in Perugia, studying Italian literature and history at the local university in order
to "master that infernal language", i.e. Italian. He returned to England in September 1966

on a British Arts Council scholarship and joined the répétiteur class at the London Opera Centre, where his fellow students included the New Zealand soprano Kiri Te Kanawa. Upon the conclusion of his training in May 1967, Jephtas landed his first contract, working as a répétiteur and accompanist with the Welsh National Opera in their 1967/68 season, during which he toured with the company in both Wales and England.

In August 1970, Jephtas was appointed vocal coach and pianist at the 18th annual Oglebay Institute opera workshop organised by Boris Goldovsky in Wheeling, West Virginia, in the USA. Several vocal coaches were employed, each with their own speciality, Jephtas's being Italian opera. During his time at the workshop, he coached Verdi's *Don Carlos*, *La traviata* and *Macbeth*, and Donizetti's *Lucia di Lammermoor*. Afterwards, he travelled to New York City for several auditions. He was offered a post as assistant conductor at the New York City Opera for 1971 on the apparent recommendation of the soprano Beverly Sills,[11] but difficulties in obtaining a work permit scuppered the opportunity.[12] It would be another six years before he was able to work there.

In the (European) summer of 1971, Jephtas travelled to Durban in South Africa, where on 7 August he gave a recital with May Abrahamse at the "Indian Cane-Grower's Hall at the M. L. Sultan's College". This was organised by a coloured cultural organisation called "Die Bruins" (literally "The Browns", referring to the skin colour of its members), who donated the proceeds of the recital to the Durban and District Community Chest. This recital was most likely performed before a wholly coloured audience. In an article of 22 August 1971, the local newspaper *The Post* reports that they performed "before a packed audience who gave the duo a two-minute standing ovation after the recital, forcing them to take four curtain calls".[13]

Jephtas returned to Italy in February 1972 to take up his first important contract in Europe. He was appointed as a répétiteur and assistant conductor for a season with the Teatro Sociale in Mantua, where he worked with some of the leading singers of the day including Plácido Domingo and Elena Suliotis. Four months later, in June 1972, Jephtas was given a contract as a répétiteur at the Zurich Opera House, beginning the following August, where he worked primarily with the conductor Nello Santi. His contract was renewed with each new season, and he held this position concurrently with a post as répétiteur with the Teatro Nacional de São Carlos in Lisbon, Portugal, where he spent several weeks in early spring each year from 1973 onwards. In September 1973, Jephtas was hired by the soprano Renata Tebaldi to accompany her and the tenor Franco Corelli for concerts at the Royal Albert Hall in London on 9 October 1973 and at the Musikvereinssaal in Vienna, Austria, on 14 October 1973.

Besides his work with the opera houses of Zurich and Lisbon, Jephtas also undertook freelance vocal coaching, both with individuals and with opera companies. During 1975, for example, he gave masterclasses to the Eoan Group in London as part of the 1975 International Festival of Youth Orchestras and Performing Arts. That same year, he coached the Swiss-American soprano Gloria Davy in Geneva; he was also engaged to coach the singers for Verdi's *La traviata* for an amateur opera company in Venice, and furthermore worked as Nello Santi's assistant at the Teatro La Fenice.

Jephtas resigned his Zurich post in 1977, and worked his final season in Lisbon the year after. It was in 1977 that he was finally able to obtain a US work permit and accepted the

---

11   Eoan Group Archive: 55:451. "Gordon Jephtas's résumé attached to correspondence: Ismail Sydow to The Commissioner for Coloured Affairs, 16 November 1971."
12   See his letter of 7 February 1972.
13   See Anon. (1971). Eoan Group Archive: uncatalogued. This newspaper gave the venue as the "Orient Hall".

Figure 1.2 Gordon Jephtas in later years in the United States.
Source: Eoan Group Archive.

longstanding offer from the New York City Opera. But after only two days in New York[14] he was offered a contract by the Lyric Opera of Chicago, which he accepted immediately. On 31 January 1979, Jephtas was appointed the artistic director of the Eoan Group back in South Africa. He was made responsible for planning, managing and co-ordinating the projects for all three sections of Eoan – dance, drama and music. The only artistic project that would come to fruition during his tenure was a recital that he gave with May Abrahamse at the Nico Malan Theatre in Cape Town on 3 March 1979. Although he officially remained in his post until October 1979, Jephtas left South Africa in May 1979 to return to the Lyric Opera of Chicago, where he stayed until 1980. It was also in 1980 that Jephtas married one Nellie M. Barno, an African American woman.[15] Although he admitted to friends that it was purely to get his green card,[16] it seems that he and Nellie remained in touch during the subsequent decade. It is not known how they got to know each other, nor what the terms of their arrangement were.

By the end of the 1970s, Jephtas had worked with a whole array of world-class operatic figures, including Luigi Alva, Piero Cappuccilli, Maria Chiara, Fiorenza Cossotto, Alfredo Kraus, Luciano Pavarotti, Frederica von Stade and many others. In 1981 he moved to the San Francisco Opera for a season. He explained in a letter to Abrahamse that he had been engaged only as a prompt, but the tenor Neil Shicoff had apparently demanded "daily 2-hour private coaching" sessions with Jephtas alone, supposedly because he was "the best there is".[17]

From 1982 to 1985, Jephtas lived in New York City and was mostly self-employed as a freelance accompanist, vocal coach and prompt. In 1985, Jephtas was appointed the opera coach and conductor of Opera Amici, a small-scale non-profit opera company in New York City founded by two of his colleagues, the soprano Barbara Christopher and the mezzo-soprano Barbara Mahajan.[18]

In 1986, Jephtas moved back to South Africa as the chorus master for the opera company run by the Performing Arts Council of the Transvaal (PACT) at the State Theatre in Pretoria.

---

14 Jephtas on occasion claimed it was after three days; see Melich (1986).
15 Their marriage was registered in Manhattan. See www.nycmarriageindex.com/, accessed August 2022.
16 Information kindly provided by Johannes Lüthi in August 2022.
17 See his letter of 22 October 1981.
18 E-mail from Barbara Mahajan, 7 October 2022.

But like his tenure at Eoan in Cape Town seven years earlier, this position too was short-lived. He soon abandoned it (without officially resigning, it seems), and returned to the USA where he worked as the chorus master and senior vocal coach at Utah Opera in Salt Lake City. One year later, in 1987, Utah Opera appointed him their first-ever "music director", though he only held this position until the end of the following year. It seems that Jephtas thereafter resumed his work as a freelance vocal coach in New York City; his correspondence with Abrahamse dwindled to almost nothing at this time.

In 1991, Jephtas returned one last time to his home country, where he was given a three-month contract by Eoan as a part-time research and development consultant, working just 3 hours per week. He was tasked with mapping out the organisational structures that would be needed to launch a performing arts school, though this never materialised. He also did some vocal coaching for the Cape Performing Arts Board and held a concert with members of the Eoan Group. He returned to the USA in 1991, and died there of Aids a year later, on 4 July 1992.

1.2 MAY ABRAHAMSE

May Abrahamse's letters to Gordon Jephtas have not survived, but those that he sent her reveal her as a vital, active partner in his world. He was a loyal friend to her throughout his life, as she was clearly loyal to him; she was the first "diva" that he loved, and he clearly adored her voice. From the beginning they had a mutual understanding of opera and of the discipline and skills required to reach a professional standard. They were both classified coloured under apartheid, and so grew up in a socio-economic and political environment that was harsh and left little space for developing the competencies they needed to realise their musical potential. Jephtas left South Africa for good in 1965 (notwithstanding occasional attempts to return and forge a career for himself back home). May Abrahamse, by contrast, continued to live and work in South Africa for the rest of her life in a difficult, isolated artistic environment, and this informs the background against which we must read this correspondence. According to his sometime Zurich flatmate Johannes Lüthi, Jephtas rarely received letters from South Africa except for those from Abrahamse. Over the years it was she who kept alive his longings for home and for his own people, and who clearly stilled his hunger for local news by providing information and gossip from the Eoan Group and about mutual friends. Jephtas regrettably did not keep her letters as she kept his; we have only his side of their correspondence.

Abrahamse was born on 6 May 1930 in District Six and was thus 13 years older than Jephtas.[19] She was one of the first soprano soloists of the Eoan Group, singing in musicals and large-scale sacred works that the Group performed in the years before they began staging operas. Her first solo role was in the comic opera *A Slave in Araby* by Alfred Silver, produced in 1949 when she was just 19, and this was followed by annual productions of works such as *The Maid in the Mountains*, *Hong Kong* and *The Gipsy Princess*,[20] all performed with orchestra under the baton of Joseph Manca in the Cape Town City Hall. Her first big role was Violetta in Giuseppe Verdi's *La traviata* in 1956. We know that Jephtas attended a performance of this production, and it is most likely that he heard her there for the first time.

---

19   Roos (2018): 53.
20   Composed by Harold Fraser-Simson, Charles Jessop and Emmerich Kálmán respectively; the last of these was an English-language version of Kálmán's operetta *Die Csárdásfürstin*. See Roos (2018): 189–190.

Little is known of Abrahamse's vocal training in these years, but what is certain is that she did not attend any conservatoire, because people of colour only had access to such facilities in exceptional circumstances (and it was in any case prohibitively expensive). A newspaper article published in 1956 shortly after her debut as Violetta noted with astonishment that this "opera star" was by day working in the "cheque room of the *Cape Times* newspaper",[21] probably doing menial administrative work. She initially received vocal tuition from the theatre producer Billie Jones, then from the singer Beatrice Gibson (neither of whom seems otherwise to have been known as a singing teacher). In later years, Abrahamse trained with the opera singer Olga Magnoni. It was during her time with Jones that Abrahamse learnt the role of Violetta, which she sang with Eoan throughout her career, also on the last occasion that the Group performed the opera, in 1975.[22]

Abrahamse sang many other roles with the Eoan Group, including Santuzza in Pietro Mascagni's *Cavalleria rusticana*, Mimì in Giacomo Puccini's *La bohème*, Butterfly in Puccini's *Madama Butterfly*, Rosalinde in Johann Strauss's *Die Fledermaus* and Nedda in Ruggero Leoncavallo's *Pagliacci*.[23] She furthermore sang in sacred works that the Group performed, such as Giuseppe Verdi's Requiem and Handel's *Messiah*, and her repertoire included many opera arias and lieder that she later featured in her recitals and other concerts.[24]

May Abrahamse married Jonathan Rushin in 1956,[25] gave birth to two daughters, Wendy and Trudy, and became a stay-at-home mother, though she occasionally also offered private singing lessons. She continued to perform with the Eoan Group, though under her maiden name. Since she and Jephtas consistently used her maiden name, we have followed their example in this book. This was unusual for someone of her circumstances at the time, especially since she was not considered a "professional" singer and did not earn her living from her art. Abrahamse's husband worked in the building industry in Durban on the south-east coast of South Africa for much of their married life, and his wife and daughters joined him there from September 1968 to September 1972. During this time, Abrahamse did not return to the Cape to perform with the Eoan Group, except in 1971 when she sang Nedda in Leoncavallo's *Pagliacci*. On 7 August 1971, she and Gordon Jephtas gave a recital together for a coloured-only audience under the auspices of "Die Bruins"[26] in the Indian Cane-Grower's Hall in Durban, as already mentioned above.[27]

The friendship between Gordon Jephtas and May Abrahamse grew from shared music making, a common cultural background and a passion for opera. Jephtas also coached her intensely, and her extant recordings prove that she continued to sing to a high standard well into her mature years. Because Jephtas spent most of these years abroad in Europe or America, he coached Abrahamse by means of letters and recorded messages on tape that they posted to each other. Jephtas's infatuation with Maria Callas and his projection of Callas onto Abrahamse becomes obvious in his letters. After hearing Callas sing Tosca at the Royal Opera House on 30 January 1964, Jephtas reported every detail of her performance in breathless rapture to Abrahamse and ended his letter with the words: "We'll make a Callas of you yet!"[28] As a singer of colour in apartheid South Africa without sustainable

---

21 Roos (2018): 52.
22 Roos (2018): 209–210.
23 See the list of works performed by the Eoan Group in Roos (2018): 187–210.
24 *Ibid*.
25 E-mail from Trudy Rushin, 19 October 2022.
26 See Jephtas's letter of 22 August 1971.
27 See Anon. (1971).
28 Letter dated 31 January 1964.

Figure 1.3 May Abrahamse during the recital that she and Jephtas gave at the Nico Malan Theatre in Cape Town in March 1979.
Source: May Abrahamse Private Collection.

income, Abrahamse did not find it easy to get good singing tuition. It is therefore ironic that she was coached through the mail by a man who was working with some of the finest singers on the international stage at the time.

The only studio recording that exists of Abrahamse is a 1974 recording of her performing with the orchestra of the South African Broadcasting Corporation.[29] This was an unusual occurrence at the height of apartheid, when interracial productions were rare. The apartheid regime was nevertheless keen to convince the world that apartheid functioned to the advantage of all members of its racially segregated population, allowing even people of colour to excel in Western art music. It is therefore difficult to know whether this recording was in acknowledgement of Abrahamse's artistry, or whether it was made essentially for political, propaganda purposes. Either way, the fact that it was made illustrates the dilemmas that people such as Jephtas and Abrahamse faced in pursuing the art that they loved under apartheid.[30]

After returning from Durban, Abrahamse remained active in the Eoan Group for many years. In 1975 she was a soloist with the Group on a tour to the United Kingdom, where they were invited to participate in the Aberdeen International Youth Festival in Scotland. She became involved with the administration of the Group after Joseph Manca retired in 1977, and subsequently served as the Secretary of the Board. In March 1979, Abrahamse and Jephtas became the first coloured classical musicians to present a recital at the Nico Malan Theatre in Cape Town, where they were received with great acclaim.[31] In the 1987-88

---

29 See Jephtas's postcard of [12] October 1973 and his letter of 28 December [1973]. On this recording Abrahamse sings "Sì, mi chiamano Mimì" and "Donde lieta uscì" from Puccini's *La bohème*, "Mercè, dilette amiche" from Verdi's *I vespri siciliani*, "Vissi d'arte" from Puccini's *Tosca* and the Afrikaans song "Heimwee" by the South African composer S. Le Roux Marais. The National Symphony Orchestra of the SABC is conducted by Anton Hartman. It is not clear whether the recording was made for a reason other than archival purposes, and there is no indication that it was ever broadcast. It was made during 1974 and can be found in the SABC Sound Archives under Catalogue number TM 421(76).

30 Abrahamse and Jephtas do not discuss this particular issue in their correspondence.

31 Roos (2018): 174-175. The Nico Malan Theatre was officially opened to all races in 1975 but, it was largely boycotted by the coloured community.

season, aged 57, Abrahamse was finally given the opportunity to sing in a professional capacity with white singers when she accepted a two-year contract as a chorus member with the Performing Arts Council of the Orange Free State in Bloemfontein.[32]

The correspondence between Abrahamse and Jephtas became less frequent during the 1980s, and the content of their letters suggests that they had grown apart. There are a number of possible reasons for this. During this time, Jephtas lived an openly gay life and became politically outspoken against apartheid. These were things that he clearly never felt able to share with Abrahamse, who steadfastly refused to discuss politics or sexual matters, considering them unconnected with music. When interviewed in 2009, she reiterated that she was never interested in politics. For her, everything "was just music, music, music".[33] Issues of sexuality or gay identity were similarly taboo. According to her daughters, Jephtas's orientation was something of which she was always aware, but that she refused to mention.[34]

Several accolades were awarded to Abrahamse in her senior years, acknowledging her stature as a soprano and her lifelong contribution to opera in South Africa. These included the Cape Tercentenary Foundation Award in 2005 for her "distinguished contribution to the Fine and Performing Arts"[35] and the KykNET Lifetime Achievement Award in 2013.[36] At the time of writing, May Abrahamse is 92 years old and has been living with Alzheimer's for more than ten years. She is currently being cared for by her daughter, Wendy Abrahams.

1.3 THE EOAN GROUP

The Eoan Group was founded in 1933 and is one of the oldest cultural organisations for the coloured community in the Cape.[37] It functioned as a home for amateur ballet, theatre and opera before and during the apartheid era, at a time when few other opportunities existed for coloured singers, dancers and actors to express themselves. The story of the Group was determined by the politics of race and class. It was initially created with the intention of socially "uplifting" a racial group in line with the "civilising" mission of the West. Helen Southern-Holt, a British immigrant, founded Eoan in District Six, a suburb just to the east of Cape Town's city centre that was home to a large coloured community, and was generally regarded as a slum. She set up elocution classes because she envisaged that "clear articulate speech"[38] would help the locals to find better employment. Drama and ballet classes were added to the burgeoning organisation, and soon a choir was created that performed in Cape Town proper. Before formal apartheid was initiated in 1948, the Eoan Group's projects and productions were funded by the government and by well-to-do white citizens. In 1939, the Group adopted a constitution that had far-reaching consequences for how it would function through the years of apartheid. It chose "we live to serve" as its motto – thus essentially emphasising servitude itself – and declared that it was a non-political organisation. This implied both that the Group's teaching and production activities constituted a service (implicitly unpaid) to each other and

---

32 Vosloo (2016).
33 Eoan History Project (2013): 23.
34 Roos (2016): 41.
35 Anon. (no date B).
36 Anon. (2013).
37 For more extensive research on the Eoan Group, including the acquisition of its archive by Stellenbosch University in 2008 that led to renewed historical appreciation of its importance, see the Eoan History Project (2013) and Roos (2018).
38 Roos (2018): 19.

to their community, and that the aims of the Group were divorced from anything political. This notion was one to which they clung in the most compromising of circumstances, though it merely exacerbated the difficult conditions under which the Group was operating, and which at the height of apartheid almost destroyed it.

Eoan came to opera via choral singing. Its choir was started by Joseph Manca (1908-1985), a (white) South African of Italian descent who was an accountant by trade and an opera lover and amateur conductor. He steadily built the choir and its soloists into an amateur opera company. In 1946 they performed Martin Shaw's cantata *The Redeemer* and moved on to operettas such as Alfred Silver's *A Slave in Araby* in 1949 and Emmerich Kálmán's *Gipsy Princess* in 1953. They also performed large-scale choral works such as Henry Maunder's *Bethlehem* in 1953 and George Frideric Handel's *Messiah* in 1954, all of them with orchestra.

Eoan's first opera production took place in March 1956 at its first-ever Arts Festival. It gave nine performances of a full-scale production of Verdi's *La traviata* at the Cape Town City Hall, sung in Italian. Manca conducted the all-white Cape Town Municipal Orchestra, and the audience was also predominantly white, with just a few seats designated for coloured attendees. The reviews were exceptionally good, if somewhat condescending, and left a favourable impression among Cape Town's cultural classes. The well-known Afrikaans critic Charlie Weich of the main Cape daily *Die Burger* wrote that, had he not seen with his own eyes what a "coloured opera company" could achieve on the night of 10 March in the City Hall, he would not have believed it. The voices of May Abrahamse as Violetta and Lionel Fourie as Germont were singled out as outstanding, as were the décor and costumes.[39]

For the next twenty years, Eoan continued to present Cape Town with Italian opera. It also held a second Arts Festival in 1962, toured the country twice (in 1960 and 1965), and was ultimately given the opportunity to perform in the United Kingdom in 1975. What started out as a humanitarian organisation had metamorphosed into a company that provided opportunities for coloured artists who were otherwise deprived of participating in the arts, and to whom performing with white artists was generally prohibited under apartheid.

The Eoan Group became an active participant on the classical arts scene in Cape Town, and the Group acquired a large following among local opera lovers who were predominantly white, but also included coloured patrons. The conditions under which they rehearsed and performed were difficult, however, and the disadvantages that they experienced because of apartheid legislation were debilitating and isolating. Eoan's singers were not familiar with the Italian language, none had access to a conservatoire education, and nobody in the company could attend opera performances by the white companies in South Africa because they were not allowed in whites-only venues. Many of them were unable to read staff notation (this also applied to several principals) and had to be taught their roles by rote. Listening to recordings was therefore important for their learning process. Most of Eoan's artists came from low-income households. But throughout these years, none of its singers, actors or dancers received any payment for their work. In fact, all their activities had to take place after working hours and over weekends because they had other, daytime jobs to make ends meet. All vocal training was undertaken by two Italians who were active on the local opera scene: Alessandro Rota and Olga Magnoni, neither of whom were employed at the College of Music at the University of Cape Town. Joseph Manca remained Eoan's music director for some three decades and was the main driving force behind its activities. The zeal with which he

---

39   Weich (1956).

Figure 1.4 Robert Trussell as Dulcamara during a rehearsal for Eoan's production of Donizetti's *L'elisir d'amore* in 1965.
Source: Cloete Breytenbach Collection, DOMUS.

managed the group was, however, problematic. He undoubtedly created opportunities for music-making for the coloured community that they would otherwise never have been given, but he was covetous of his position and protective of his "musical children", as he often called them, and who he clearly did not want to grow into musical "adults" who might be able to assume control of their own affairs. Jephtas's letters to May Abrahamse frequently refer to their problems with Manca and his paternalism.

By 1971, the Group's repertoire included 10 operas: Verdi's *La traviata*, *Rigoletto* and *Il trovatore*, Bizet's *Carmen*, Puccini's *Madama Butterfly* and *La bohème*, Donizetti's *L'elisir d'amore*, Rossini's *Il barbiere di Siviglia*, Leoncavallo's *Pagliacci* and Mascagni's *Cavalleria rusticana*. In the late 1960s, the Group also gave the first South African productions of two Rodgers and Hammerstein musicals, *Oklahoma!* and *South Pacific*, and of *Carmen Jones*, Hammerstein's adaptation of Bizet.[40] Eoan also had active ballet and drama sections that performed to great acclaim. In 1962, Eoan premiered a new ballet, *The Square*, depicting gang life in District Six. It was composed by Stanley Glasser, a lecturer at Cape Town University, and was written specifically for Johaar Mosaval, at the time a principal dancer at the Royal Ballet in London. Eoan's humanitarian work also continued with after-school classes for children and literacy classes for adults.

Eoan's artistic successes did not alleviate its chronic funding problems. Sustaining an ever-growing amateur arts company required considerable financial resources, despite the fact that none of its artists was being paid. The Group had accepted funds from the government before formal apartheid began in 1948, and it continued to do so until 1956. The more politically aware members of Eoan were unhappy about this, as were many in the wider coloured community, because it meant that the Group was viewed as politically tainted, even during these early years, and despite maintaining an officially non-political stance. After the success of the 1956 Arts Festival, Eoan managed to function without government

---

40   See the list of performances in Roos (2018): 187-210.

Figure 1.5 The Joseph Stone Auditorium on Klipfontein Road in Athlone in 1969.
Source: Revel Fox and Partners Architects.

funding for several years. But in the longer term it simply proved unable to survive financially on its own. In 1964, the Group re-applied for government funding. By this time, grand apartheid was in full swing, which meant that state funds came with many more strings attached. Eoan had to agree to perform only before racially segregated audiences, it had to apply for permits to sing at all venues, and it had to invite government dignitaries to its events. Soon afterwards, the Group was evicted from its home in District Six – which was now designated a "whites-only" area – and relocated to the coloured suburb of Athlone on the eastern side of the Kromboom River that separated it from the white, middle-class suburb of Rondebosch to the west. In November 1969, the Group moved into its own premises, the Eoan Group Cultural Centre, today called the Joseph Stone Auditorium.[41] The subsidies that the Group received were miniscule compared to the amounts received by "white" opera companies such as the one run by the Cape Performing Arts Board. Just two years later, in May 1971, the whites-only Nico Malan Theatre opened in Cape Town: a state-of-the-art theatre complex, fully funded by the government, which cost ZAR 11.5 million – almost one hundred times more than the ZAR 120,000 that the authorities had paid for the Joseph Stone Auditorium. Nevertheless, simply accepting money from the authorities meant that the Eoan Group began to be regarded as politically compromised by members of the coloured community, especially from the late 1970s onwards.[42] This placed the Group in an impossible position, because if it had not accepted government funding, it would have been unable to perform at all.[43]

In the early 1970s, the number of opera productions staged by Eoan began to dwindle. It held its final opera season in 1975, which featured a production of Verdi's *La traviata* with

41   See Pistorius and Roos (2021): 102–131.
42   This process of political alienation took place over many years and is described at length in Roos (2018), with a summary of the Group's political problems on p. 179.
43   The tragic implications of this position have been explored in a documentary film on the Eoan Group by Aryan Kaganof, entitled *An Inconsolable Memory* (2014), which can be viewed here: https://vimeo.com/111217435, accessed 9 November 2022.

May Abrahamse as Violetta. Shortly afterwards, the group travelled to the United Kingdom to take part in the Aberdeen International Youth Festival. Manca resigned in 1977 due to ill health, after which the opera section of the group slowly disintegrated, despite Gordon Jephtas briefly accepting the post of its director in 1979. By 1980, all opera activities by Eoan had come to a complete halt.

The Eoan Group's story offers a prime example of how race and politics impinged on the arts in apartheid South Africa. It illustrates the difficulties faced by artists of colour, who strove to use their art to rise "above" politics, only to find themselves the victims of the compromises that this entailed. After racial segregation was officially ended in 1994, Eoan continued to function as a small-scale ballet and drama company, today called the Eoan Group School of Performing Arts,[44] still situated in Athlone, just outside Cape Town.

1.4 THE POLITICS OF COLOURED IDENTITY

In South Africa, the term "coloured" has specialised meanings. Unlike in most parts of the world, "coloured" in South Africa is not used to describe people who are phenotypically "not white", nor is it understood as derogatory in the same way as in the African-American context. On one level, "coloured" in a South African context denotes a person perceived to be of mixed racial ancestry.[45] On another, under the perverse system that was apartheid, "coloured" referred to a collective of people who were artificially grouped together because they did not fit easily into racial categories such as "white", "black" or "Indian".

According to the historian Mohamed Adhikari, an abiding popular perception of South African "colouredness" (as a race) is that it originated almost immediately after the onset of Dutch colonisation at the Cape in the 17th century as a result of sexual relations between European men and indigenous women or imported slaves.[46] Throughout history, the idea of racial "purity" has repeatedly enjoyed favour, while racial "mixing" has been met with disfavour (Nazi Germany and the Jim Crow era in the southern states of the USA being just two relatively recent examples). Colouredness in South Africa, according to the sociologist Zimitri Erasmus, was treated similarly and became stigmatised as a "race" that is "'lacking', supplementary, excessive, inferior or simply non-existent".[47] Another pejorative historical claim was that coloured individuals were "deficient in positive qualities associated with racial purity and handicapped by negative ones derived from racial mixture".[48] When the National Party came to power in South Africa in 1948, it continued the colonial legacy of racism towards the country's coloured population, treating them as possessing a "residual, in-between or lesser identity".[49] In a 1983 interview, Marike de Klerk, the wife of the then minister (and future President) F. W. de Klerk, offered an opinion that clearly reflected official thinking: "[Coloureds] are a negative group. The definition of a coloured in the population register is someone that is not black, and is not white and is also not an Indian, in other words a no-person [*sic*]. They are the leftovers. They are the people that were left after the nations were sorted out. They are the rest".[50]

---

44   See Eoan Group School of Performing Arts, www.eoangroup.com/, accessed 26 October 2022.
45   Adhikari (2009): viii.
46   Adhikari (2009): xi-xii.
47   Erasmus (2001): 16.
48   Adhikari (2005): 14.
49   Erasmus (2001): 16.
50   De Klerk, as cited in Adhikari (2005): 13.

Coloured people during apartheid enjoyed certain privileges above their black counterparts that in part could be ascribed to their being supposedly more "'civilised' and partly descended from European colonists", unlike black South Africans.[51] Coloureds were not as privileged as whites, but were supported with better housing, secondary and tertiary education than black South Africans, while also being exempt from certain curfews, pass laws and other restrictions applicable only to blacks. Erasmus explains it aptly: "For me, growing up coloured meant knowing that I was *not only* not white, but *less than white*; *not only* not black, but *better than black* …".[52] In this sense, the idea that "white is better" was an obvious conclusion to draw at the time. Although all "non-whites" remained officially inferior to whites, being classified "coloured" was without doubt more advantageous than being classified "black". In an article entitled "South African finds life away from home", published on 5 October 1986 in *The Salt Lake Tribune*, Gordon Jephtas explained his own experience to its reporter: "The first thing a child learns in South Africa is color … You are told that whites are superior[,] Coloured people not quite as superior and the black man is an animal. It is something that is in the air. You feel it everywhere".[53]

This was fundamental to the divide-and-rule tactic created by the apartheid regime to separate "non-white" groups from each other and prevent them from forming a united front in any struggle against racism and exploitation.[54] In today's South Africa there are no more laws on the statute books that discriminate on the basis of race. Socio-economic differences remain, however, and individuals from different racial and cultural groups still self-identify as coloured, black or white, etc., even though the post-apartheid South African constitution promotes diversity and encourages the pursuit of an equitable society.

While the category "coloured" enjoyed an "elevated" class status under apartheid, both Adhikari and Erasmus agree that some coloured individuals at the time internalised negativity and resentment towards their own identity, leaving them with feelings of shame and discomfort. This seems to have been the case with Gordon Jephtas. During the first twelve years of his correspondence with May Abrahamse, who was herself a member of the coloured community, Jephtas is repeatedly negative towards his identity, making bitter remarks about the handicap of his colouredness. He views it as an obstacle – more mental than physical – and frequently blames his coloured nature for preventing him from standing up for himself. In a letter of 26 February 1972, he explained to Abrahamse that this "coloured nature that I was born with and live with for 28 years isn't that easy to shake off", and in a letter written just over a year later, on 4 April 1973, he complained "I forget, we are not human, we're coloured, not even black". Jephtas had clearly internalised, to some extent, the status conferred on coloureds under apartheid as summed up by Marike de Klerk above. However, from 1975 onwards, Jephtas's letters suggest that he had begun to reconcile himself with being coloured, for his self-disparaging comments now dwindle. It seems that the longer he was outside apartheid South Africa, the better he was able to accept his own identity, even reaching a state of pride in it, and (in his own words of 13 June 1975), asserting that "we coloureds have something to offer".

---

51   Adhikari (2009): xi.
52   Erasmus (2001): 1.
53   Jephtas, as cited in Melich (1986). The spellings color/coloured are original.
54   See, e.g. Adhikari (2005): 35.

2. ENGLAND, SOUTH AFRICA AND WALES

2.1 "... THINGS ARE SO DEPRESSING"

In December 1963, Jephtas embarked on a three-month trip to Europe: his first journey abroad. He was 20 years old, had just graduated with a Teacher's Licentiate Diploma from the College of Music at the University of Cape Town, and was eager to attend as many opera performances as possible in order to "continue studying opera", as he described it in his letters to Abrahamse. It remains unknown who provided the money for the trip. Jephtas flew to Rome, then travelled via Germany to England where he visited his childhood friend Didi Sydow, whom Eoan had sponsored to train with the Royal Ballet in London (she was the daughter of Ismail Sydow, the secretary of the Eoan Board and Joseph Manca's right-hand man).[55] It was here that Jephtas first heard his ultimate "diva", Maria Callas, when she sang Tosca in Franco Zeffirelli's production of Puccini's opera at Covent Garden in January 1964. Jephtas saw it twice, queuing for hours in the winter cold to obtain his tickets. He was instantly infatuated with Callas and reported every detail of her performances in his letters to Abrahamse. It was, he wrote on 31 January 1964, "the most thrilling and exciting experience of my life". During this visit, he also heard singers such as Joan Sutherland, Anna Moffo and Elisabeth Schwarzkopf. Before returning home, he spent a few weeks in Milan and attended opera performances at La Scala where he heard singers such as Giulietta Simionato, Giuseppe Di Stefano and Mirella Freni. These initial experiences of Europe, its opera houses and its opera stars made a huge impression on Jephtas, who until now had been compelled to listen to records or dress rehearsals at the UCT Opera School if he wanted to hear singers other than those of the Eoan Group (as a coloured man, he was not allowed to attend opera performances sung by whites).

Jephtas returned to South Africa in mid-March 1964. The Group had no opera season planned for that year, but was already preparing for its national tour lined up for the following year, and Jephtas helped with rehearsals over the coming months. He also travelled with the Group on its South African tour from July to September 1965. In October 1965, Jephtas took a ship from Durban to England with the intention of studying there, though he as yet had no plans for where or what to study. Again, the source of his funding remains obscure. He returned to South Africa several times over the ensuing years, but never again settled there permanently. The nature of his work as a vocal coach also meant that Jephtas led a nomadic existence for much of his life.

Jephtas stayed in London until May 1966, though he disliked the cold, grey weather. He attended as many opera performances as possible and made ends meet by working as a music copyist for the publishing company Boosey & Hawkes.[56] He spent June to August 1966 studying Italian at the University of Perugia – eventually attaining a fluency in Italian that proved invaluable in years to come – then returned to London in September to enrol at the London Opera Centre with a scholarship from the British Arts Council.[57] This was an intense learning period, during which he had to master vast swathes of the operatic repertoire in a short time, becoming acquainted with operatic styles that had hitherto been unfamiliar to him. The Opera Centre was also used by the Royal Opera House as a rehearsal space, which enabled Jephtas to observe much behind-the-scenes activity. The productions

---

55 See Jephtas's letter of 28 December 1963. Didi Sydow was supposed to return to South Africa to teach ballet for Eoan, but never did; she married a white Australian, and such "mixed" marriages were still banned in South Africa.
56 Davids (2021): 10.
57 *Ibid.*

he was able to observe in this way included Luchino Visconti's "black and white" production of *La traviata* with Mirella Freni, Renato Cioni and Piero Cappuccilli, which generated much international attention[58] and was also subjected to a detailed report by Jephtas in a letter to Abrahamse of 30 March 1967. Abrahamse had sung the title role of this opera many times, though she was by necessity familiar only with Alessandro Rota as stage director, whose ideas Jephtas now described as "thirty years out of date".[59]

After completing his studies at the Opera Centre, Jephtas joined Welsh National Opera as the pianist on their "Opera for All" tour of Wales and middle England from June 1967 to April 1968, playing for Smetana's *Two Widows*, Donizetti's *Don Pasquale* and Rossini's *Cenerentola* in a total of over 70 performances in schools and church halls from Blaenau Ffestiniog to Merthyr Tydfil, Scunthorpe, Stevenage and Skegness.[60] Jephtas had been delighted to experience the higher operatic standards that Europe offered when compared to his native South Africa – with Callas naturally at the top of his list – though he also expressed disappointment at the many "Manca-type" conductors whom he encountered and at the nonchalance of the singers he worked with, complaining to Abrahamse in a letter of 16 October 1967 that "... things are so depressing – no artistic achievement or attainment involved. Everyone is a prima donna and tries to be the star and ART goes for a holiday, or better into exile".

After his contract with Welsh National Opera came to an end, Jephtas returned to Cape Town for several months to assist with preparing the principal singers for the Eoan Group's forthcoming Eighth Opera Season, which was due to start in October 1968. Abrahamse and Jephtas did not see each other during this visit because she was living in Durban at the time. However, the season was cancelled at the eleventh hour – apparently because of insufficient preparation caused by several singers falling ill with the seasonal flu. This caused a major dent to the Group's reputation. Jephtas returned to Europe, but fell into a depression lasting several months. He tried to enrol for music studies in Rome, Milan and Barcelona, but left each of these cities without achieving anything concrete. In early 1969 he settled in Milan, where he already knew Joseph Gabriels, a tenor formerly of the Eoan Group, and earned his money from teaching English to foreign nationals at the local Shenker Institute.

Throughout his life, Jephtas was prone to bouts of depression and listlessness, particularly after having visited South Africa or after having had disagreements with the Eoan Group and its management (his relations with the Group over the years seem indeed to have been more fraught than pleasant). Jephtas was ambitious, immensely talented, and wanted Manca and his colleagues to acknowledge his achievements. He was also sensitive to the situation of his fellow coloured artists in South Africa. But his feelings were seldom reciprocated, he often felt rejected and misunderstood by his peers at home, and this merely fuelled his melancholy. Jephtas's repeated problems with work permits in Europe and the USA similarly exacerbated his tendency to depression, and he would then often rail against the subservient attitude with which he felt indoctrinated through his upbringing as a person of colour in South Africa. He saw May Abrahamse as the only person in the Eoan community who truly understood him, and who knew what it meant to be an artist. His letters to her also describe in detail the chaotic circumstances that led to the cancellation of Eoan's 1968 season, and he frequently complained to her about what he saw as the Group's low artistic standards. The longer he lived and worked abroad, the deeper the divide grew between him and Eoan's management.

---

58   See, e.g., Heyworth (1967).
59   Letter dated 11 May 1974.
60   Information kindly provided by Ian Douglas of Welsh National Opera, e-mail of 8 March 2021.

1

c/o Overseas Visitors Club, 180, Earl's Court Road, London S.W.5 [United Kingdom][61]

28 December 1963.

My dear May,

This very morning I received your touching Christmas card. How kind and thoughtful of you - - thank you so very, very much.

I am hoping to hear all about the [Eoan] concerts *soon* (from you). I can hardly wait. However, I hope they were successful and satisfactory, though knowing your musical ideals I guess that you are not satisfied. But believe me, not being entirely satisfied with one's performances is the only way of improving one's abilities especially in an organization such as ours and a country like South Africa.

But to tell you all since leaving home. We landed at Rome 13 hours after leaving Johannesburg - at 5.40 a.m. A ridiculous hour, I agree. This was followed by a long drive into the city (about 50 mins) and I discovered that in Rome there are also streets, with houses (nice ones as well as grim-looking ones), pavements, trees and sand. Very much like it is at home, the only difference being that the motor-vehicles travel on the opposite side of the road, that is, they do not go on the left as in Cape Town, but instead on the right. Confusing, no doubt. After checking into the hotel recommended by Fiasconaro,[62] I wandered down the street. Although the sun was shining it was damn cold. I expect that it is cold in the morning in Cape Town also, but I must admit that I have never roamed the streets of Cape Town so early in the morning. Of course, things were still pretty quiet. I watched the shop-keepers opening up for the day and the early-risers going to work. How exciting it seemed - the cobbled streets, the funny-looking trams and the mini-cars driving along furiously. And there I stood in the Piazza Barberini with all the buildings towering above me.

I returned to the hotel for breakfast and met a South African pianist, Helga Bassel[63] (you may have heard of her). She and her family had also just come and much to our surprise we discovered that we were on the same flight from Africa. Of course, the next thing to do was to go to the Opera House. I was duly disappointed with the building - it seemed out of place with the surroundings being the most modern building in comparison to the others. However, I ventured in but had another shock coming - said the gentleman in the ticket box (in Italian, of course) - "Sorry, the opera season does not start until Christmas but there is a performance of *Iris* in commemoration of Mascagni's birthday on Monday with Tullio Serafin conducting."

---

61   The addresses given for the letters are in each case taken from the envelope where one exists. The dates given are as stated in the actual letter, though they have been standardised here in the format "28 December 1963". Where Jephtas includes a place with the date in his letter, we have retained this.

62   Gregorio Fiasconaro (1915-1994), South African baritone of Italian birth, the first director of the Opera School of the University of Cape Town (hereinafter UCT) and director of Eoan's productions between 1958 and 1962.

63   Helga Basel, also "Bassel", or "Uys" (1908-1969), German-South-African pianist, the mother of pianist Tessa Uys and satirist Pieter-Dirk Uys. She fled the Nazi regime in 1936 and settled in South Africa. She suffered from bipolar disorder and committed suicide in 1969.

Hard luck - on Monday I was to be in London. So I stalked out feeling grim and lousy and saw there was to be [a] piano recital at the University. Off I went but by the time I found the place (walking) the recital was just about over. However, no need to worry - by walking I managed to see something of the city and also a chance to exercise my Italian. Of course, I made great use of this and stopped every second Italian to ask "where I was" or "how to get there". Not that I always understood everything they replied (they speak at a fantastic speed) but I learned. Having failed in musical entertainment I then decided to go to see the *Hamlet* produced by [Franco] Zeffirelli[64] - the top Italian producer who also produced [Joan] Sutherland's[65] first and now-famous *Lucia* [*di Lammermoor*, by Donizetti]. An excellent production by all means. Very good actors, stagecraft to marvel and gape at and truly great directing. Towards the end of the play, Ophelia, one of the characters, has a mad scene. I have never seen or imagined any mad scene so well and exquisitely done - a real lesson. The performance started at 9.30 p.m. and finished just after 1.00 a.m.

Abroad one has to tip everybody - especially in theatres - almost beyond comprehension. My seat cost L 700 (about 7/6 [7 UK shillings and 6 pence]) which was right up under the ceiling; leaving your coat costs L 80 with a tip makes it L 100 and then you have to tip the usherette a percentage of the ticket cost. I feel quite sorry for the richer people who sit in the expensive seats.

Next morning, Sunday, I decided that I had had enough of Rome and thought I might have better luck with opera in Milan. So I trekked to the airways office and two hours later I was on my way to Milan. [On arrival] I left my suitcase at the large station where I had a chummy conversation with the porter. Then off, I ventured to find somewhere to stay. Suddenly, it occurred to me - "to hell with it, why not stay near La Scala" - and anyway, living in a rich place meant I could smoke my cigars. So I booked in at the hotel right next door to La Scala where all the singers like Leontyne Price[66] etc live, at the handsome rate of L 5000 per day with breakfast. This was great fun - I bathed to my heart's delight. You must remember that I had last bathed in Cape Town. So, of course, I needed no provocation. This was the procedure. I would go down-stairs for a drink then come back and have a bath, then I would go out and look around La Scala, come back to [the] hotel and bath - and so it went on. Anyway, my luck was out because it was Sunday and no performances at La Scala. The season opened the night before with Giulietta Simionato[67] in [Mascagni's] *Cavalleria* [*rusticana*] and Mirella Freni,[68] this new soprano making a name for herself, in *Amico Fritz*, another Mascagni opera. But as they say, third time lucky, I spotted a newspaper advertisement - an operatic recital in commemoration of Verdi's birth at 9.15 p.m. Good, I thought, just what I want. So at 5:00 I went out to get supper and to get there in time to buy a seat.

To do this I had to get a bus to go to another part of the town. What a wonderful experience to go on a Milanese bus. Everybody stands and all the buses are always full so you have to push your way in as well as out. What amazed me, was that nobody minded. There were women in the best of fur coats and high bouffant hair-styles in the middle of the squash and they weren't particularly perturbed nor were their hair-styles or clothes spoilt. I got to like these buses that I went on them almost as often as having a bath. Oh yes, the women dress

64   Franco Zeffirelli (1923-2019), Italian opera and film director.
65   Joan Sutherland (1926-2010), Australian soprano.
66   Leontyne Price (*1927), African-American soprano.
67   Giulietta Simionato (1910-2010), Italian mezzo-soprano.
68   Mirella Freni (1935-2020), Italian soprano.

very smartly and look very elegant and the men even more so, and the streets are always crowded – the population spend, or seem to at any rate, all their time on the streets – but it is wonderful.

Anyway, to get back to the concert. When I eventually found the place and having walked around in the cold for hours, I learnt that admission was by invitation only – miserable. Wanting to do nothing but die, I got on a bus and watched folk-dancing from Yugoslavia for a while and returned to the hotel where I saw the last act of [Puccini's *Madama*] *Butterfly* on television. Only now does this act make sense to me. You know all that music when Butterfly is not singing, well, Antonietta Stella[69] used all this music for her interpretation & dramatizing which was highly effective and convincing. I wish you could have seen her. I wish I could describe in detail but we will get technically involved. However, she worked in socks only – no shoes! And the child, Trouble,[70] had black hair and brown eyes. Anyway, I could not stay for the next performance in La Scala (as much as I would have like to) [...].

I got... into London as scheduled and booked into an hotel which I happily discovered was only two blocks from Didi[71] – though 2 tube stations. After a week I decided that I could no longer stay at the hotel (finance is running pretty low) and for another week I stayed with S. African friends on the other side of London, but as all my things were at Didi's I would have to take a tube (a quick ten-minute journey) to Didi's in order to brush my teeth. Then my friends departed for Amsterdam and I moved into a hostel at 11/- [11 shillings] per day. Now Didi and I found a flat which we hope to move into today or tomorrow. Lucky we were, because rooms are difficult to find unless you can pay 12-16 guineas a week.[72] Now at least, we have a place her father can move into when he comes.

I have been to one concert which cost 30/- for the seat – a big conductor, Otto Klemperer.[73] The place was packed and Klemperer as old as the hills dithered on stage with a walking stick and everybody went mad. I found it a strain watching this man who could be suffering of Parkinson's Disease, but he does surely produce wonderful sound – and what exquisite playing.

[Puccini's] *Tosca* was already completely sold out when I came, but we may get black market seats if we go to the actual performances. Callas[74] is the rave and very much reigning – those fortunate ones who heard and saw her recital earlier this year go into hysterics when they describe the performance. Operas at Covent Garden now are [Richard Strauss's] *The Rosenkavalier*, [Shostakovich's] *Katarina Ismailova*[75] and [Britten's] *Billy Budd*. Not very interesting so I have not been, though I did go and watched one act of [Tchaikovsky's ballet] *Swan Lake* last week.

Living here is fantastically and unbelievably expensive – I must get a job or I'll be penniless soon. I desperately want to go back to Milan and stay for a longer time and to learn Italian. I loved Milan best of all – much more to see and do.

69   Antonietta Stella (1929-2022), Italian soprano.
70   He is probably referring to Cio-Cio-San's child Dolore in Puccini's *Madama Butterfly*, whose name means "troubles" or "sorrow".
71   Didi Sydow, the daughter of Ismail and Carmen Sydow, had been a ballet dancer for the Eoan Group. The group provided her with a bursary to study at the Royal Ballet in London beginning in late 1962. See Roos (2018): 83. Jephtas had lived with the Sydows and knew Didi well. See his letter of 28 August 1967.
72   A guinea was equivalent to 21 shillings. See the explanations of currency in the section "Editorial approach and terminology" above.
73   Otto Klemperer (1885-1973), German conductor.
74   Maria Callas (1923-1977), Greek soprano.
75   The name given to the revised version of the opera *Lady Macbeth of Mtsensk*.

Didi is shouting to go out so for now enjoy yourselves. I miss you and all the singers – can you believe it. Write to the address I give because they will forward any mail in case we go to the Continent while Didi is on holiday.

Bye for now

Write soon – Gordon

OVERSEAS VISITOR'S CLUB

180, EARL'S COURT ROAD

LONDON. S.W.5.

P.S. Didi has just reminded me that the main purpose in writing to you was to tell you about some Jamaicans we recently met. […]

Both Didi and I thought and expected that the West Indians were people with natures and minds like our people – we were pleasantly shocked. First of all, they are much better bred, spoken and read than we could hope for. They have a fantastic command of language and whereas our people very often have difficulty in saying what they think merely because they have not a command of English nor Afrikaans, these people can present a logical and under-standable point of view with the utmost facility and ease. The family in case consisted of a mother and father, two sons (one of which is studying hotel managing) and a grandmother. Their living conditions are entirely different – a much more Westernized approach – a search for comfort and pleasant surroundings – rather a delightfully furnished living room than living in the kitchen as we do. Also there is not such a big gap between parent and child – the whole family enjoys a gin or whisky and together they would listen to swinging music and the entire family would make perceptive criticism of what they are hearing – the sort of criticism we leave to specialists – and they can do the same with the *Messiah* or a Brahms Concerto. I have heard this and these people are not even amateur musicians. While we were there, they discussed radiography, compared American and English economics.

Yes it is fantastic – Didi and I just marvelled. Perhaps if our people were less interested in skin colour and hair quality they could reach the same intellectual status – but will they!!!!

2

Overseas Visitors Club, 180, Earl's Court Road, London S.W.5 [United Kingdom]

Friday, 17 January [1964]

My dear May,

Your letter of this morning was the most pleasant surprise of the week. I had thought that perhaps you could not remember my surname. However, many thanks and what charming and amusing letters you write – must be a hidden talent of yours. Anyway, I am trying to be very good and instead of paying you back with your own coins, I am answering practically imme-diately. But I had better not talk too soon because I am still on page one. It takes me hours to write letters and it is about 2.00 a.m. now. So if anything does not make sense to you, you must guess that I am falling asleep.

Tomorrow Mr. Sydow arrives and I hope that it will not be too cold. At the week-end it snowed – none at Christmas, though. It was lovely and [I] spent a lot of time walking in the snow. Didi thought I was going mad because I braved it in my shirt sleeves and sandals – very courageous, I agree. Today the sun was shining ever so meekly but by English standards it was a glorious day – brrrrr!!

My English has become worse since I have come here and though I am pleased therefore that very few people have recognized me as South African merely because they think that I have no South African accent (they expect me to say, 'I em from Sout Efrica, men' – do you get it). Everybody, especially in cafes insist that I am Continental – mostly Spanish, though sometimes Italian with the result that I am almost obliged to speak in such a manner – eet ees ver-r-ry cold-d-d to-day-ee. Quite funny, but I am enjoying it. On the other hand, my English (and Afrikaans) swearing vocabulary has improved and enlarged beyond recognition. Of course, I lose no opportunity to holler the most expressive Afrikaans whenever I feel the need to. My favourite target has been the weather – of course, nobody understands, but I get tremendous satisfaction out of shouting "poep-hol" [arsehole] or such a word when walking in the cold. [...]

Oh I forgot to mention. Didi and I moved into apartments about a week ago. The flat we found was much too smelly and dirty so now we found two adjacent rooms – one is a smallish bedroom and [the] other is a sitting room which can sleep two and it has [a] television and radio which is more than most. At any rate, it is clean and doesn't smell. We share the kitchen and bathroom with 3 residents on the same floor – 1st floor. It is amazing but the standard of living here is low and the cost of living is exceedingly high.

As I had anticipated last night, it is now Saturday 5.30 p.m. Mr. Sydow has arrived and more or less settled in and is at present resting. He has been intrigued by the television and has spent the greater part of the afternoon watching the Saturday afternoon wrestling.[76]

Needless to say we were overjoyed to see him. Unfortunately Didi has been put to bed by her doctor and has been for the past week, so she was unable to meet him at the air-port. Thank heavens it was not too cold. Said Mr. Sydow as he came through the gates "It is not cold, what lovely weather". The flight he said was pleasant and very comfortable and both Didi and I reciprocate your love and kisses.

But to get back where I have left off. Callas is the talk of the town at the moment – she still reigns supreme in spite of Sutherland. She opens on Tuesday evening and is to sing 6 performances of *Tosca* between then and 5 February. All the performances were already sold out long before I arrived here but thanks to some engineering on the part of Johaar[77] I managed to get one seat only for 5 February. I can hardly wait and only hope that she doesn't get laryngitis or something like that. I implored Johaar to get me to a rehearsal and I would have gone this morning if Mr. Sydow had not arrived – such a pity. As a compromise Johaar spent an entire afternoon with me in the artists' canteen backstage hoping that Callas would appear but my luck was out. Apparently she does often, when rehearsing, have something to eat there. However, Cillario[78] who is conducting the Callas performances did appear. Backstage everybody talks and breathes Callas and yet, one realizes from the stage chatter that Callas is but human and a person who does eat, sleep, etc. Eavesdropping on two stage hands who were having lunch at the table next door I heard –

"Madame (as they refer to her) will be in on Saturday morning".

---

76 Television was not introduced in South Africa until 1976.
77 The South African ballet dancer Johaar Mosaval (*1928) moved to England in 1951 and was a principal dancer at Sadler's Wells at the time that Jephtas wrote this letter.
78 Carlo Felice Cillario (1915–2007), Argentinian-born Italian conductor.

"Of course, she will be singing down but she is so nice when she sings down and so cleverly done, too!"

Of course, there is antagonism as well. Two gentlemen were very annoyed because "whenever Callas is around everything revolves around her and the management could hardly care less about anything else". Apparently a call was changed from 9.30 to 11.00 to suit Callas and these gentlemen turned up at 9.30 because they had not been informed of the change. I have met and seen several of the soloists of the Opera Company, like Geraint Evans,[79] while they were having their lunch. What impressed me greatly was the no-fuss, no-compliment attitude in the Opera House.

I had hoped to see much opera but Covent Garden is only offering *Der Rosenkavalier*, *Billy Budd*, *Tosca* and [Verdi's] *Rigoletto* during my stay. The 1st two I have seen and though I may not have completely liked what I saw, mainly because I am not completely familiar and conversant with those works. But I have learnt a lot and it has been a thrilling experience. The Sadler's Wells are at present doing *Carmen* which I must make an effort to see esp[ecially] now that I have some money. [...]

Two nights ago I saw Schwarzkopf[80] at a Richard Strauss Centenary Concert. She sang the closing scene from *Capriccio*, one of R. Strauss's operas. She appeared in [a] costume lent by the Vienna State Opera complete with wig and all - a beautiful costume. You know I have always thought of Schw[arzkopf] in terms of purity in singing - never a bum note, never flunking on top notes and always producing a ravishing sound. However, I have since had to change my opinion - perhaps it was an off-night vocally. She does not have a big voice and perhaps she sounded forced at times because of the large orchestra (150 players) and the mass of orch[estral] sound she had to penetrate. But on the other hand we assume that she does not know of any orch[estra] as large as the Cape Town one. Very German [as] a singer and produces many pure nasal sounds which to my ears are not very pleasant. She flunked many notes esp[ecially] top ones but she also produced many good ones. On a few occasions I even noticed that she breathed by jerking her shoulders. Her stage presence is what impressed me most. During the very long orch[estral] intro, although she did not visibly use her body, I could notice that she was entirely in the music, living every sound and visualizing in her mind's eye every movement she does when on the operatic stage. It was quite wonderful. The aria ends with another long orch[estral] interlude and in the opera the Countess has left the stage. Here again she stood so still that she invoked the impression of not being there. The ovation was fantastic - perhaps because she is Schw[arzkopf] or perhaps they thought she was good. The applause was wine to her and she knows how to take it. The audience surged towards the stage and she accepted kisses from the public members with perfect charm & ease even if she did not expect anybody to embrace her.

Hullo there!

It is Sunday and the time roundabout 11.30 p.m. So permit me to continue this lengthy epistle. To come back to Schwarzkopf. I managed to get within six feet of her during the surge towards the stage - I could almost count her teeth when smiling. She is even more beautiful from near and sports the most ravishing and exquisite complexion - I suppose she can afford it.

---

79   Geraint Evans (1922-1992), Welsh bass-baritone.
80   Elisabeth Schwarzkopf (1915-2006), German-British soprano.

We have this evening listened to the [Eoan] tape. As you have surmised it does speak for itself, but I was overjoyed to hear some familiar voices even though some of it is pretty embarrassing.

But let's start at the beginning – the chorus sounds feeble and somewhat inaudible but as both you and Mr. Sydow pointed out, they were very few in number. Alie[81] spared me the embarrassment of having to listen to the applause given to the various artists or should I say, items, but the little bits I did hear sounded thoroughly enthusiastic. And audience enthusiasm may well be regarded as an important feature. However, I find it difficult to analyse whether the applause is just complimentary because of the cause and circumstances or whether they really enjoyed what they had just heard. I wonder.

Pat's[82] *Ernani* [by Verdi] sounds good – I dare not use too complimentary adjectives. The voice sounds full and easy but this feeling is lost during Musetta's Waltz Song which I found both forced and industrious – far too much obvious effort. The art of good vocalization, I imagine, is the ability to disguise the effort required to make and produce a sound. Yes, I think that she was pushing too much and consequently singing slightly out of pitch. But then I found that every-body with only two exceptions, had more intonation trouble than usually. It was good to hear the soprano in the quartet for a change. Of course, as regards the musical observance I was appalled but considering that she had no *Rigoletto* score, never really studied the part and that she had stepped in on the last minute I found it admirable – venturingly, I would say, excellent.

Vera's[83] voice sounds more than sumptuous but again pitch trouble especially in the "Ai nostri monti" which was somewhat painful to listen to. Vera again would profit greatly if she would make more effort when singing esp[ecially] top notes. I found her Adalgisa [in Bellini's *Norma*] appealing but wonder why she sings it like a coloratura soprano and in the other arias makes sounds like a basso buffo. The entire duet I found much easier to listen to than the previous version. Your Norma is cute and charming – but I think Norma ought to be brutal and cruel. You make her sensitive, kind and tender and not without effect. Thank God you sing E flat rather than E natural in the cadenza.

That Gabriels[84] got through "Vesti la giubba"[85] without any major mishaps and anxious moments was a relief. He sounds good and the voice free but sometimes the tempos [were] laboured and ruined his best moments. Jimmy[86] tries to sing like a bass and probably would be successful if the quantity of voice and physical stature were not against him. A rather embarrassing top C which made me shudder from sheer exhaustion. I am sorry that none of Ruth's[87] arias are not on the tape because I wonder what I would think of her singing after not having heard it for some time. You know, now I feel I can listen to the singers with a fresh approach and perceptively. Working with them all the time one gets used to certain mannerisms and vocal eccentricities, objectionable or not, and does not hear the vocal sound in the same way as those who do not hear the same singers quite so often.

I can't say that I like this "Miserere"[88] mainly because I find no point or logical reasoning behind the performance. I would say there are 3 facets to consider, namely (a) Leonora

---

81   Alie Sydow, the adopted son of Ismail and Carmen Sydow, was probably recording the performance.
82   Patricia van Graan, Eoan soprano.
83   Vera Gow, Eoan soprano.
84   Joseph Gabriels, Eoan's most famous tenor soloist. Gabriels moved to Milan in 1967 and made his debut at the Metropolitan Opera House in New York in February 1971. Roos (2018): 140-143.
85   Canio's aria in Leoncavallo's *Pagliacci*.
86   James Momberg, Eoan tenor.
87   Ruth Goodwin, Eoan soprano. Goodwin had by this time left the Group.
88   From Verdi's *Il trovatore*. Jephtas is commenting on Abrahamse's singing.

giving vent to her suffering, (b) the death-drone of the male chorus [and] (c) Manrico repenting and calling for Leonora but still very much the hero. To my mind these facets are very much opposed and together they form a unity rather than forming a unity with everybody singing in this same manner. You know the bit you sing – "Di te, di te scordarmi" sounds like a Viennese Waltz from [Johann Strauss's] *Fledermaus*. Yes granted it is in 3 time but, if I remember correctly, it is in 6/8 or 12/8 and not 3/4. And there is a difference. But it is not your fault. Sorry, it seems I need another book. [...]

I shall raise the Union Jack when you are able to execute the trill in "D'amor" starting with 3 notes, a trill and then a turn of four notes instead of the painful wobble we have to contend with. Admittedly it is infinitely better than Tebaldi[89] who simply does not bother to trill, but however, it is still objectionable. Somehow the aria sounds uncomfortable because the compromise between you and the conductor [i.e. Joseph Manca[90]] does not quite come off. It will teach us never to fight verbally about a singing matter with him because it only aggravates the eventual performance. If only he was more rational. But let's not get involved in that unpleasant business. When I started listening to the tape during *Ernani* I suddenly found myself listening carefully to the orchestra and for a moment I thought that here was going to be some dynamic support but, it lasted for one second only. The orchestra does not support the phrase leading to the top C (in "D'amor") and then your desired effect is ruined. But why this scooping up to some notes and this German guttural production in the middle of one of (perhaps?) the most Italian of Italian arias. "Ritorna vincitor"[91] sounds dramatic and histrionic – jolly good for you?!! [...] The contrast between the different section [and] changes in mood need to be strongly marked and exaggerated. Only if the performer exaggerates and blows everything up beyond normality does the listener perceive any difference. We must bear in mind that our listeners are not specialized but rather musically illiterate. You try very hard and admirably to get this difference but the accompaniment lets you down again – not only as far as tempi, which are in fact, a matter of opinion, are concerned but also orchestral colour. How exquisite and dynamically exciting your "Ritorna vincitor" could be if the orchestra gave as much as you. But still, we can't have everything. Can we? [...]

To cheer you up – Last night I heard a tape of a *Lucia* broadcast of Sutherland. She does not sound nearly as wonderful as on the records where conditions probably are ideal – she can do things over & over until she gets what she wants, microphones are placed where her voice sounds to best advantage and probably has an echo chamber as well. The voice sounds almost common-place and not nearly as resonant as we hear on the records. She at times sounds horribly dull and so frightfully English. I had suspected that something like this would happen.

I only hope that Callas does not let me down. In a few minutes I hope to go down to Covent Garden to try for her autograph. Her first performance is this evening and they usually come to the theatre in the afternoon.

Another day has passed. It is Wed[nesday] and Madame has made her appearance – the morning papers are full of raves – I feel so pleased and happy for her, don't you? My ambition to see her has now become an obsession – You['ve] never seen anything like it – I run about in an absolutely neurotic state and wish it was the fifth of Feb. today.

---

89   Renata Tebaldi (1922-2004), Italian soprano.
90   Joseph Manca (1908-1985), South African musician, music director and conductor of the Eoan Group. See Chapter 1.3, The Eoan Group.
91   Aria from Verdi's *Aida*.

Hoping to see *Rigoletto* with Anna Moffo[92] and [Verdi's] *Aida* with [Galina] Vishnevskaya,[93] and also the *Golden Girl from the West* - Puccini. Tried to get into [Bizet's] *Carmen* but no luck.

No Callas autograph yet - but I must keep on trying.

Today I have a shocking cold - rather unpleasant.

This morning I went out to buy all the newspapers and returned with about ten - and those are not the lot. Since I have been devouring what they say about Callas - [I'll] tell you about it when we are together which isn't too long as you say.

Love - kiss Trudy & Wendy.

G.

3

Overseas Visitors Club, 180, Earl's Court Road, London S.W.5 [United Kingdom]

Friday, 31 January [1964]

My dear May,

Last night by sheer determination I got in at Covent Garden and saw *Tosca*. This I would easily describe as being the most thrilling and exciting experience of my life. But to start at the beginning and hope you are not bored by my lengthy epistle.

Last Monday was the 3rd *Tosca* performance of the season and I just could not stand the suspense of having to wait until the 5th [of February] before I could see my famous lady. So with much determination and borrowed money I arrived at Covent Garden at 12 noon on this day, only to be confronted by a notice reading as follows "There are 42 standing tickets at 14/- each which will be sold at 7 p.m. on the day of the performance on the basis of one ticket per person in the queue". I looked down the road and saw a queue of at least 50 persons each hoping to get in. So taking my courage in both hands I joined the rest of the crowd and [was] given No. 64. After 7 hours standing the doors opened and the 1st 42 were admitted and the rest hopefully waited for return tickets. By this time the queue had increased in magnitude, loquacious and fighting fans and hysteria. In the meantime I was, in the course of order nearing the fatal door which would decide my destiny for Monday evening. Eventually I was 3rd from the door and uttered a quick prayer to the Madonna. Just then the commissioner returned and I armed myself with the borrowed £10 prepared to buy the returned ticket he was bound to offer. Instead he uttered in a large voice "Ladies and Gentlemen, there is nothing more for tonight. You are wasting your time by waiting. Next performance is on Thursday". I could have cried but I was not the only one; several were howling their eyes out and the most doleful atmosphere infected the disappointed crowd.

So with twice as much determination I got to the Opera House at *6.45am.* on Thursday morning and joined the queue at No. 35 assured of a standing ticket. This queue started on Wednesday at 2.00 p.m. Anyway, what was left to do was to sit on the pavement for the next 12 hours the only [consolation] being the assurance of seeing Callas. But 12 hours is a long time and although the sun made an occasional appearance it was nevertheless cold and at about

---

92   Anna Moffo (1932-2006), American soprano.
93   Galina Vishnevskaya (1926-2012), Russian soprano.

11 a.m. my feet were like blocks of ice. The only remedy was to nip into the pub opposite for a quick brandy. This became a routine and after every hour I went along and downed a brandy. With the stuff costing 3/- a tot, needless to say, it was an expensive day – but believe me it was absolutely necessary. Actually it worked quite well because the person in front of me kept my place while I went on my frequent drinking spree. Of course, I kept his place when he found it necessary to do likewise. At 5.15 [p.m.] I went for my penultimate drink and spotted a group of people hanging around the stage door. I needed no invitation to investigate. Yes, you guessed correctly, they were waiting for Callas. After ½ hour, at exactly 5.45 [p.m.] a large Rolls Royce moved in right next to the pavement and the 25 or so people lauded the occupants with "Brava". Chaperoned heavily, Callas emerged from the back seat and [was] ushered in by her chaperone. She was completely self-possessed and dressed in a fur hat & coat. She flashed a smile – the crowd went mad and now shouted "Brava Maria" – Maria – Hearing her name she half-turned and smiled and was gone. What we spent ½ hour waiting for was over in exactly 2 seconds. If only the male chaperone was not so tall and fat I might have been able to see more of her. However, I was happy with a glimpse – of course, she looked beautiful. But then I am prejudiced!

To come to the actual performance. The best singing came from the tenor, Renato Cioni.[94] This singer has sung a lot with Sutherland in the same way as Di Stefano[95] and Callas. He hasn't a large voice like Gabriels say, but it helps because he can therefore sing the most beautiful sotto and mezzo-voce. His top register comes with great ease and [he] did some brilliant phrasing. It was very intelligent singing.

Tito Gobbi[96] sang Scarpia and frankly disappointing. He has tremendous histrionic ability but I don't like the way he sings – very white sounds which to me are much too non-masculine for a baritone. I found him very ugly – looks like a fat farmer. Also as he appears on stage mostly with Tosca one's attention is riveted to the star and perhaps it is because I have a Fiasconaro-Scarpia image. I don't know.

The production by Zeffirelli is magnificent. He is extremely imaginative and has a fantastic eye for detail. I have now seen two of his productions and I have great admiration for his work. On Tuesday evening we hope to see his *Rigoletto* with Anna Moffo singing Gilda.

And now for Callas – she was everything I desire and wish for in a singer. Vocally she is having a fantastic battle and sings almost purely on technique. Her top notes wobble so much that it sounds like an excellent trill – anything above A flat is fatal. But more of this later. Her first entrance could so easily have been greeted with applause because her appearance is what the entire auditorium waits for after curtain-rise, but the audience are immediately attracted by her intensity and literally forget to cheer. Callas did not act, in fact she was not Callas but Tosca. How she has the ability to [evoke] such an impression is almost uncanny. She also has a fantastic eye for detail. She immediately portrays Tosca as the jealous lover, a woman conceited and vane. Her vanity she gets across by almost persistently putting the scarf on her head into place – you know the way women finger their hair. When Cavaradossi sings about her beautiful eyes after she questioned the colour of the eyes in the painting, you can see her entire body loving the compliments and thriving on it. Her acting is not "grand-dame, prima-donna" in manner, but very realistic – almost childish. Very little of what I thought was true operatic tradition. Large and big gestures were used only when absolutely necessary which

---

94   Renato Cioni (1929-2014), Italian tenor.
95   Giuseppe Di Stefano (1921-2008), Italian tenor.
96   Tito Gobbi (1913-1984), Italian baritone.

gave it more meaning and impact. In both acts she wore an Empire-hive dress with a long following train - pink chiffon with an orange shawl in Act I and red velvet in Act 2. She knows how to wear her clothes; for instance in the last act she wears a black, wide cloak over the red dress. She sweeps across the stage like a dress model. You know, I always notice that actresses avoid mishaps by preventing them. Let me try and explain - when an actress wearing a long frock prepares to walk or run she almost instinctively lifts her dress so as not to trip. But very often, say when angry, a woman would not think about her dress and might almost trip. This Callas did excellently - she plunged ahead and if she trips - well she is just going to trip - such attack. Also when angry she sits herself down on a chair, but she doesn't sit prettily but instead her legs are wide apart. In the 3rd act the tenor again compliments her hands - she listens for a while, walks up to him and teasingly slapping his cheek obviously expressing the joy she was deriving from the situation. Towards the end of Act II she only thinks of killing him (Scarpia) when he says "Tosca finalmente mia". You can see how revolting she finds him & the thought of having to sleep with him. It so suddenly dawns on her to commit a murder that not even she, Tosca, realizes what she has done until she sees the blood on the knife. Before throwing herself off the parapet she has to run up a long flight of stairs while being pursued. She trips, rolls down the stairs falls, runs. And does she run and sing.

She has a small voice but because of her technique can produce big sounds by darkening the voice. The difference between the different registers is very uneven - I sometimes found it amusing. Lots of chest - from the stomach. When she shouts "Assassino" or a succession of "Muoris" at Scarpia she really shouts without thinking of having to preserve her throat for the next phrase.

"Vissi d'arte" was for most part sung standing up - actually she was supporting herself on the back of a chair. No sofa. I now see what context this aria is in. She sings it with practically no over-emotionalism and only during the latter half when she sits on the chair does she make it desperate. The high B flat is sung sitting down - a very embarrassing wobble. The A flat wobbled went out of tune and consequently the G wobbled and moved further from the required pitch. No attempt to make a diminuendo from A flat to G. At the end a long pause and crescendo on the "ri" of "rimuneri". Well it makes two people who have extreme difficulty with this damned aria - May Abrahamse and Callas. Well you can't have everything cream and honey.

Her curtain calls are perfectly timed - she does not take a call until the applause convinces her of the necessity. She appears very relaxed, and almost arrogant - she just stands and looks at the audience as if saying "Klap julle donders[97] - Come to my feet". After several minutes she would lower her head only and each time would curtsy a little lower. She also is coy - she flung a kiss at the audience and burst into laughter at her actions. When the conductor tripped over the train of her dress, she made no attempt to rescue him or the dress, but burst into childish laughter while he was freeing himself.

After the performance the street outside was packed with about 500 fans all shouting, "Brava Maria" when she got into her car while she smiled and blew kisses. Magnificent.

If I write another page I won't be able to pay for the postage.

Bye for now.

Practise please - slow trills.

Gordon.

P.S. We'll make a Callas of you yet!!

---

97   Afrikaans: "Clap, you bastards".

O.V.C. [Overseas Visitors Club], 180, Earl's Court Road, London S.W.5 [United Kingdom]

Wednesday, 5 February [1964]

My dear May,

This must [be] a good week for you with the lucky stars because if I remember correctly I have just two days ago sent you one. But as a special effort this comes as a reply to your most entertaining letters of yesterday. I shall have to write as small as I can because there is so much I want to say and so little paper and [I am] as usual stone broke.

I have 10 minutes ago returned from Callas so please compare this to what I have written earlier.

This time I sat in the gods up against the ceiling. Callas was magnificent – I can hardly imagine her being anything but magnificent. Her acting just bowls one over even during the most agonizing and painful vocal emissions. But let me try and relate the sort of acting she does. She often clasps her mouth with her hands when afraid or horrified. Her hands are extremely expressive but her entire body, face, eyes and even lips are under complete control and co-ordination. She uses loud, audible breaths often to indicate sorrow and pain – in "Vissi d'arte" for instance when she sings "Nell'ora del dolore" – she also uses it but much more loudly and a deeper breath when she addresses Scarpia in bitter anger. Whereas on her gramophone recordings she does not make extraneous noises like sobbing and laughing, she certainly does when on stage. When she sings "io piango" on a long, slow phrase in [the] first act she makes a terrific crescendo on "go" building up the tension and then bursts into spontaneous crying and sobbing. But she does not put her face in her hands like most sopranos would but instead fidgets around in her bag for a handkerchief to dab her eyes – especially when she suddenly realizes that there are other people in the church. The scene after she has killed Scarpia and she has to put the candles beside his body and the crucifix on his chest, she breathes in short, audible gasps of terror. In fact, she starts breathing like that from the moment she realizes she is a murderess. And she doesn't dash for the candles immediately like most Toscas do, but being fear-stricken her first impetus is to run away. She runs to the bed to collect her gloves and bag and when she runs to a chair to collect her stole she suddenly stops and I could actually see what she was thinking – her Roman Catholic upbringing – she drops her personal possessions when she remembers God and rushes around trying to blow out the candles. She takes the last two candles and moves swiftly over to Scarpia but just as she is two feet away from him she remembers he is dead. All humans are scared of dead bodies – she approaches him slowly and scared stiff and if she could run away she gladly would but her religion takes the upper hand and she must therefore deposit the candles. As she puts down each candle I could see her whole body trembling. She ran about looking for this crucifix and she drops this on his chest almost without looking – too scared. When she drops it she lets out a deep scream of horror. Having satisfied her religious conscience she runs like a madman to find her things and makes for the door. And during all this there were gasps of terror continuously – fantastic.

Before she kills him he is writing and she finds she must do something to arrest her attention even if only for a minute. Her eye falls on a glass of wine on Scarpia's supper table. She makes for this glass and drinks – but she doesn't trust Scarpia for a moment so she turns around to see where he is in the room, with the glass still in her mouth. [T]hen I noticed her short-sightedness – she lowers her glass very slowly with both hands holding the glass. Her supporting hand reached the table but the glass travelled below the table level – she had misjudged the distance. Also at the 1st performance I saw, I again noticed this. At the very end of the opera she is pursued by the police. When she realizes this she runs around in circles in a panic and has to make for the stairs to jump off the parapet. Well on this occasion she ran slap bang into the arms of her pursuer but being very quick thinking she pushed him over (really hard) and ran in the other direction where she found the steps. This evening this did not happen.

She did put in one or two more "Marios" after she discovers her lover has really been shot. The shriek she lets off when she makes this discovery is really telling. There were many things in this evening's performance which were not there last week & vice versa.

It would seem that every performance of the same role differs greatly in detail. She does faithfully adhere to the producer's basic moves so that there are no accidents but the details vary. She does not beforehand work out a detailed set of movements which would appear studied and not spontaneous. She seems to have a perfect knowledge of the character – she makes a detailed account of nationality, physical and mental make-up. She discovers what makes Tosca tick: how Tosca thinks and when she is on stage she is Tosca and thinks like Tosca. It is difficult to explain but that is what I make of it.

The voice itself is not big – not in the sense that I imagined but then when you consider that all the singers at Covent Garden have to sing through the orchestral sound of at least, I counted, 120 players playing full out it makes things somewhat different. We [i.e. Eoan] with only 50 or so musicians in the orchestra should have no problems (?). A great deal of her sounds are chest notes and from the stomach – I could feel it – dark chesty sounds which I adore. So I'm sorry to inform you that this year you will have to learn to sing from your stomach. I have always been mad about such sounds and the fact that Callas does them so well and effectively has merely increased my interest to no mean end. She uses and manipulates several different qualities of sound to expose and emphasize her points. Very, very white sounds for moments of childishness, flirting moments and for moments when she sings of love she makes the most tender of sounds in a peculiar "veiled" tone. This is mostly in her middle register – the note is neither dark nor white but covered and has the most stunning effect. She never sings the same note twice in the same way if the context is different. Everything takes so much meaning and even if your Italian is very bad you immediately understand what she is saying and why. For instance, I never knew what "Ma falle gli occhi neri" meant but now I know it's "but make her eyes black". She is perfectly free of mannerisms like stepping back on high notes or wriggling her hips when singing semi-quavers. No, everything is governed by the dramatic situation and if she has been walking up-stage for some or other reason and she has to sing she makes no attempt to turn around and sing to the audience – she sings facing upstage very often and she is heard. Apparently she is the only singer who does this. I am rather in favour of this because I get very cross when singers obviously turn their heads to the audience when they have a singing cue. What also struck me was her spontaneous singing – you know the second act where Tosca merely sings "Ah" then nothing for 12 bars and another "Ah" going higher in pitch. Now most sopranos would start getting ready to sing the next "Ah" as soon as they finished the previous one. But with Callas you can see it only occurs to her to sing at the very moment she has to. It is amazing how she manages to fill her music when she is not singing and with other singers you can see how they wait for their next cue.

Her "Vissi d'arte" was as bad as last time if not worse - she had to cut her high B flat short because it became unmanageable, but her body was working hard so one didn't mind. She tried a diminuendo at the end - it didn't come off. I could write a book about her vocal faults and difficulties but they don't matter because she has the knack of incorporating her faults to inflict the drama. If she were any other singer singing as badly (as opposed to bel canto) she would in all probability have been booed.

Her curtain calls - there were calls after each act but these she took almost reluctantly for fear of becoming Callas & not Tosca.

At the end only the 3 principals took calls - Cioni, the tenor, Callas and Cillario the conductor. Then the tenor by himself. The curtain would then be raised, but she keeps the audience waiting. She doesn't take a single call unless she is sure they want her. She walks on nobly and just stands like a Greek goddess looking at the auditorium for several, long minutes. The essence of dignity. About 20 lilies came down from the gallery and landed around her - and now she lowered her head only - a posy of flowers landed near her feet. She looked at it surprised, dropped down and gracefully lifted it up, looked at it, toyed with it and raised it to her breast. The audience went mad. All this time the commissioner was waiting to hand her the bouquets and when she saw him she jogged her shoulder in surprise, laughed almost child-ishly and took the bouquets. At this point flowers came pouring on the stage from all sides of the auditorium - a thrilling moment. Within minutes she was surrounded by flowers - little bou-quets, single flowers. She chose this moment to drop into a semi-curtsey and still the flowers came raining down on her. While she was in her curtsey they landed on her head, her back - it was fantastically exciting. She gently removed those flowers which remained on her body when [she] again stood erect, kissed them, fondled them. But she is not selfish - she stretched her arm indicating her two colleagues - they joined her and she stooped down to pick up flowers to give to them. Of course, when they saw this, they both stooped down as well for flowers to give to her but she would not have their flowers - she got in first and gave each a posy - charming.

After the second act when Gobbi took his final curtain calls she dropped him a low curtsey to express her gratitude and to indicate that the applause was for him.

But to get back to the end - eventually she was blowing a kiss or two to the raving audience - but she was always flanked by tenor and conductor.

I suspect that she is really shy of applause - because whatever she did, did not strike me as from her heart - I could almost sense her wishing that it was all over.

However, it [gives] me great pleasure to tell you that an idol does not have clay feet but feet of gold. "Brava Maria" I repeat after the audience. My only wish was that you could have been here. Now to get on to answering your letter [...]

Callas's autograph - not a chance. She doesn't wear glasses in public and therefore can-not see a thing. I tried to take her picture as I got quite close to her, but the crowd was so restless I couldn't hold the camera still for long enough. She is dark skinned (as compared to local residents), has black hair and a long nose - she looks in real life just like the picture on the wall in my room. By the way, I am still waiting for that picture of yours - please, I must put it up near Callas the moment I get back! promise!!! Thank Trudy and Wendy for the messages. Ask Trudy if she wants chocolates with centres or with brandy or rum. Dear Wendy - I wish I had the money to buy a house and scooter. I have just bought two more books on Callas and I am stone-broke. In desperation I have had to write to my mother for money as much as I hated it. I have been resisting the temptation [of] buying records but I can't hold out much longer - my resistance diminishes every time I pass a record shop.

The concert now being the 25ᵗʰ April gives us more time but not very much.[98] But we must be thankful [for] small mercies. What distresses me is having to sing "popular arias" - perhaps I must avoid fights with Dr. Manca for diplomatic relationships - don't you think. I have a few ideas but let's discuss them when we are together.

I hope *Showboat*[99] is going well and I do hope to be back in time for it. *San Maratto*[100] sounds a good idea. I don't know the work at all. What is the new oratorio to be - the Puccini mass. No, I don't think so because it is for tenor, baritone and bass - no soprano.

I've heard about Gigi [i.e. Gregorio Fiasconaro] - I was expecting a resignation from him and I don't really blame him. I am disappointed about his pettiness but like you I have a soft spot for him. [...]

One of the notices in our lavatory - "Here we must all come to do those things which have to be done, but before you go one more thing. Lift the seat, use the brush, pull the chain and shut the door."

No more paper, love - Gordon

5

Paris, Thursday, 27 February [1964]

My dear May -

Thank you so much for your very interesting (and entertaining) letter of the 15ᵗʰ. But before divulging my latest activities, permit me to answer your letter.

Callas - I still cannot forget her performance and every subsequent performances of opera (*Rigoletto* and *Aida*) I kept on wondering how she would have done it. Often, some little detail of her acting or how she sang a certain phrase would suddenly occur to me. Needless to say, my preoccupied humming in the bath and the street has enhanced a great deal of the Puccini opera. Damage, as you say, has been the result of her singing mixed-up roles, but coming to think of it now, she has always had a wobble. Listen to the recording you have of her singing "Ah! fors'è lui", "Qui la voce", "The Liebestod".[101]

This particular recording was made very early in her career for as you know, she only sang Wagner at the start of her career and never again. To me it seems that the art of opera singing can be divided into two sections - (a) beautiful singing, that is, making smooth and pure vocal sound - in fact, bel canto. Therefore this interpreter will have little cohesion between sound and action because the drama has changing emotions: or else he or she will make no attempt at acting. The latter seems the case, in my opinion, with most opera in England and especially English singers.

---

98   A concert to be given by the Eoan Group after Jephtas's return to South Africa in mid-March 1964.
99   The Eoan Group choir took part in a production of the musical *Showboat* by Jerome Kern and Oscar Hammerstein in the Alhambra Theatre in Cape Town in March 1964. This production, by the Johannesburg Operatic and Dramatic Society, was touring the country and required a choir representing African-American workers. It was one of the very few productions in which the Eoan Group participated that was not under Joseph Manca's control. See Roos (2018): 102.
100   Manca composed an operetta, *San Maratto*, in 1932 (when he was 24 years old) that was performed in the same year with the Cape Town Municipal Orchestra under the direction of William Pickerill. See Malan (1984). In later years, the Eoan Group choir sang parts of this work.
101   From Verdi's *La traviata*, Bellini's *I Puritani* and Wagner's *Tristan und Isolde* respectively.

(b) Performing with equal emphasis on the vocal side (and here I include the musical side) and the verse – the drama. Therefore, in this category there is no beautiful singing. Anyway, not in the sense of bel canto – and Callas I place in this category – but then I am prejudiced. She is very slim figured – you'll have to go on a severe diet to match her biological curves. It is difficult to judge her height especially when looking down on her. She must be of medium height because there was no obvious difference between her height and the other singers. Incidentally, she wore high-heeled shoes – not stiletto, but period. But today, I saw a picture of her taken with another woman and she appears quite tall. This article (today's newspaper) says that she will marry Onassis if the Vatican and Pope give their approval – she was married to Meneghini by Italian and Catholic rites. Otherwise, the article continues, Callas will be "Miss". She does "drop" characterization at curtain call – I may have led you to understand otherwise. It is difficult to really describe her curtain calls – she doesn't appear vivacious, bubbling and effervescent like Schwarzkopf but does project some warmth and remains very dignified though somewhat reluctant. I think it takes time to "drop" characterization for her, because she does become more relaxed as the calls increase.

Showboat will have opened by the time you get this. You must be thriving on the "no-responsibility" kick. Any professional jealousy – I'm only pulling your leg, of course. I can well imagine what the music is like because these American musicals are all written in the same sort of way. *Secretly*, I must admit that I care very little for musicals because I find the singing-dialogue very often illogical. But this is a personal whim – musical singing and work is excellent experience for opera singers and especially aspirant or would-be opera singers. [...]

I sense that the discreet note regarding your choice of arias is a "dig" in some direction (?) So perhaps under the circumstances you should study "Quando me'n vò"[102] and "O mio babino caro"*!!!*[103] It would make the choice more popular than can ever be hoped for. Actually, I had thought of several things you should or could study – but obscure [ones] like Spontini's *La vestale*. What about looking at "Madre, pietosa Vergine" from [Verdi's] *Forza del destino* or the "Morrò" from [Verdi's] *Un ballo [in] maschera*. Then there's still "Qui Radamès verrà.... O patria mia".[104] (How are your top Cs?) Anyway, let me know what arias are to be studied.

Yes, I have heard about *Carmen*[105] – but whether it will happen is another matter. Who is the proposed Carmen? [...]

Mr. Sydow's Labarang[106] was pleasant and very interesting. He tells me that the Mosque was so full (in fact, it is a converted house) that hundreds had to stand outside in the wet and mud. Most of these people knelt on newspapers and he was very touched when a young student took off his overcoat and laid it in the mud as a praying mat for him (Mr. Sydow). Further, Didi and I arranged to meet him at some people for lunch. Something went wrong in the arrangements and we thought that he had got lost. But lo and behold, at 5.00 p.m. he rolls up in a car ever so calm and nonchalant – he teamed up with some others and went visiting other Moslem families! Bless him!

As you may have noticed – I have left London. Actually the three of us got on a train and went down to Barcelona (Spain) for 3 days and we have just this morning arrived in Paris until

---

102 Aria from Puccini's *La bohème*.
103 Aria from Puccini's *Gianni Schicchi*.
104 From *Aida* by Verdi.
105 Eoan performed Bizet's *Carmen* in 1965 while on tour through the Republic of South Africa.
106 The end of Ramadan, more commonly called Eid, which took place this year while Sydow (a Muslim) was visiting Didi and Jephtas in London.

the end of the week. Then we shall be going back to London before coming home. Actually, I don't think I am going back to London, but rather on to Milan.

Spain is a country after my own heart. As a matter of fact, we all fell in love with Barcelona almost instantly after setting foot down. The town is large by our standards and it is filled with Gothic and Mediaeval architecture – very large, colossal buildings, very ornate and full of detail. But Spain is a relatively poor country judging from the currency only – 1 peseta is valued at 1½d; but each peseta consists of 100 centimos. You work out what the value of 1 centimo is. A peseta is quite valuable – tea and coffee is expensive but wine 3 pesetas per bottle – therefore much cheaper to drink wine, which all Spaniards have with their meals. Cigarettes 9d for 20. The food is cheap, very varied and very well prepared and a lot of it is consumed at each meal-time. Because of this (I gather) the women are all plump and fat, especially around the hip area – it occurred to me that if you were living in Spain you would not be upset by your shape. Language difficulties no doubt arose, but somehow we got by on English, elementary Italian and frantic gesticulation. The people are typical to the Latin temperament – unrestrained (as opposed to the snobbish English), coarse, vulgar and impulsive. I adored and marvelled at their manners and behaviour – governed purely by their emotions. [...] The entertainment we had – music-hall and very slap-stick – was pleasant though not of a very high standard. They sing very well – the pressure they exert on their vocal chords and throat is quite extraordinary – must be made of steel. The sounds they make are wonderfully spine-chilling and biting – all singers could learn much from their Spanish counterparts.

This evening we saw the Folies Bergère[107] – basically, it is nothing but an exotic and fashionable display of clothes with aid of music and dancing. Fantastic costumes – the sort of thing one imagines or sees on film. For instance they did a subtle skit on the Opera – *Traviata* was one scene and the women (and they're pretty) appeared in such voluminous and bulky gowns that I felt sure that only 3 such dresses would block out the City Hall stage. Incidentally we spoke to Basil Poole[108] after the show – you know of course, that he is dancing with the Folies. Paris is damned costly and a shock after Spain – coffee = 2/8, a plain omelette = 12/- – just the end. At the opera there is [Puccini's] *La bohème*, *Tosca*, [Rossini's] *Barber of Seville* and [Gounod's] *Faust* – I'll let you know which I go to.

I am very cross with you for sending me money, though I must admit, that at least I could get some more books and things – thank you so much, it really was very thoughtful of you. I trust you received the book on Callas in fairly one piece – I had been carrying that around for some weeks not being able to afford the postage so the first thing I did was to change those postal orders and send off the book. [...]

Am running out of paper. Use the same address as before when replying and the Club will forward the letter to me wherever I land up. For now "Au Revoir" and "Merci beaucoup" – Kiss Wendy and Trudy.

Gordon.

---

107   A cabaret in Paris.
108   Brother of the ballet dancer David Poole (1925-1991).

6

[Aerogram posted from Italy. Address given by hand at the close of the letter: Pensionato studentesco, via Porpora 44, Milano.]

Thursday, 5 March [1964]

My dear May,

Outside it is snowing and miserable, so to keep warm I am writing letters. *Showboat* must be well on its way and if I remember correctly, will be opening shortly – Anyway, all the luck in the world. I am thinking of you all. [...]

At last I am in Italy and I am very happy. Of course, language difficulties arise and mainly because the local people speak so quickly and I take such a long time to translate. But, my Italian improves slowly if not surely.

Of course, I have been to La Scala. It is such an elegant Opera House and contributes greatly to the social life of Milan. Oddly enough, Milan is not the big cultural town I thought it would be, but more of an industrial and commercial centre. But the opera is excellent. The theatre is large and besides the stalls, it has in a semi-arena 4 tiers of boxes and two tiers of gallery. The thing amongst the wealthy Milanese is to own a box where they come dressed in all their finery and expensive stones and either try to see who else is in the theatre and to wave to their friends. – I personally find this degenerative but it is essential to the Milanese social life. These people hardly ever applaud, though I daresay they know the operas. The audience in the gallery are the ones that matter to the performing artist because they decide whether the artist is good or bad, and they are the ones that show their approval with applause. And how discriminate they are – and do they know the operas – each note, each word. The first night I went to the opening of [Boito's] *Mefistofele* with Raina Kabaivanska[109] (soprano), Nicolai Ghiaurov[110] (bass) and Carlo Bergonzi[111] (tenor). All first nights are big social affairs and the audience dress to no mean end – I have never seen so much flowing velvets and gold lamés in my life. I felt a bit of a fool in the gallery because I was the only one who did not know every bar of the opera. I did not even know how many acts there were to be – 5 by the way, and finished at 1.30 a.m. The acoustics in La Scala are the best I have heard and although the orchestra is at least 200 strong and sit in front of the stage and not under, the singers are never drowned even in the loudest passages. My biggest disappointment was Carlo Bergonzi who turned out to be a light (very light) tenor and not dramatic as I had thought judging from his gramophone records. But he is very sensitive, articulates very well and a good musician. The bass stole the performance – what a voice, quite stunning and breathtaking but the soprano, apart from not articulating sang fff from beginning to end – thank heavens she did not have much to sing. What really amazed me was the chorus – they produce such sonorous sound and always dark sound and never [with a] white edgy tone like the famous choir we know[112] – even on the high notes the women cover well. One has to hear it to really notice the astounding difference. Careful note is made of all markings in the score – when written pp they sing pp and not ff. Breath control is very cultivated and to hear a body

---

109 Raina Kabaivanska (*1934), Bulgarian soprano.
110 Nicolai Ghiaurov (1929–2004), Bulgarian bass.
111 Carlo Bergonzi (1924–2014), Italian tenor.
112 The Eoan Group choir.

of singers execute some fantastic phrasing is the most wonderful thing anybody can wish for. Very disciplined and when they have a long high note, they don't peter out but the end of the note has the same quality as the beginning. How wonderful it was to hear "Inneggiamo" from *Cavalleria*[113] the next night start mp as written with all the marked crescendi. Giulietta Simionato sang Santuzza – and can she sing. The astonishing thing is, that when I heard her at La Scala the voice sounded big and rich though at Covent Garden in *Aida* her voice sounded very small and subtle. She and Mirella Freni are the idols of La Scala at present. The name Tebaldi is not breathed, while Callas is referred to whenever somebody's acting is lousy. Leontyne Price is held in greatest esteem – everybody thinks she is fabulous. Perhaps she is clever by not appearing on the Continent too often. This season she has only been singing in America from what I gather. But back to *Cavalleria* – the tenor made a balls up of his opening phrase in "O Lola, ch'ai di latti" and the gallery did not hesitate to let know their disapproval – I heard several agonizing and disappointed "No's" and such negative words. When they like a certain note sung, they do not hesitate to shout "Bravo" and they pass audible comments to the person behind or in front whether they know him or not. Simionato had many deserved "brava's" and after her "Voi lo sapete, o mamma" which she sang exquisitely the gallery went hysterical with "Brava" and some were even crying because it was so good. Anything below C above middle C she sings in chest voice – like a large double bass. Just the sound I am mad about; and like Callas she uses different kinds of voice for every different emotion. Her acting is subtle and has much less point and meaning than Callas but is better than most I have seen. All her shouting at Turridu [in Mascagni's *Cavalleria rusticana*] was done in chest voice – very, very effective.

She also did some marvellous phrasing and the gallery noticed it and approved with "Brava". The audience do not miss a thing – a change of words if it sounds bad gets unhesitant disapproval. Also they do not hesitate to hum or sing with, when they feel bored and tired of listening. How different to what we are accustomed to. Turiddu was not very responsive but he sang his "Mama" aria very well. The baritone received the most disapproval because the gallery did not like the way he closed his throat on top notes.

I very much want to go to Parma where I believe all singers are whistled and boo'd at, and if you are not boo'd then you're good. Somebody tells me that Anna Moffo was whistled at so much in *Traviata* that she collapsed and refused to sing after the second act. Parma is about 50 miles from here – I should be able to go if I eat less. [...]

Kiss Trudy and Wendy.

Auguri molti[114]

Gordon

P.S. I don't know whether to call you Signora or Signorina so perhaps I had better use neither. [...]

---

113   The Easter hymn from the opera *Cavalleria rusticana* by Pietro Mascagni.
114   Italian: "best wishes".

7

Pensionato Studentesco, Via Porpora 44, Milan, Italy

Friday, 13 March [19]64 / Milano

My dear May,

Thank you so much for your letter which did find me, but not in London as expected.

About the Callas book – I am so pleased that first of all you received it (I hope in not too bad condition) and that it pleased you. Perhaps you will be disappointed by the recording, because it does really show how badly she sings – that fatal wobbling, but if you do not raise your hopes too high, I think you will be able to learn a lot from it instead of being let-down. Anyway, soon we shall see. [...]

5 feet 9 inches makes Callas sound very tall – perhaps she is, I don't know, but I do remember that she didn't seem much taller or shorter than anybody else.

When you receive this you will already be half-way through your *Showboat* run. I do hope it was the success we hope[d] it to be. At any rate, enjoy the experience and *good-luck* to all for the remaining performances. As everybody has now stopped thinking of the Operatic Concert with *Showboat* being on – I agree, because it is often better to think of one thing at a time – it does not leave very much time before the actual concert, and does mean hard work – very hard work, if the concert is to be good. I am pleased that you are back with Magnoni[115] – as you know I do not have complete confidence in her, but she is, I think, the only one in Cape Town who can still help. Of course, you will feel exhausted after scaling, especially when you have hardly done any for years – Am I right? That you were even feeling faint means that Magnoni was really making you work – that is a blessing by itself. I see what you mean about, "Madre, pietosa Vergine"[116] – I don't know the aria that well to be able to make any dogmatic statements, but I did gather when looking at it that it would need sustaining powers – not only because of the long legato phrases but also it is rather lengthy. The *Mefistofele* I am not so keen about because in my opinion the aria has little histrionic content for you – and we need the histrionics as much as the music. Apart from this, the aria has never made much sense to me and now after seeing the opera a few times, it makes even less sense – BUT there is no harm learning it. Now which of the two arias from [Francesco Cilea's *Adriana*] *Lecouvreur* is the one you like – "Poveri fiori" or "Io son l'umile". Incidentally what about "Qui Radames verrà!" What a pity your record player has conked in – it always happens when one really needs it – shit!

You say *Carmen* is in the bag – but if I know Dr. [Manca], it might easily be out of the bag as quickly as it came in. My Carmen – Vera [Gow] – yes, she has all the voice though it will need far more control – but to me as important, the histrionics – no, she hasn't. But I do not know *Carmen* well at all – I shall have to learn it. What about you singing Carmen? [...]

I had to avoid being home for my birthday like the plague because I couldn't take the fuss – it is very conceited of me to even think that there might have been any fuss, but anyway, just in case. I must admit that it did need much engineering on my part, but I was reasonably successful because I spent the first few hours of my 21st birthday seeing *Mefistofele* at La Scala – it only ended at 1.30 a.m. [...]

---

115 Olga Magnoni, a vocal teacher who trained many Eoan singers.
116 Aria from Verdi's *La forza del destino*.

Figure 2.1 Gordon Jephtas and Patricia van Graan during a rehearsal in the Cape Town City Hall, surrounded by chorus members of the Eoan Group in 1965. Source: Cloete Breytenbach Collection, DOMUS.

On Wednesday evening [I] stood through the opening performance of [Donizetti's] *L'elisir d'amore* with Giuseppe di Stefano, Mirella Freni and Rolando Panerai.[117] Di Stefano is tremendously popular at La Scala and so far has been the only singer to get applause on his first entrance. He is very much like Fiasconaro on stage, the same sort of build and presence. Although not as good an actor as Gigi [Fiasconaro] he certainly sings, protrudes his bottom lip like Gigi – but what amazes me is that he sings all the time with a *very* open throat – clear sound. To me he sounded excellent though everybody says he was much better 5 years ago. After his "Una furtiva lagrima", the gallery stopped the performance for over 15 min[utes] shouting "Bravo Pipo" as he is nicknamed. The other big delight of the evening was Freni – she is lovely. She sounds to me like I imagine Sutherland sounds on stage and she sings like Sutherland mostly in the mouth. I suspect that she has been working with Sutherland's husband, and as she is only about 25, she is the soprano to be watched. [...]

See you then next week

Regards to all – Love, Gordon.

---

117   Rolando Panerai (1924-2019), Italian baritone.

Admiral Hotel, 139 Crescent St, Overport, Durban [South Africa].

19 July 1965

Dear May,

Many, many thanks for your interesting letter of some weeks ago. Here there is so much to do and so much that needs seeing to that I am afraid the writing of letters has most unfortunately to be neglected – my apologies. However, how are things with you – how's the throat? I trust, of course, that you are shutting up completely – NO TALKING. It must be trying.

[Puccini's] *Turandot*[118] must have been very good judging from your apt writing about it. I wish I could have seen it – a good change would be so welcome especially if it's different to the five[119] we are involved with.

Tonight is [the] first performance here of *Trovatore* and Wed[nesday] is *Elisir*. So far we've had *Carmen*, *Traviata* and *Bohème*. Judging from the applause the audiences loved it all as seems usual. The critics scathed *Carmen* – found everything conceivably wrong with the entire business – from Don José[120] described as being much, much too fat and thin-voiced and Carmen[121] – not sultry or passionate enough right down to the tiniest detail of production was under execution. The only redeeming features being Susan & Yvonne.[122]

Traviata has been enthusiastically received and whereas in [Johannesburg] Patricia [van Graan] was the soprano darling of the public, here Winifried [du Plessis] is the rave followed with fantastic compliments. But isn't it fantastic to watch how a little success goes to people's heads. Everyone in the company walks around with the air that Callas, Gobbi and di Stefano have nothing on them and that they can do no wrong. A sad state of affairs when artistic standards are considered. A human failing!

Naturally everyone has had his or her share of sore throats, colds, temperament to the point of absolute distraction. But that's to be expected.

Generally everybody's working hard – many rehearsals because [of] different orchestras and stages. Also there are Operatic Concerts to contend with. – A hard life which is not made easier by the complication made by those individuals who consider themselves to be "stars" – and believe me the number of these have been tripled since [we left] C[ape] Town.

We are travelling without producer – makes no difference because productions are still the same – dreadful!!!! Looking at the stage this very moment I see one horrible straight line in what should be an exciting climax in *Elisir*. [...]

Anyway, I have a cue coming up, so must run off.

Best wishes to you.
Look after yourself,
Yours, Gordon.
XXX for Trudy & Wendy.

---

118 The UCT Opera Company performed Puccini's *Turandot* in the Cape Town City Hall in June 1965. Talbot (1978): 169. It is not clear whether Abrahamse attended a performance or the dress rehearsal and if she had to obtain special permission to attend as a coloured person. See also Jephtas's letter of 22 October 1981 in this regard.
119 Eoan was presenting five operas during this tour: Verdi's *La traviata* and *Il trovatore*, Bizet's *Carmen*, Donizetti's *L'elisir d'amore* and Puccini's *La bohème*.
120 Sung by Joseph Gabriels.
121 Sung by Vera Gow.
122 Susan Arendse sang the role of Frasquita and Yvonne Jansen sang the role of Mercedes.

Schneckenburgerstr 17/111, Munich, Germany
[This letter was written aboard the ocean liner "Africa" from the Lloyd Triestino Line en route from Cape Town to Europe.]

"Africa"
22 October 1965

Dear May,

[...] I am on my way to Italy on an Italian ship for a year's extended study (and work, I'm afraid) on the Continent and England. I did have every intention of writing to you when the tour so abruptly ended but the sudden hustle and bustle which comes about when one prepares to leave the country and also procrastination prevented me from actually getting down to it. [...]

I left Cape Town last Saturday and [am] travelling [along the] East Coast on a ship that tosses around like a dinky and is full of Moslem pilgrims on route to Mecca. I thought I would be able to brush up my dormant Italian on this voyage, but I find I'm learning Arabic instead – and it's backwards too.

The Moslems are in splendid Cape Town behaviour doing all the same things they do in their homes I suppose – putting their [cigarette] ash in the wash-basin, using the cabins for laundry, banging doors and making a general racket. Every now and then some official from the ship makes a request to them – please to wear a jacket to dinner & please not to speak too loudly in the dining-room, please to be punctual for meals – then they all have a caucus meeting and say how terribly nice of the official to tell them. Of course, the official usually [uses] some white lie as an excuse which really means "It's damn civilized manners!" [...]

Feel sorry for me? Yes and No. Yes, because they make an infernal racket and reek of sweat, and No because their ignorance amuses me. One of [them] doesn't even know his home address – I ask you?!!

But to come to the crux of this letter. You have several Callas recordings of mine. Would you be interested to take them over? I'm not prepared to take more than ⅓ [of] the original prices. As you can guess I need funds because I have nothing very definite overseas and would hate to be poverty-stricken.

Think about it and if you would like to own them good; and if you can't afford it, keep them till I get back to S.A. There's no great hurry and I only get to Europe Nov. 9th. Anyway, write because I'd like to hear from you.

Regards to all,
Kiss the children,
Love –
Gordon.

My address from 10th November for about a month:
8, MÜNCHEN, 8
SCHNECKENBURGERSTR. 17/111
(DEUTSCHLAND)
[...]

49, AVONMORE RD, LONDON, W.14.[123]

18 December, 1965

My dear May,

Thank you so very much for your very interesting letter which afforded me much pleasure and delight. But I do feel rather guilty to notice that it was written well over a month ago which is a frightfully long time to leave a letter unanswered. Actually, I did have a reason for not replying before. Having been rather unsettled in my whereabouts and immediate [sic] I thought it best to put off writing until such time as I will [be] sure of my position. Well, at last I am reasonably settled, for a few months anyway – about six. Arrived here in London a week ago during which time I have managed to secure some sort of accommodation which I must admit I am not very enthusiastic nor happy about, but it will have to do for the time being. [...]

During my 5 weeks in Munich I went to the opera more often than my pocket allowed but came to the disheartening conclusion that to find an opera performance in the manner of Callas, so that it makes sense visually, dramatically and musically, one really has to go a long way. The Germans have very healthy appetites for art and are able to give enthusiastic receptions to what to me has been no more than mediocre. The productions mounted in Munich are only productions as such – very good sets, good planning, excellent crowd grouping, well devised lighting, but the opposing forces just don't fuse to make a uniform presentation and performance: To me it always [remains] three separate entities – the production (the producer), the singing (artists) and the orchestra (conductor) just stuck together hoping that somehow the result would mean something to a member of the audience. Perhaps I remember too much about Callas/Gobbi/Zeffirelli['s] *Tosca* – but that in all honesty was a performance where everybody had worked together and not against [each other] in order to produce a performance full of truth and not just visual beauty, a few very stagey poses and singing. I find it continually harder to watch a singer singing "Io tremo" but looking nothing like being afraid or making an attempt at being afraid. I think this traditional manner, alla Rota,[124] where the singer just stands put and sings, occasionally lifts his arms to the high heavens whether music and situation demands it or not, is still very prevalent especially amongst singers.

I saw a performance of *Traviata* with Hilde Gueden[125] in Munich. She received much star treatment and an ovation which I thought the Germans would be incapable of – I wonder what they would do after seeing Callas. Probably go completely berserk. But to get back to *Traviata* – as this was a special occasion, the company who normally sings everything including *Traviata* in German, sang in Italian; so it was perfectly understandable when in the 3rd Act the Barone inadvertently sang "Germont ist hier" and then quickly recollecting himself continued "Il vedete". But I found it hard to forgive Gueden who got her Italian words all confused and in the wrong order in the drinking song and even worse, got all tongue-tied when reading the letter in Act IV. After all she had been singing nothing but *Traviata* for weeks all over Germany. Being the guest star she wore her own costumes – shocking pink for Act I; blue in Act II and white in Act III. Her voice in both quality and timbre reminded me very much of

---

123   Jephtas had already moved to private lodgings but still used the aerogram from the hotel where he had just stayed, the Regent Palace Hotel, Piccadilly Circus, London, W1.
124   Alessandro Rota, longstanding friend of Manca and director of many of Eoan's opera productions.
125   Hilde Gueden, also Güden (1917-1988), Austrian soprano.

Ruth's,[126] and when she just skipped notes in the "Sempre libera" – the coloratura obviously proving way beyond her – she reminded me even more of Ruth. I saw the same production some days before with the soprano who had sung the opening night and therefore had all the rehearsals, so it was rather obvious that Gueden had not had a rehearsal in this particular production and continually landed on the wrong part of the stage in relation to everybody else. In the second act she became so exasperated by this that she just plonked herself in a chair and sang almost the whole duet with Germont without getting up. She did make some ravishing mezza voce sounds especially in "Dite [al]la giovine".[127] That is the one thing the Eoan singers just cannot do – that is mezza-voce singing – rather strange!

You want to know whether I'm over here on a bursary from the Group. Thank heavens, I'm not on a bursary from them or anybody else because I would not be able to do what I want with some thought of obligation at the back of my mind. About not being at a music school – I am not keen on studying in England and there is very little information to be had in Cape Town on continental schools – hence my month in Germany to look around and see what gives. Studying on the Continent really costs little, but the living is the main problem!

I am very happy indeed that you are once again in shape to sing. How I wish that the Group would produce an opera with an ideal dramatic-music part for you – like [Cherubini's] *Medea* or [Donizetti's] *Anna Bolena*. You are the only singing-actress in Cape Town who could really give the public something that will satisfy – with an excellent director and musical director. It is my greatest sorrow that the officials, music and otherwise, do not want to think along these lines. If this could be done it would be making ART and not the perpetual involvement with unnecessary and energy wasting petty things. I am very keen to have all details about your singing. I didn't manage to see Gigi [Fiasconaro] – missed him both in Cape Town and also Durban, but I heard all the favourable things about his *Aida*. About the *Rondine*[128] – I'm afraid I've made a mess up there because I catalogued it with the Group's music. As a compromise I'll send you another copy within a few weeks. [...]

Merry Christmas & Happy New Year to you and your family. Kisses to Trudy and Wendy. Love. Write soon – Gordon.

---

126 Ruth Goodwin, Eoan soprano soloist who sang the role of Violetta in Eoan's productions of *La traviata* between 1956 and 1962. She and May Abrahamse often sang on alternate nights.
127 Aria from *La traviata*, Act 2.
128 He probably means an aria from *La rondine* by Puccini that Abrahamse was studying at the time.

11

22, Monmouth Road, London W.2.

Sunday, 27 March [1966]

My dear May,

I was so pleased to receive your letter which was the pleasure of the week. [...] I moved at the end of January because it was the rainy season and there was a leak in my room, the kettle provided had holes and the window couldn't close and no matter how much newspapers and other articles I shoved into the [cracks], I still suffered the blowing gusts comparable only to the South-Easter.[129] So as I had no desire to die of bronchitis or pneumonia (so unromantic), I thought it better to move to a house with a tendency for tuberculosis rather. And mind you, I've not made a bad choice because whenever I climb the two flights of stairs to my humble but very untidy room my lungs feel as if they have collapsed. [...] What am I studying – at the moment German of all things and with a thick tongue like mine it is almost impossible to pronounce. Also delving into the History of Art and learning operas – it takes the best part of a week learning one – so far *Aida*, [Verdi's] *Don Carlos*, [Bellini's] *Norma*, [Rossini's] *Cenerentola*. Have been sitting with thick volumes of 15th-century Spain for *Don Carlos* to get some of the background. Covent Garden will be doing the Visconti[130] production soon. To obtain use of a piano I have to use one of the practising studios at 5/- [5 shillings] an hour which tends on being costly, so I depend mostly on libraries, etc. [...]

I'm overjoyed that you are recovering vocally – it really makes me happy. As you say you do only ½ hour a week and more lately 10 minutes scales a day, don't rush it because it will be far more rewarding in the end to persevere now and get all the workings into action by slow process of elimination. What you say about up and forward producing more resonant sound is perfectly true – and it keeps clear of the throat. I'm pleased that you have discovered this principle for yourself because now you yourself are able to appreciate the benefit of it. The trouble about singing light and practically white is that the voice lies in the throat more which leads to complications. Keep on working at it in the way you have discovered – and slowly.

You ask about Callas – she is in the same vocal difficulty as you and also working away at it in quiet solitude as she said in a review that she is now working 8 hours a day correcting her technique because her resonating chambers are full of pus with the result that she couldn't hear herself and was forcing the voice. But above all, the fact that you feel that you are improving vocally pleases me beyond words. *Aida* has some of the most beautiful music imaginable to sing but I imagine taxing because she has so much to do. My advice to you before you accept the part[131] is to get a score and the records and to go into detail about the complexities of the part and then if you are sure your throat can take the whole opera you could acknowledge your acceptance. Your instrument now is delicate and needs careful care. I don't know when exactly this *Aida* is to be except [in] 1967 – the later, the better it would be for your throat. [...]

I saw Sutherland in concert – she is monstrously huge and wore a wide black flowing coat over a white gown which made her look 6 feet broad compared to her husband[132] who

129 He means the strong wind characteristic of the Cape in South Africa.
130 Luchino Visconti (1906-1976), Italian theatre, opera and cinema director.
131 Manca's plans to produce *Aida* never materialised.
132 Richard Bonynge (*1930), Australian conductor, husband to Joan Sutherland.

is lean and looked more in character with the music than she. But my God, when she opens her mouth one really has an object lesson in bel canto – a smooth legato, full blooded tone, firm sound from bottom to top (with the exception of E flat and above (high) which change their colour). And it's not a white voice but round and wonderfully full. But she has no sense for words, and quite frankly her recitatives would have been fearfully boring if it weren't that one was enchanted by the sounds. In the more passionate moments, her gestures consisted of raising her left hand and stretching her five fat little fingers. She does evoke great excitement in scales and those famous trills and [is] very down to earth. I got this impression with her curtain calls – well, if you didn't like it tough luck, but I had a whale of a time, now let me go and take my shoes off – as opposed to Callas who appeared slowly with a look of innocence and did you really like it!

Sorry, no more space – Regards & love – Gordon.
(When you answer, I'll be able to complete this one.)

12

22, Monmouth Road, London W.2.

Friday, 1 April [1966]

My dear May,
Armed with a writing pad this time (miniature pad that it might be), I hope to answer your letter cards which have now reached me after a tour of the world of inner London. Perhaps I'd refrain from vulgar comments about that housekeeper and be thankful that I have received them. [...]
Yes, I hope to do quite a bit of opera going now that Cov[ent] Garden has finally completed its Wagner cycle. This week I saw *Iphigenie* (Gluck) – another of the Callas operas. The music quite frankly was boring and more so because it wasn't well sung – the mezzo (leading role) had a cold and got her vocal cords into a mess and at times produced frightening sounds. It is quite a dramatic sort of plot with Iphigenie having to stab her brother etc. which would be just up the Callas line. Unfortunately this lady had been doing the Wagner as well and somehow forgot that the Wagner cycle was over, so consequently still indulged in the erect and arch-backed stances. The tenor – twice the current size of [Joseph] Gabriels with a voice like Samaai's[133] made me want to laugh because it seemed uncanny for such a big body to produce such a small voice. The production was extremely interesting – producers tend to be better than singers these days. This coming week I want to see [Richard Strauss's] *Elektra*, and I ought to see *Butterfly* to see what they make of it. You ask about Gueden's acting – she not only sounded like Ruth, but disconcertingly also acted like her – no better and no worse. It was really a I-am-the-prima-donna performance.
I quite agree with Magnoni that if you work hard at your singing it will kill whatever depression may come your way. I hope you are now over that feeling, though my God, I know what it's like to be depressed. You have no idea how many such attacks come my way and usually

---

133   Gerald Samaai, Eoan tenor. He was younger than Gabriels and sang solo roles only after Gabriels had left the company.

coincide with moments when I recall some or other incident that might have happened during my work as repetiteur – all those hours of rehearsal wasted because Manca didn't know whether "Stride la vampa"[134] came at the beginning of *Trovatore* or the end. And then *Carmen* – which you were spared.[135] But don't let me get on that subject or I'll get all bitchy. [...]

Have heard the Callas recording of *Aida* which is filled with remarkable phrasing and even better declamation of the words. When you propose to work through the part I earnestly suggest you use her recording because above all she is musically correct all the way through compared to both [Leontyne] Price and [Renata] Tebaldi who make semiquavers into crotchets for the sake of beauty of sound. Callas gets beautiful colour on the word "*parola*" in "l'empia parola"[136] in "Ritorna vincitor". The section "I sacri nomi di padre... d'amante" for instance the conductor (old [Tullio] Serafin) takes much slower so she has a better chance to show the meaning of the words. But not everything is good – "Patria mia" has bad moments – but the total sum obliterates deficiencies. Also "Sventurata, che dissi" has meaningful overtones.

Getting writer's cramp. Love to the children.

Regards to your family.
All the best.
Gordon.

P.S. The idea of raising money on your own is wonderful though frankly I'm beginning to get very very bored with this "no money in the bank".[137] Hope you can arrange something and that you get co-operation. Tons of luck.

13

22, Monmouth Road, London. W.2.

9 May 1966.

My dear May,

Thanks a lot for your delightful letter which surely was the pleasure of last week. But you must excuse me for not answering sooner – but the usual laziness for written utterances and I've been opera going more, of which I'll write after answering your letter. [...]

But while my memory is yet fresh, let me tell you about the things I've seen – hoping not to be too boring. Firstly then, naturally, Miss Callas. She appeared briefly in a programme covering Visconti who was here producing *Der Rosenkavalier* at Covent Garden. She was interviewed in Paris and appeared looking rather thin in the face and the cheeks rather prominently sunken. However, completely composed and very, very cultured she chatted about Visconti who had just before (unknown to her) said that she is a great actress. Anyway, in this deep voice which I wrote about before she mentioned [Bellini's] *Sonnambula*, *Traviata*, *Vestale* which they had done together. I quote ad lib. what I remember – "Luchino (Visconti)

---

134   Azucena's aria from Verdi's *Il trovatore*, Act 2.
135   Eoan performed Bizet's *Carmen* on the tour for the first time. It was their only-ever production for which they did not receive positive reviews. They never staged the work in Cape Town again.
136   *Aida*, Act 1.
137   He is probably referring to lack of funds at the Eoan Group, which was a constant problem.

spoilt me terribly! – and not only the prima donna, he spoilt everybody in the company. It was in *Traviata* that he really taught me to act, and the one great thing he taught me was never to move unless I had deep and *profound* reason. Opera can be ridiculous and I only hope that Luchino has artists who respond to his direction because of what use is an excellent producer with artists who couldn't bother. At Scala there never was any need for us in the company to reproach him and he never needed to reproach us because we all worked very hard at a time when we were all at the age and spirit to do so". I could not help but feel a twang of grief at her last remark, because Callas seems to have lost courage to come on stage again, and she must miss terribly those times when she was able to work and strive for more perfection in times less antagonistic than now. The programme showed Visconti at work as well – everything is planned to the minutest detail and [he] works rather like [Alessandro] Rota – that is, literally pushing the singers and speaking and coaxing them while they're singing. The big difference is that he knows what he wants whereas Rota did not. [...]

I managed to get into the dress rehearsal for *Rosenkavalier* which lasted from 10 a.m. – 4 p.m. But Visconti would not work with an audience – so each act was played straight through and then the curtain was drawn and he would make changes or rehearse what he wanted behind the curtain for an hour or so! During the acts he sat in the auditorium quietly looking at the stage through binoculars for most of the time. He struck me as a quiet, but highly intelligent and perhaps unyielding [man] of tremendous aristocratic bearing and quiet yet striking dignity. No flamboyance in the manner of the honourable Dr. of C. Town.[138] The actual prod[uction] of *Rosenkavalier* was largely interesting, a spectacle besieged with painstaking detail, and much cause for wonderment to me. Of course, I swotted the opera before hand but still find it a very complex and too-Teutonic work to get even with it.

I saw also Strauss's *Elektra* which is in one act and had this notice outside – "Latecomers will not be admitted until the interval" – there wasn't an interval! Anyway, I heard a young Norwegian soprano who replaced someone who was indisposed. This girl, according to the papers only 22, has the biggest and most thrilling voice I've ever heard – the only one that comes near to what I think a dramatic soprano is. It was really an eye-opener (and ear-opener).[139] Elektra played by Amy Shuard[140] gave such an exciting and well-timed performance that I went back to see more performances. [...]

Then *Madama Butterfly* with a Covent Garden favourite – Elizabeth Vaughan.[141] But alas! this was a terrific bore and the only thing that kept me in the theatre was the hope that I would see something interesting in the production – but this was even worse! So I left the theatre feeling rather disillusioned only to return to see *Tosca*. The much raved about Marie Collier[142] sang abominably badly but for some soaring top A's, B's and C's which became so boring not even to mention the ridiculous circumstances. Of course, it was fatal to go after the Callas impression and no doubt the soprano must feel the strain of having to compete with so great an artist as Callas. Collier can act – purely as a mechanical force. However, I could concentrate on other things which I missed with Callas around. So I had a good sniff, judging the

---

138   In 1963 Joseph Manca received an honorary doctorate from the University of Cape Town "in recognition of his work for the cultural progress and upliftment of the Coloured Community". Roos (2018): 94-96.
139   Jephtas does not provide the name of this singer, but it was probably Berit Lindholm (*1934) from Sweden, who is listed in Covent Garden's online database as having sung Chrysothemis. She was 32 at the time, not 22. See www.rohcollections.org.uk/performances.aspx, accessed 6 November 2022.
140   Amy Shuard (1924-1975), English soprano.
141   Elizabeth Vaughan (*1937), Welsh soprano, later mezzo-soprano.
142   Marie Collier (1927-1971), Australian soprano.

angles of the chairs in the first act, count the number of steps in the last, and seep in all the other details from the remnants of Zeffirelli's production. And the tenor [Renato Cioni], who sang with Callas. I noticed for the first time because he was really good!!

Elizabeth Schwarzkopf came on Friday and gave a German song recital. Beautiful as ever, wearing a fabulous light green flowing dress of chiffon she enchanted the audience with songs of Strauss, Brahms and Wolf. And what an artist – [in] one song she was an 8 year-old girl singing about the mouse-trap. The next song she was a gipsy girl snaking coyly, then vulgarly and brusquely – all this in the voice. I'd hate to think what all the traditional singing teachers were thinking of this exhortation of vocal means. Perhaps the most fantastic thing was how she is able to create the mood of the song with a flash across the face, sadness, love, regret, fear of old age, youth – and all this without any gestures!!! I always wondered how art-songs ought to be performed – and now I know. The woman is so professional even though she may be a bit past [it] as everybody says[143] – but only in pure vocal terms – and what does that matter. To me it doesn't matter! The artistry matters and it's fantastic how people run for the real artists!

Accompanied by the famous Gerald Moore[144] at the piano I felt quite ashamed of my past efforts at this sort of thing. The man was excellent – and she made a tremendous fuss of him! At last, I feel that there are some people in the world, like these two, who care about Art and perform Art with little care about personal success. And this in itself procures for them much success. It was wonderful to witness, the absolute sincerity – and I dared not think of prevalent conditions in the Eoan Group where it *is* possible to work in such a manner, but hampered by political, spiritual and other trivial muck that occupies the minds of people [who] cannot care 1 inch about the art, but their personal, public image or other such outrageous things. How I wish things could be otherwise there and instead of working with the aim that our cultural efforts will obscure or obliterate the political and ethnic problems of the country – why not work in the pursuit of perfecting an art for which the company has so much to offer! [...] [Regarding] *Aida* – September next year is a long way from now – get a score from the library and listen to it – then learn the part *without singing* necessarily, study the psychology of the character, the declamation of the words, the music in detail. Then nearer the time, should you feel capable of getting through the whole opera, and decide you want and can do it, you won't have to rush with learning – because rushing is dangerous as we know so well. I shall, when you inform me that you have a score, and starting to study the part send you lists of my observations and whatever ideas I have accumulated. I have been studying the score and am still at odds with *Aida* – but only time will solve this and I shall learn more on hearing your comments. But whatever you do, *don't stop working*.

I hear relatively little about Eoan activities and in fact, haven't heard from the Sydows for weeks. All I know, is that *Traviata* is being rehearsed for the 31 May – please go and see it and send me an objective account. I hear costumes are being changed, etc, etc. But why *Traviata*!!!!! Am especially eager to know about the production as I don't think Manca [is] even slightly capable – [he] can hardly conduct the damn opera! But I believe one can be pleasantly surprised.

Am off to Italy determined to master that infernal language some time after 3 June – 4 months to Perugia University to do Italian Literature and History. God know where the money is coming from! However, the University has accepted me and I'm going. I may well

143   Schwarzkopf was only 50 at the time of this concert.
144   Gerald Moore (1899–1987), English-Canadian pianist.

stay here until 10 June in order to see Visconti's *Don Carlos*, but must get to Spoleto in July to hear a singer called Montserrat Caballé[145] about whom much speculation is going on! And also Richter[146] is coming there. The money! Thank God, Spoleto is near Perugia. [I] move out of this room end of this month. No more paper! Love to Trudy, Wendy & family.

Bless you! And remember WORK – Gordon.

P.S. Found another sheet –
Get whatever information and pictures from libraries on *Eleonora Duse*, Italian tragic actress of about 1840 – you will learn much by just looking at her pictures. At the moment I'm delving into her life absorbing as much as humanly possible.

Love – G

14

Universita Italiana per Stranieri, Palazzo Gallenga, Piazza Fortebraccio, Perugia. (Italia)
[Jephtas was writing from London on the eve of his departure to Italy and put his address-to-be in Perugia as his return address.]

Friday, 10 June [1966]

My dear May,

Thanks a lot for your delightful letter and looking at it once again I feel rather relieved for not having taken too much time over replying as seems to have become wont with me. […]

Am definitely leaving England tomorrow, with the sea-men's strike in full swing, crossing the dicey English Channel has become an inconvenient affair because would-be sailors like myself have to be content on waiting on some or other foreign ship to do the crossing in what has been an English precedence. But this delay has suited me advantageously because I've been able to see and *hear* Sutherland at Covent Garden on Wed[nesday] and have managed to obtain a gallery seat for tonight's performance of the much hailed Visconti production of *Don Carlos*. The production itself must be no less than 5 years old but nevertheless still carries the laurel of being the best all-round production Covent Garden has ever done. Well, let's hope that it does not disappoint.

About Sutherland – there can be no doubt that she knows everything there is to know about vocal technique and what is more important perhaps, she knows how to use it.

The opera was Donizetti's *Figlia del reggimento* sung in French with spoken dialogues as originally intended. The plot, a comic one, revolves around an orphan girl who had been adopted by the French army, she is then claimed by a long-lost wealthy relative who persists in having her learn the finer and more sophisticated things like dancing and [singing]. The second act consists of a very lengthy, and with Sutherland very interesting, dancing/singing lesson. She has tremendous confidence and I could only marvel at her grace in the dancing lesson and then how she has used the scales [and] trills to become comic in the second act. She is not much of an actress, but my God she tries and the result is more than delightful. She has the advantage of having a good director who works out things that she can bring off,

145 Montserrat Caballé (1933-2018), Spanish soprano.
146 Sviatoslav Richter (1915-1997), Soviet pianist.

and she has a designer who creates her into a less huge figure on stage. She is a big woman as I've said before and with the average small-size tenor she would look quite comical, but thank heavens her clothes are designed to give her more line and sophistication - no bulky underskirts to make her look like a barrel, nor any unnecessary adornments or trimmings to increase her heaviness. Her experience she uses to great advantage and I am still in seventh heaven when I recall those absolutely clear trills, her ability to sing/hit a high D without effort or preparation - and full-blooded sound which she can hold for any length of time. I would love to see her in her customary tragic roles to really assess her. No, I can safely say that I shall always make an effort to go and hear [her] sing because she is always interesting - never dull as most singers. Amy Shuard in *Ballo* and *Turandot* - not only my opinion but generally - not any good. She had such bad clothes and sang abominably. She was in grave difficulties with the Verdi exposed vocal line. In Strauss she was terrific, singing a full-blooded C with huge orchestral backing, but hitting an unaccompanied high B flat in Verdi proved too much for her. Her acting did not once convey any meaning and the entire production irritated me especially as I had taken the trouble to study the score. Her Turandot fared much better - but her voice was somehow too small. Franco Corelli[147] sang Calaf. A real belting Italian tenor with little interest in anything or anyone else around him. I think his Hollywoodian good looks earn him more fame.

I don't think I shall hear Caballé (new singer of Callas temperament), nor Richter (Russian pianist) because my finances are in a very grave state - (please don't mention this to those at home because they'd worry themselves to death). No more paper. Shall attempt to write next week. Shall be at address in Perugia from 1 July.

Love - Gordon.

15

Universita Italiana per Stranieri, Piazza Fortebraccio, Perugia. Italia.

10 July 1966

My dear May,

Thanks so much for your delightful letters of last week, which are always such a joy to read. [...]

Perugia is a real country town, with narrow winding streets, far too many stair-cases and hillocks to climb but with a great number of 10th, 12th and 15th Century examples of architecture. It is essentially a University town with its inhabitants making good use of this facet, by letting rooms to students. Admittedly, it doesn't cost much especially compared to London where I paid £5 a week for a small room. [...]

Last week I hitched down to Spoleto to hear the Caballé woman. So all very well, after 3 hours of hitching and much walking (about 50 miles) I arrived in Spoleto only to discover that Caballé was not singing because of illness. The rumour was though, that her fee was much too high and the management refused to relent. Well, in order to hear her, I was prepared to live on 2 apples which I had for the day so that I would have money for the ticket. By this time I was so angry and hungry that I had a meal and returned to Perugia without

---

147   Franco Corelli (1921-2003), Italian tenor.

wanting or bothering to go to the concert with her substitute – some unknown English sounding name. Tough luck! [...]

I have been talking to many people about opera here in Italy and everybody places Callas in a category by herself, way above everything else because she is unique in her own art and nobody has yet been able to surpass what she has done. And these people I chatted to saw her in most of the operas she has done – *Medea, Norma, Lucia, Traviata*, etc. Of course, there are people in the Callas school and Leyla Gencer,[148] a Turkish soprano, is one. But my friends pointed out that although she works in the manner of Callas – Callas is still unique. Anyway, Gencer is singing *Aida* at Verona next week and I believe this is very good. I want to go if I have the courage to hitch the 150 miles and have the money. Sutherland has the reputation also here of being the best singing voice with many "pity" [*sic*] that she hasn't the "tiger" of La Callas because she wants to do *Norma*. But there are other singers who are taking [a] place amongst [the] beautiful voice category, namely another Greek [soprano] of only 24, Elena Suliotis,[149] but [she] is considered cold, inexperienced but with possibilities. Tebaldi is rumoured to return to La Scala next season and this gives me hope that Callas will return the following season. I hope so and I am almost sure because from what I gather from people who know Callas, it is exactly the sort of situation Callas thrives on.

My greatest disappointment has been putting off Serafin with whom I had an appointment but couldn't afford it because he wants £10 per lesson, and I would have to go to Rome. I hoped just to see him and talk to him about opera, so I wrote asking whether I could come later. So now I'm looking for a job here even just to have one session with him. *But please, not a word about this to anyone!* I can just imagine Manca and others being pleased about such a failure of my intentions. [...] My finances [are] the touchiest point of my life. I've no income and living now on what I saved in England where I did manage to work copying music but hating it. I dare not write home about not having much money because my mother would die of heart failure and the Sydows would get the group to give me an allowance which at all costs *I don't want.* I think I prefer my present struggle because this way I feel more appreciative of what I have and [am] INDEPENDENT and therefore [am] able to do as I please. Thanks for the note about *Traviata*[150] – had not heard anything about it but what you wrote and in London saw a review in the *Argus*[151] – the usual praise but no critical survey. That it wasn't too bad is better than nothing and not more than expected. No more space. For now "arrivederci".
Love to Trudy & Wendy and your folks.

Love Gordon.

---

148   Ayşe Leyla Gencer (1928-2008), Turkish soprano, active mostly in Italy.
149   Elena Suliotis, also Souliotis (1943-2004), Greek soprano.
150   The Group presented a special performance of Verdi's *La traviata* for the 5th Anniversary Festival of the Republic of South Africa. Roos (2018): 201-202.
151   A Cape Town newspaper.

16

Universita Italiana per Stranieri, Piazza Fortebraccio, Perugia. Italia.

Wednesday, 24 August [1966]

My dear May,

Today, feeling down in the dumps musically, both for my lack of musical activity and cul-mination of opera going in Italy, I was walking up one of the very narrow alleys of which Perugia consists for the most part, when from a little electrical shop I heard strains of the very final scene of *Trovatore* with Callas. It was a broadcast, and the recording the one both of us know so well, with di Stefano and von Karajan. Naturally, I stopped and went into the shop and [was] given the permission by the kindly middle-aged woman to stay and hear it all. And what a thrill! Isn't Callas magnificent – listening to her intense and vibrant performance once again brought back my joy for music. Last time I heard her (on record of course) was in England – then many weeks ago now. But thinking and deliberating about it I find it strange that whenever music starts losing its significance for me, it is always this tremendous Callas that convinces me that it is an Art, worthy of every respect. And stranger even, is that it is a singer who can convince me when I am essentially one of "those" who believe that singers do not care about music or the art, but more about their voices and their own person.

But after all this preamble I must apologize for my bad manners not thanking you for your letters in the first place. THANKS!! When the huge and thick envelope arrived, I excitedly set-tled myself down to a few hours of stimulating reading, but only to find realms of blank airmail sheets. I hadn't thought that you would really carry out your threat to send me some writing paper – thanks! And then the bank-draft. How very kind of you, and although I have absolute-ly no recollection that you owe me any money, I was certainly happy to know the feeling of "being in the money". Actually I felt rather a millionaire and was just on the verge of running to the nearest art-and-book-shop when my better nature stopped me. THANKS. You maintain that [it] is in lieu of books and records I gave you, but I gave them to you knowing that you would really appreciate and find happiness from them. So then, let's not go into a battering exchange. Promise? Alright.

Now that I have all this paper at my disposal I can really get down to writing all that I am thinking of. True, as you say, I have at times not answered most of your questions, but to tell the truth, whenever I write to you, I have so much to say and get carried away and then when I want to answer your letter I find no more writing space or that my hands are tired of holding these ridiculous things one uses to write with. So then I think, "Oh hang, I'll have to leave it for next time" and so the procrastination goes on until it reaches the point of no retrieve. [...]

My Italian is truly rock bottom – and not nearly fluent. I find it extremely difficult to think in Italian and spend my time translating to and from English in conversation, and so always remember things that have been said in a conversation in English. My vocabulary is non-existent, and being all involved in grammatical laws and syntax, which is rather complicated, doesn't help matters. Italy has an entirely different code of class distinction and one of the main facets of this is the language or rather the grammar used by individuals. The language is full of very subtle distinctions which I am still very busy trying to identify on hearing in con-versation with Italians. And then to get the true feel of the idioms of the language I now feel one has to spend some years in the country. [...]

The poor old future of the Eoan Group. Yes, I have heard about this courageous suspension of activities.[152] How will the honourable musical director [i.e. Manca] survive without an audience to preen himself in front of. It seems then that the audience will have to be the Groupers who will have to attend countless and inconsequential meetings and lay their appreciation of his activities at his feet while he in turn will repeatedly mention his last performances, which will have been the best (Verdi should even be grateful) and all the fantastic plans for the future, running down the activities of other music groups in Cape Town. Such seems the natural trend of events. I only wish that this slack period (which I don't believe for one moment that it would be so) would be used to improve the technical *and* vocal accomplishments of the singers. But knowing them, it won't happen. Perhaps this is when I wish that I were there to get really stuck into hard, solid work – but then I have discovered that this is not nearly fruitful unless it has everybody's cooperation (including the much learned doctor [Manca]). This building[153] forms a great part of planning and I've heard much about it from varying sources, and if words were to produce things then this building ought to be out of this world – with equipment to suit a dream. Thank God there is no communication between Manca and myself because I'd hate to hear his exhortations and how much he has done. I personally have my doubts about this affair. Not that I don't expect the building to arise one day, which I suspect will be a make-shift affair and within a few years will be a black sheep like Ochberg Hall,[154] inadequate to house the activities of the Group satisfactorily, but what I wonder about is how the building will keep itself once established. If it is to be a College of Music where will the students, the money and the lecturers come from? Let's hope that the committees are considering all these things. And yet, I may be pleasantly surprised?

Why do I want to come back? I don't know that I do. At present I am still sorting out myself as regards this matter and have not reached any satisfactory conclusion, but a lot of mixed ideas. South Africa is my country as much as any other's and no matter what, my roots are fixed there and it isn't easy to break away from such strong roots. Europe is free, in the racial sense, but the place is packed with people in the rat race which accompanies every avenue for success. But I feel out of place – I don't understand the mentality of the people, how they think and why they think. People here are steeped in culture – which is not only [to] do [with what] they learn at schools, it is all around them and the effects of the world-wars are still evident. I then, am much of a rough diamond, uncultured, etc, etc, and how long will it take to adapt myself to this entirely new code of living? I don't know. If I were to return to S.A. no sooner will I have got there, when I will probably want to get away. Difficult no? I would like to spend my life making music and a big attempt even though it can be no more than a drop in an ocean, to raise the standard of music performance above the standard of the Manca-mentality. But this depends so much on participation of others – I am no conductor, no musical director. However, I have more chance of doing this at home than here!!! My only personal [armour] against racial South Africa then will be whatever recognition I can win here – but it is so hard. I don't know – my thoughts are just too mixed on the matter. But, in fact, I am not returning to South Africa just yet. I return

---

152   It is unclear why activities were suspended in this specific instance, but documents in the Eoan Archive mention Manca's plans to expand the scope of the group. Such initiatives on his part often resulted in a temporary suspension of the Group's activities. It was also in 1966 that District Six was declared a white area, and plans were being made to provide the Group with a new home in the coloured suburb of Athlone that could feature a broad range of educational and cultural activities.

153   Plans for a new building, the Eoan Group Cultural Centre in Athlone, were formally tabled during the 1966 AGM. See "Minutes of the 32nd AGM held on 29 September 1966", 6-7. Eoan Group Archive: 1:3.

154   The Ochberg Hall was the home of the Eoan Group when they were still in District Six. It was an old church building in Hanover Street.

to England to take up a scholarship which I won for a year at the London Opera Centre starting end of September. Have just heard of it and only just written home, so don't know what the reaction will be. Thank heaven, I don't feel the slightest obligation to the Group as I felt after leaving University[155] for instance. Though as you mentioned, this idea of me remaining abroad for another 2 years has been subtly indicated to me from that direction. But just an indication – but it hardly matters to me. My mother is probably going to be the biggest problem and I've tried to put my case as clearly as possible and hope she follows and understands. Then I hope this extra-time abroad will make me decide one way or another – do I want to go back or not!

Deep down, the only responsibility that I feel strongly, is an allegiance to the singers. Speaking purely objectively, I think they have so much talent, which can produce worthwhile results and realizing just how much this music-making (excluding the personal acclaim) means to them in the midst of oppression makes me want to continue working with them – if only to produce these few hours of escape from the brutality of the reality. Perhaps this is the strongest link that is pulling me homewards.

Thurs 25 [August] [...]

Remembering now, you asked what Schwarzkopf did with her hands when singing. Her right hand was usually resting on the piano and the left relaxed by her side, and sometimes she put the left hand on the piano lid behind her forming a V – but always very relaxed. Perhaps the nicest thing was that she instead of nodding her head at the accompanist when ready to start, during the applause she would lower her head, and would raise her head, looking slightly upwards, with [the] entire expression of [the] next song on her face, to indicate that she was ready to start. One song I remember had a long quiet introduction and I shall never forget her stillness during it all so as not to detract attention from the musical sounds, almost atmospheric, of the piano. She hardly ever clasped her hands in front of her – only between songs when acknowledging applause. Talking about this, I was just the other day talking to someone who had seen Callas in concert in London. Her gestures, according to this person, were not necessarily big but always had strength and point. She sang the *Macbeth* sleep-walking scene and walked off at the end – but produced such a fantastic effect with her timing, and made the audience believe, half through the walk, that she was stopping walking having forgotten something, singing the high D flat bit, but in fact was moving all the time. [...]

Am happy that you are working on the voice and that you are feeling much less of the previous strain which is surely a sign of goodness. What's this about not having technique? Nonsense! You have a technique that most singers (and I include the celebrated ones of Europe) would give their eye teeth to have. Perhaps, then what you mean is that singing rapid scales and arpeggios has never come easily to you. But to whom has it come easily, only a few isolated cases. Just think Sutherland spent more than 8 years at it, and what about Callas. [...]

I hope the concerts at Bellville [on the outskirts of Cape Town] are successful but this idea of not preparing and practising with an accompanist makes me so angry. It is just this Manca mentality. If anything is to be presented to an audience, it must have careful preparation. And you know how important rehearsing is. My blood curdles when I think of those concerts when singers arrive, and then accompanist and perhaps without having laid eyes on each other, they proceed to give a joint effort at pleasing the audience and usually fail. If I could just raise the mentality of people above this I would die happy and contented. [...]

---

155 Jephtas obtained a Teacher's Licentiate Diploma in Music at the College of Music at the University of Cape Town in 1963. The Eoan Group funded his training, but did not support him financially for his studies abroad.

It wouldn't cost Manca anything to think that he is on a par with La Scala. But Scala is Scala and Eoan is Eoan. One cannot compare cognac with Coca-cola, because even though both are drinkable, they're not nearly the same. [...]

But better collect my thoughts and I may even have this lengthy epistle dispatched to you within a day or so with a bit of luck. Oh yes, my opera going! I may have mentioned before that there are two singers who enjoy the Callasian reputation of being singing-actresses, and naturally, I couldn't miss either of them at any cost. First came Magda Olivero,[156] an aged singer (57) who now only sings *Adriana Lecouvreur* - in fact, she makes an annual tour of Italy in the part, and has the reputation for being its best and foremost interpreter. It is an opera which both Callas and Tebaldi have sung at Scala (I think). The opera is not one that comes off easily, because although it has frequent broad and sweeping melodies it is rather considered a bad imitation of the more famous Puccini. The opera revolves mostly around the great actress, Adrianna, with a love intrigue (naturally) and some peculiar political conspiracy. For most of the first two acts Olivero struck me as being overrated because the gestures were stagey and not at all convincing. Every actress feels certain things in different ways, but the one who can convince that what she is doing is valid is great - a hesitant in-between produces confusion in the audience. [...] One thing that bothered me immensely was that in the last act she comes out of bed in a nightdress but beautifully combed hair - it reminded me of the Eoan production of *Traviata* in Act IV when Violetta climbs out of bed, but looking as if she had instead been at the hairdressers! But with all Olivero's greatness she could not bring the opera above its often moments of boredom.

Next came Leyla Gencer in *Aida*. I trekked the 250 [*recte* 175] miles to the open-air theatre in Verona in the heat and open road and having got there at 5.30 (after 8 hours) found that it was "house full". This meant spending every penny on a black-market ticket at 3 times the price - no food. The performance started at 9.30 p.m. but already at 7.00 when the gates opened there were thousands eager to claim a good seat - they're unnumbered. Such enthusiasm. And by 9.30 there were 25,000 people - I won't have believed it if I hadn't been there.

The production is spectacular and gigantic - no elephants this time. Only two horses, whereas Zeffirelli's Scala production boasts 6 horses. The scenery when lit was tremendously effective and even though the Nile came cascading down like the Victoria Falls, it was nonetheless an experience to see. The stage bore thousands [of singers], and in the triumphant scene it was a blaze of colour with fidgety and itchy Italian guards. [Carlo] Bergonzi sang Radamès - what a stylish singer he is - a small voice for [a] dramatic tenor but always pleasing. But talk about looking funny - he looked an absolute scream in his costume and his acting consisted mostly of a few steps forward or a change of direction on a high note.

Gencer as Aida was not nearly what I expected - all too sexy - alla Jayne Mansfield, making every endeavour to strike poses like [a] strip-tease artist. Yes, she did show more reaction to proceedings going on around her, like the mention of her father, or Amneris calling her "sister". But she was always Gencer and never Aida. The voice is not a very happy one and the rumour is that she doesn't make recordings because it sounds too awful. [...]

The bright star of the evening was the mezzo, Fiorenza Cossotto,[157] who has a clear ringing voice, a very minimum of gestures, but whenever she did anything it was clear why she did so. She has a very free voice and a diaphragm like a bag of potatoes in the beginning but deserved the honours she won.

---

156 Magda Olivero (1910-2014), Italian soprano.
157 Fiorenza Cossotto (*1935), Italian mezzo-soprano, who later sang Amneris in the 1974 EMI recording of *Aida* under Muti.

I came away feeling baffled because at the best of time Aida's costumes looked richer than Amneris's - rich golds upon red and black background. And when Aida's father arrives he looks a real ruffian. Doesn't make sense to me! [...]

My appointment with Serafin[158] I'm hoping to keep, but there's no chance of him charging any less, because if Callas was his most talented student and had to pay through her neck he would hardly do it for nothing in my case. Only Callas had a rich husband. But there are so many things which I need clearing on re the realization of composer's written page which if anybody, only he can help. Perhaps my greatest disappointment in the Group has been that Manca never was the sort of person I could turn to with my purely musical problems and incomprehensions. Anyway, let's see what happens.

Keep up working on the voice and don't forget about the *Norma*, and let's hear from you before I leave Italy.

Lots of love.

Yours.

Gordon.

And THANKS again.

P.S. I hope you have not been bored by this lengthy [divulging].

17

11, Arundel Gardens, London. W.11., England

22 November [1966]

My dear May,

No, I haven't forgotten you. How can I possibly forget my favourite soprano second only to Callas. How are things with you? What are you doing? I have been itching to hear from you and had been putting off writing because I just did not have a permanent address until just some days ago. I spent 7 weeks looking for a room where I can have a piano; and you can imagine the faces of prospective landladies change dramatically on the mere utterance of the first syllable of the word "piano". Because people here live in such close proximity of each other, one is forced to consider neighbours - though I often wonder if neighbours reciprocate that same consideration. Now I'm looking for a piano to buy within my pocket and my very maximum is £4. Sounds ridiculous but I'm told this is more than possible at the larger street markets held each Saturday, with only one snag which is that such luck does not happen every time. So I need to choose my Saturday with the help of the "Stars". The other alternative is to watch the newspapers for those advertising to give away pianos free because they need the space or for some such reason. But there are so many daily papers I just couldn't be bothered with having to make the choice between the elite, snobbish *Times* or its opponent on the other end of the pole - the vulgar *Daily Mail*. So I still don't have an instrument but who knows within the next 7 weeks my luck may change.

Thanks awfully for your letter which I got as I was making my exit from Perugia. Do I miss it? Yes I do because with the sunshine it was the nearest to being home in Cape Town and here now it is oh so cold. My teeth have not stopped chattering for days. This very instant

---

158   Tullio Serafin (1878-1968), Italian conductor.

I'm warming in front of a paraffin effort – but my legs are scorching and my ears like ice. This climactic condition does drive on home-sickness and I am having more spells of this than I dare admit in one breath. The inconsistency and dissatisfaction of human nature in my case alone, causes much speculation. Were I to be home now I'd probably want to be here. Oh dear, what a mess.

Again I must thank you for being so kind to me in Perugia keeping my head above the water level with S.A. rands. I was deeply touched by this and felt so hopeless at my inadequacy of expressing my sentiments at the time. But you know what I mean – I hope.

I am deliberately stalling to write about the Opera Centre and my studies as such because I want first to hear of your activities and will then write a lengthy episode of my impressions and dealings with [this] place. This much I will say now – I have to work like a devil – the pace is fantastic and in the short period of not even two months I have to work through [Mussorgsky's] *Boris Godunov*, [Mozart's] *The Marriage of Figaro*, [Beethoven's] *Fidelio*, [Richard Strauss's] *Capriccio* [and] [Verdi's] *Falstaff*. This week I'm on *Rigoletto*, *Rosenkavalier*, *Barber of Seville*, *Queen of Spades* (Tchaikovsky) and a modern one by Wolf-Ferrari. How do I manage? Actually I don't. But more of this next [time] – so write soon and then I'll be able to have a good moaning session in your direction.

How did "Friends of Italy"[159] go? I heard of several other events. Write and tell all. What [did] you sing – your interpretation, breaths, etc – everything you can manage to write in words. Until then

much love and regards to all.
Gordon.

18

11, Arundel Gardens, London. W.11., [England]

Sunday, 11 December [1966]

My dear May,

Thanks so much for the ever-so-interesting letters of the week, which have provided thrilling reading pleasure and a tinge of nostalgia for Cape Town. But without any facetious preamble, I'd better get on and with luck you might have this reply by Christmas. [...]

Your change of address surprised me even though I do now remember that your folks were waiting for a council house. But where is this Heideveld[160] place – in the vicinity of Athlone? I feel quite alien. I'm sorry that the whole thing is a bit of an inconvenience but perhaps it is a consolation to mention that in this hemisphere even stair-case landings are converted into rooms in which one cooks, lives and sleeps!

Yes, I finally got a piano last week at the colossal fee of £2 a month. And what a performance it was to get it up the stair-case. Anyway, it's happily installed and though not the best of instruments it is at least relatively in tune. [...]

---

159   He probably refers to an operatic concert. Since people of Italian descent were involved with the Group (such as Manca, Rota, Fiasconaro and Magnoni), Eoan probably often sang within the Italian community.
160   Heideveld was a new residential area on the Cape Flats designated for the coloured community under apartheid.

I am thrilled that you are thinking of making a tape for my purpose. As a matter of fact, just last week I wrote to Mr. Sydow requesting the same.[161] I would then be delighted to have 2 tapes, so doing, then not treading on anybody's toes. Could you then arrange to sing different things on your tape and another choice on Mr. Sydow's when he gets around to it which I don't think will be until after *Oklahoma*.[162] Would it not be possible to make your tape with available singers as soon as possible (what about over the holidays?) because I am really anxious to hear several things that I have been wondering about. I have a recorder at the Centre. And it would be easier to make a 2-track recording. [...]

So we come now to the bit I've been threatening to write about – my studies.

First about the Opera Centre – it is housed in a converted old Cinema (like Sadler's Wells Opera) situated in the East End of London which is the permanent place of the Cockney inhabitants and West Indian immigrants and a large contingent of Indian and Pakistani business dealers. The area is equivalent to our District Six in atmosphere and slummy conditions. All this means it is miles out of the way and takes a full hour of both underground train and then bus to arrive there. The building although reorganized inside stands much the same as when it was a cinema. [...]

Some 50 students attend daily of which 4 are in the stage-management course with ambitions to produce eventually; 4 in the repetiteur's class with ambitions to be mostly great conductors. The rest then are singers – a large number of sopranos – decreasing down the line to 3 basses. Most come from Australia or thereabout. It is true that more than half the singing crowd in London are Australian. Then there is [a] Maori girl[163] with an exciting voice – like Vera [Gow] in manner and disposition – working as a soprano but really has mezzo-soprano tendencies. The voice is warm, largish and expressive yet she sings mostly like Mimi.[164] A South African girl, Noreen Hastings,[165] who won the Mimi Coertse scholarship – you may remember her – we were at College[166] together and she sang in *Silas Marner*[167] years ago at [the] Little Theatre. Now she is a dramatic soprano and singing Leonora in the *Trovatore* Garden scene for end-of-term.

The singers spend their days at acting, make-up and fencing classes. Then there are language classes – and coaching sessions with repetiteurs from the Opera Houses who come in a few days a week. The term is spent mostly preparing for end of term or for master classes with an international figure. Last term Paul Schoeffield[168] from Vienna who I had not heard of until then – he produced and coached scenes from *Capriccio*, [Mozart's] *Don Giovanni* and the *Rigoletto* Quartet. Next term is Jani Strasser,[169] top man from Glyndebourne whom I've never heard of before, and there's talk of Richard Bonynge and [Joan] Sutherland coming the term after.

(Monday evening – [I] had to lay off last night for writer's cramp.) We repetiteurs have a 3-hour session on Monday and Tuesday mornings with a senior repetiteur from Covent Garden/Sadler's Wells or a conductor who discusses a complete work in 3 or 4 sessions. In most of the sessions I have not gained much except have my sight-reading ability sent for a

161   He probably asked Sydow to send him a tape of the soloists and the choir.
162   Eoan performed Rodgers and Hammerstein's *Oklahoma!* in January 1967.
163   Probably Kiri Te Kanawa (*1944), who arrived at the Opera Centre in 1966.
164   Mimi Coertse (*1932), South African soprano.
165   Probably Noreen Berry, (1931-2012), South African mezzo-soprano.
166   The College of Music at the University of Cape Town.
167   An opera by the South African/British composer John Joubert (1927-2019).
168   It is unclear to whom Jephtas is referring, as he has presumably misspelt the name; it can hardly have been Paul Scofield the actor (1922-2008).
169   Hungarian opera coach active at the Glyndebourne Opera from 1937 onwards.

Burton[170] – my reading I fear to admit is appalling. One plays and the others sing the parts as allotted by the particular person in charge. This is not a very pleasant situation when on a frosty Monday morning one has to sing Gilda. I have already had to sing Leonore's "Abscheulicher" from *Fidelio* 3 times in a row. It's fun once one has accepted the ugly sounds and uses bags [of] imagination. The attitude is a general lackadaisical one but the pace goes on. Most of the others read well and can scan through a work, but frankly I prefer to spend more time on a piece and at least get to know it well. So I have been trying to get as much preparation in as possible by getting up at 7 a.m. and doing 2 hours work before classes at 10 a.m. The rest of the time is spent with coaching for about 12 hours for the week and playing or conducting rehearsals. When the conductor arrives on the scene we are allotted a turn to take his notes during rehearsals – so far I've not yet played a production rehearsal but only taking notes – things like the tenor should sing C sharp and not D in this bar. The conductor usually leaves as promptly as he arrives if not before and then whoever is on the notes schedule conducts – not that any attention is paid to one, but it's good practise. The singers imagine themselves as the world's next greats and so [are] difficult to get on with. We are considered students only by them – but this suits me fine because I can save my speaking voice and get through a lot of music unknown to me. Italian and German pronunciations are appalling but nobody cares and believe it or not they are allowed to get away with more than you at home.

Naturally, I am appalled and have only scorn for those responsible but am relieved that with the top artists this is not so. Fortunately, I have been able to watch rehearsals with Renato Cioni (who sang in the Callas *Tosca*) and more lately Nicolai Gedda[171] (who recorded *Carmen* with Callas). These fellows know their work and get on with it – don't have involved discussions about what they think Verdi or Berlioz ought to have written but try to find the truth in what has been written. Lower down the line working conditions are rather different – conductors who prefer to talk about "when I was conducting *Puritani* at Wexford, etc…" [or] "this morning I was playing Bach's 2-part inventions" – singers who imagine themselves greater creative geniuses than the composers whose music they are singing and wanting to change everything at will.

All rather like Manca – and the approach to opera at the Centre is exactly like his – just lots of notes near enough to what has been written and the voice, voice and more voice.[172] Perhaps when I have learnt that the so-called professional world is largely [full] of Manca-types who delight in preening themselves before audiences, life will be more tolerable. Therefore I have no desire to work professionally in this country unless in the very top and with my limited capabilities that is just impossible.

Working conditions are much the same as in the Group and singers make no less errors on stage. The only difference I have noticed is that the initial rehearsals go at a quicker pace because everybody reads music – but this has no advantage on the end-product and after all that is what matters.

Where do I fit into all [of this?] – just a desire to learn as much as possible from everybody, listen, keep my ears open and my mouth shut. This is working for now and I hope this attitude lasts.

We have free passes to opera performances but I've just not had the time to go.

I must finish this and get it posted if you are to get it by the end of the week.

---

170 English slang: "gone missing".
171 Nicolai Gedda (1925–2017), Swedish tenor.
172 The saying "voice, voice, voice" as the prime prerequisite of a singer is variously attributed to Rossini and Verdi.

Write soon – and I'll be very grateful to have that tape as soon as you can make it. [I am going] on holiday from 18 December and back to work on 2 January already.
Much love to Trudy and Wendy,
and your family.
Love
Gordon.

[P.S.] End of term things are: garden scene from *Trovatore*; garden scene from *Falstaff*; a scene from the Mozart *Idomeneo* and [Ermanno] Wolf-Ferrari's *Inquisitive Women* in English. The others in Italian. I'm on percussion playing in the orchestra for this lot – that is when I don't miss the cue after counting 179 or so bars.
    Love.

19

11, Arundel Gardens, London. W.11., England.

Sunday, 5 February [1967]

[...] My dear May,
    Thank you ever so much for your most readable and delight-packed letter of the other day which was most certainly worth waiting for; I must admit having anticipated a bit of a break in our correspondence because of the festive season, etc, so not to worry! Oh yes, thanks ever so much for your card at Christmas.
    Your account of *Oklahoma* is so breathtaking that I can only heave a sigh of relief at the thought that I might have been involved in it were I in C. Town. As a matter of fact, I do rather dislike musical comedy outside [Bernstein's] *West Side Story* and perhaps [Lerner and Loewe's] *My Fair Lady* mainly because the relationship between music and dialogue doesn't convince me over much of either's worth, and because such a work has little intrinsic worth it has and needs to be brilliantly staged for which only the Americans have the dollars. Mr. Sydow consequently sent me a programme, which I thought had ravishing photos of Pat, Winnie and one or two of the others – but what a pain when the chorus and dance groups appear later on. Also so many new faces that I am feeling already distressingly out of touch. And also a newspaper cutting of Pat with her factory associates[173] getting the prima donna treatment. [...]
    The end-of-term things went as successfully as they could with nothing to rave about. There were odd moments of enjoyable singing. Noreen Hastings scored among the highest with her *Trovatore* scene. A nice dark sound which she seems so intent on darkening that it worries the listener. She insisted on singing the high D flat in the "Tacea la notte" cadenza – the note is not comfortable in her present compass and I haven't yet understood why the thousands of coaches, producers, conductors and their assistants didn't make her rather sing a B flat or C well than D flat badly. She does show her teeth and wore a fabulous empire-styled costume but couldn't manage the train well enough. During this period at the Centre what worried me most was that

---

173   This refers to a newspaper article in the Cape, featuring Eoan singers in their daytime environment, many of whom worked in clothes factories.

as the performances drew nearer there were increasingly more people interfering with production and music handing out advice and above all asserting their self-importance. However, if this led to better performances, good – but it seemed to confuse the issue rather. The performers did not know whom to listen to with the result that what they produced was invariably a mediocre and uncomfortably mid-way. For instance, the Director of the Centre had been away ill for the whole of the term, arrived one week before [the performances], immediately started running rehearsals which already had [a] producer and conductor in charge – he often stopped proceedings and peered over [the] orchestra to advise violin-players how to play this or that passage. This really was the conductor's business, not his no matter how much the sound may have annoyed him. He is beyond doubt a knowledgeable man but there is a great difference between imparting knowledge and showing off how much one knows. He is an aspiring conductor having worked at length in New Zealand but not good enough for Covent Garden and now is intent on arranging all the Centre's productions around him on the rostrum. A perfectly disagreeable state of affairs, but proves to me that there are mostly "Mancas" in this business who bluff their way around talking about – "respirational relationship with vocal sound emittance" – which doesn't enhance performances there nor make them better. Just yesterday morning I was on call for the mid-term rehearsals for a modern Czechoslovakian work. The producer after some moments commented [saying] something like "I prefer that someone who knows some music should tell me ..." (a compliment, if anything), to which Mr. Director replied "I have a great knowledge of music", between gritted teeth. This then indicates the run of the place.

The Sutherlands' visit to [the] Centre is at the moment still as much likely as unlikely with nothing finalised. I do hope they do come. This term a man from Glyndebourne Opera, Jani Strasser is coming and I have fortunately been allocated this job. He is a great ensemble coach and is doing many obscure scenes from Cimarosa's *Secret Marriage* to Meyerbeer's *L'Etoile du Nord*. The man is a non-entity to me but has much reputation on hearsay. But this is not till March. [...]

No news about Callas, except that the senior Covent Garden repetiteur, called [Norman] Feasey is the only man she rehearses with when in London is reported to say that she has tremendous drive and intelligence. I have had classes with this man on *Rigoletto* – and he was most revealing. He may come back to do [Wagner's] *Tristan* and then perhaps I may have the chance to speak to him of Callas. Yes, she has recorded *Forza*.[174] I'll scout around and let you know what I find. [...]

I got into Birgit Nilsson's[175] *Turandot* after queueing for 5 hours in the beastly cold and getting a standing seat for £1 – (far too expensive), (Callas was only 14/- and worth more). The production was an old one dating to many years ago. She wore her own head-dress and fingernail attachments but local costumes. I always imagined her as a huge tall woman, but in fact she's no taller than Sophia Andrews[176] but has this regal bearing which gives her extra height and breadth. She has a huge voice which is very white in colour and fearfully strident. [The] moments when there was a full orchestra and chorus at fortissimo behind and she on a high note were thrilling because she just pierced through the battery of sound as if it was the easiest thing in the world and made one appreciate that she is considered the greatest Wagnerian soprano of the day. And as the evening progressed more and more I wished that she would stick to German opera. The voice is not warm enough for the very exposed passages of Italian

---

174 *La forza del destino* by Giuseppe Verdi. This recording was made in 1954.
175 Birgit Nilsson (1918-2005), Swedish soprano.
176 Sophia Andrews, Eoan mezzo-soprano, active from 1958 to 1972.

opera. It is a piercing sound and therefore not what one could call beautiful. Her Italian is not impeccable and not without trace of a Swedish accent. Her vocal technique and stamina need more than admiration and she attacks every sound from above as opposed to Italianate singers who attack everything from below. She makes a worthy attempt at acting and succeeds most of the time. The Calaf was American James McCracken[177] who is at least 1½ [times] the size of [Joseph] Gabriels and sang with satisfying mastery and I would like to hear more of him.

Then came Dietrich Fischer-Dieskau[178] who is currently singing *Arabella* (Richard Strauss). What a magnificent artist in the Callas, Schwarzkopf class who has an amazing vocal artistry and everything one can want. Much vivid acting with foot-stamping Polish mazurka moments. But what I liked most was that there wasn't spasms of acting and then spasms of singing as so often happens but a fantastic whole. The female was Joan Carlyle[179] who makes the most beautiful head sounds I have ever heard and the part suited her admirably. This by the way was [the] dress-rehearsal which is usually on the morning 2 days before opening night. Carlyle who is quite 36 or more looks very young from out front, and most of the singers at Covent Garden and elsewhere are in that age-group. What I'm trying to say is that Manca's idea of 21-year olds is for the birds.[180] The rehearsal started [at] 10.30 [and went on] until 2.30 and though Dieskau sang from the word go, she only started giving voice in the last act. I tried to get into performances but no luck. Now he is to sing *Falstaff* and with tons of luck I may just get a standing seat.

One of the advantages of being at the Opera Centre is to be able to watch production rehearsals of Covent Garden which are held at the Centre. Latterly, Solti[181] (musical director and brilliant conductor) was rehearsing Gwyneth Jones[182] in *Fidelio* which was very rewarding to watch. She has a huge voice, dark in colour - is quite unaffected and there are hopes that she will become a great singer [if she] hangs around. She may well. The present day idea is that the legend of Callas will divide in three ways, Suliotis, Caballé and Welsh Gwyneth Jones. One hopes. These singers are good and could perhaps achieve 1/10 of what Callas has, and that would be a lot. I heard Jones in *Don Carlos* - not an intense actress and beauty of the voice comes first and not always well under control. The sounds come in wallops of a lot a noise and then less. She sang quite remarkably at rehearsals always in full voice although only once [in] her big piece - "Abscheulicher".[183] Solti is a dynamic man who knows how to get what he wants. Suliotis comes from South America and spent a year in Milan before branching out. She has possibilities but those who have seen her say she's inexperienced (naturally) but makes thrilling dramatic sounds from the chest to D flat high above. Caballé is Spanish and just issued a recital record - sings Bellini and other florid music. Have heard some of the record and though she makes nice sounds she struck me as undisciplined. The story goes that when she came to sing at Glyndebourne to sing in *Rosenkavalier* she arrived 10 days before without having looked at the part. A bad stroke of unprofessionalism and what peeved everybody involved was [that] everybody else went raving when she appeared on stage. Talking about professionalism - the general idea of this much talked about and over-rated situation strikes me as one of not wasting time because it costs money. At the Centre they continually talk about it and say you can't do that or this - and spending more time talking about it instead of just getting on with it without all this talk. [...]

---

177   James McCracken (1926–1988), American tenor.
178   Dietrich Fischer-Dieskau (1925-2012), German baritone.
179   Joan Carlyle (1931-2021), English soprano.
180   Manca often used young singers to sing technically advanced roles, which was at times detrimental to their voices.
181   Georg Solti (1912-1997), British-Hungarian conductor.
182   Gwyneth Jones (*1936), Welsh soprano.
183   A scene from Beethoven's opera *Fidelio*.

After all this moaning and complaining I'd rather prefer to work in a place like home where one can make an attempt to produce serious art than amongst this run-of-the-mill non-chalance. Only on the highest levels (which are rare) is what one can call Art. And now I appreciate Callas's views on this very subject.

Covent Garden issued a scarf autographed by Sutherland and Callas and so, feeling good I thought I'd get you one until they told me it costs £4.10.0 because it's silk. So the most I can do is write about my good intentions. Sorry! [...]

Am pleased that you are working on your volume stop, but why "Madre, pietosa Vergine"[184] - there are many more other interesting pieces. Believe me, Vera's sound volume is unusual and one doesn't find it easily - what I mean is that it is not an everyday occurrence. Most singers here have much less than you. But I am pleased that you have diminished all inhibitions and that's shaping well. Keep me in touch please.

You can subscribe to the *Opera Magazine* and have it sent to you monthly directly from here. Do join as soon as you can because it's a good and useful magazine. For 12 issues (that is, one year) the subscription rate is £3.0.0. Individual copies cost 3/6 (here). If you then send postal orders to: Opera, Rolls House Publishing Company Ltd., Rolls House, Breams Buildings, London, E.C.4, they will send each volume direct to you every month. Make clear that you want "Opera" because they publish also other music magazines (I think). Alright? Let's know what happens.

Much love and write soon.

Yours,

Gordon.

Best wishes to your family, kisses for Trudy & Wendy.

 20

11, Arundel Gardens, London. W.11., England.

Thursday, 30 March [1967]

My dear May,

Well a month has passed by since you wrote to me! How the time rushes by - please let me apologize for the procrastination (a vice that governs my life most malevolently). [...]

Traviata has come and gone.[185] Were you involved? And how did it go? By the time you get this, the operatic concert will be hanging in the air.[186] Do your very best with the "Pace"[187] aria - I have heard only the most fantastic reports about how well you sing the piece. And so you will do it even better. Remember from me before you go on stage = GOOD LUCK AND "ART". [...]

Am thrilled about your plans to do the *Otello* arias - and don't learn a single note or word without being fully aware of the meaning and so doing you will get Verdi's intention. Promise? (I am making you promise so many things. Am I being hard?) [...]

---

184 An aria sung by Leonora in Verdi's opera *La forza del destino*.
185 Eoan presented a once-off performance for government dignitaries on 14 March 1967. Roos (2018): 202.
186 Eoan gave many concerts with operatic excerpts between their opera seasons.
187 He is probably referring to the aria "Pace, pace, mio Dio" from Verdi's *La forza del destino*.

Yes, warmer weather has made a bleak appearance but without much impact. I ventured outdoors only once without a coat (but still wearing the other multiple of woollen garments which as you know I need no invitation to wear in the fiercest Cape sunshine). But my courage or better my chattering teeth failed me and after only 10 steps down the road I hastily returned for my "Boston-blanket". [...]

Before I forget – as you had increased the status of my humble abode to "Mansions" some of your correspondence made a near tour of the world before getting into my expectant hands. My vanity is absolutely delighted by your subconscious raise in the social ladder (which in England plays a more important part than the over-publicized no-integration laws in S[outh] A[frica]) but my genuine anxiety to receive your news as soon as possible overrules my ego.

We come then eventually to *Traviata*. This is to be a new Covent Garden production with all the designs in black and white – costumes and set. The only splash of colour in Act I is to be red camellias. This alone is causing much dissension and the general talk is – it won't be *Traviata*. The adventurousness appeals to me no end. The conductor is Giulini[188] – a tall aristocratic looking person, quiet but breathing authority without ever needing to let anybody know his high position. He gives the impression of being a simple man who prefers to do the job and try again, rather than talk and talk about his greatness or past successes. He arrives for the very first rehearsal unlike most others who have deputies and [he] knows the piece – and well – every single word from memory. Visconti and he work hand in hand to an astonishing and revealing degree each complementing the other. Giulini watches every move and finds out every motivation behind each stage action. The partnership is fantastic. Violetta is Mirella Freni from Scala, Alfredo [is sung by] Renato Cioni and Germont [by] Piero Cappuccilli.[189] The rest are Covent Garden singers, etc. [...]

Freni is not Callas but she takes [to the] production without fuss unlike most others who find the need to protect their shortcomings. I was touched by the method of work – and this is what I treasured most and meant so much to me. They were searching for a truth and this made opera worth it for me. The greatest lesson was watching Visconti who was pensive and absorbed in concentration and what a revelation when he demonstrated. He showed Violetta's weakness in Act 3 by flopping into Anina's arms with uncanny realness. This experience alone has made the Opera Centre worth it for me.

Now they have moved to the Covent Garden stage for the next fortnight, so I shan't be able to watch any more rehearsals but must go to performances.

I wanted badly to talk to Visconti but couldn't get to him. He sat at a table next to mine in the canteen but was too busy talking to Giulini and Cioni. I wanted so badly to ask so many things and [about] Callas – but did not have the presumption to do the former and thought it better not to [ask] about Callas who was his greatest Violetta at such a time. So I'm thankful for having seen him work. [...]

Am feeling quite exhausted already. So I'll close now and if you write soon I shall have recovered enough from the writer's cramp to write another epistle.

Much love to Trudy & Wendy and your family.

    Bye for now.

        Love,

           Gordon.

---

188   Carlo Maria Giulini (1914–2005), Italian conductor.
189   Piero Cappuccilli (1926–2005), Italian baritone.

21

11, Arundel Gardens, London. W.11., England.

Sunday, 14 May [1967]

My dear May,

Your breath-taking running commentary of back-stage at the Operatic Concert was so scintillating that I needed time in order to find something of such equal to catapult back. But, the days have been ticking by (at the normal, ferocious rapidity, I may add) and I can hardly say that I have found anything to compete with your literary exercise.

Before forgetting – many thanks for the enclosed newspaper reviews. During the past I have not been so fortunate as on this occasion because as inevitable, everybody[190] thought someone else would let me have all the "dope", with the result that I never had any. So this time I boxed clever (or so I thought) and made a special trip to South Africa House[191] a day or so after the concert to scan the newspapers for all information. So feeling very pleased [with] myself I came home to find your letter with write-ups and a week [later] the same from Mr. Sydow. One is not allowed to win in life, though frankly, it is much more satisfying to have many than none, wouldn't you say? [...]

I also got copies of the programme – I must have complained furiously last time. What a long programme it seemed – 13 items in [the] 2nd half. Couldn't help thinking that the new motto must be they-want-opera-so-we'll-give-them-opera. Opera fans could hardly complain about the pound of flesh. I find [it] hard to believe that the Maestro [i.e. Joseph Manca] did not make his after-the-soloist trips back and from the Green Room – an improvement for the better!

Funny you mention the solitude of after a concert – I think most people experience it – and really it always appears such an anti-climax to me. But I think I know exactly how you must feel.

It is so very gratifying to know that your throat troubles are now over and when I think that we will be able to work together again I get so excited and thrilled that I want to come home immediately.

No, actually I finish the term at the end of July – and unfortunately no more bursaries are coming my way, so we'll just wait and see. [...]

Among the other operas I have been seeing were *Cavalleria* and [Leoncavallo's] *Pagliacci*. Both were Zeffirelli productions and an education in itself. The soprano in *Pagliacci*, Joan Carlyle, was by far the most satisfying because of her lack of mannerisms and identification with the role – none of the normal "now-I'm-singing-I-must-face-the-audience, now-I'm-not-singing-I-can-look-away-or-even-turn-my-back".

We come to *Traviata*. Yes, I saw it 3 times in all. One dress rehearsal, one performance on television and the first performance. I thought the black and white sets worked well except the 1st act which somehow lost atmosphere. There were splashes of colour in the costumes juxtaposed over the basic black and white. Violetta's first dress was black with a white rose outline – Act 2 white basically mottled with black, Act 3 – white adorned with dark red (plum) leaves. In the same way the gypsies and Spanish dancers had splashes of colour. Act III – Flora's act is the best realization of anything I have ever seen – and in this act Visconti triumphed. There was a cohesion between movement, costume, voice, orchestra, set and even hair-styles.

---

190   Colleagues and friends in the Eoan Group and at home.
191   The High Commission of South Africa, located on Trafalgar Square in London.

The impression was greatly moving and an experience which does not come often. [...] But the star and revealing light par excellence was Giulini - no I-am-the-great attitude. I never realized [that] purely orchestral playing could enhance every emotion of each character so much - he was not accompanying and beating time or pointing fingers - he was Violetta, Germont, Alfredo, Marchese - each character. Already in the overture one felt the pathos of the whole situation to come - it was no longer a piece of music before the opera starts, but part of it. During the "Dite alla giovine" one could feel him crying and the orchestra produced just that sound of desperation and later on one could feel exactly what Alfredo's anger was in the single bar before "Ogni suo aver tal femmina". To just have watched Giulini's face one could see the whole of *Traviata* - every mood. After Callas, I have learnt more from him in this single opera about music - and I'm grateful. [...]

Of the actual singers there was much which was good, though I was somewhat unhappy because none were able to sustain the greatness instilled by these two great artists because they just lacked that extra bit of personality and strength. [Mirella] Freni did marvellously - but without Visconti directly in front [of her] to coax every conviction, she paled at times in things like swallowing for a breath or such. [...]

On the opening night of *Traviata* I made my way to the Opera House in the quest for a standing ticket and just by co-incidence bought a newspaper *en route* only to find a picture of Madame the Tiger [i.e. Maria Callas] across the front page. She was in London suing for a ship. Immediately it occurred to me that she might come to the performance. There were no standing seats left but I hung around. This was 6 p.m. A crowd was gathering and the furs and diamonds were rolling. About 10 mins. before starting (7.20) a smart car stopped with a dark elegant woman climbing out. Suddenly there was an uproar of "Viva Maria", "Maria", "Violetta" - and there was Callas, elegant, gracious in a green evening dress - slim and beaming from ear to ear. She was swept through the doors - and her entry provoked instantaneous applause and more "Marias". Well I had to get in and spent £4.10.0 (my whole week's allowance) on a returned seat and proceeded to see Callas and *Traviata*. Luckily I had a good view of her - she was one tier up flanked by the Opera administrator and public relations man. She clapped and applauded like everyone else - got rounds of applause in the first interval in the bar. The next interval she stayed in her seat, powdered her nose, and talked to her chaperone and clutched a pair of glasses which she only put on when the curtain went up. By this time the entire house knew that Callas was there. And though it is impossible to get into the lower section of the house from the gallery which is where all the fans were, some people came to ask her for autographs. But what good grace she has. She indicated that they get the autographs of the artists performing and offered to shake their hands instead. I was watching from my vantage point, aided with binoculars provided for easier vision of the stage. And Callas did not disappoint as a person. People were peering at her from all angles, but she couldn't see a thing without her glasses. I sauntered up nearer and though I had [an] excellent opportunity to speak to her - but what could I say to her? Just as well - because she remains "God" for me and one cannot approach "God". She went backstage after the performance and half-an-hour later left by a side door escorted by Onassis this time with the crowd thronging and imploring her to come back and sing to which she replied simply, but charmingly "Yes, thank you" with that radiant smile. It was an occasion and I didn't mind the ten days of starvation that followed for me ...

It's nearly 2a.m. I have so much yet to write about and I want to get this off tonight. (Wishful thinking.) And as I don't use a pen all that often these days the physical sensation of writing is foreign.

I *hope* that you by now made arrangements for the *Opera Magazine*. Another big favour you are to do for me. If my pocket suited my wishes then you would already be in possession of these two records I want you to own and find.

The first called –

Presenting Montserrat Caballé

(R.C.A. Victor RB 6647) – she sings "Casta Diva", and from [Bellini's] *Il pirata*, [Donizetti's] *Lucrezia Borgia*, etc.

And the second –

Callas Mad Scenes –

arias from *Anna Bolena*, [Ambroise Thomas's] *Hamlet* and *Pirata*.

Promise to get these ([from] Hans Kramer)[192] as soon as you can. I am keen to hear your view of Caballé.

My life has been inundated with a concert with two singers up North (Liverpool) where they did English and American Art songs and [the] *Traviata* Germont-Violetta duet. I made another study of that part and for the first time knew what every word meant and implied, and realized how great Verdi is. Later this week I'm involved with *Don Giovanni* (Mozart) excerpts at the Centre and although the spasmodic complimentary gestures in my direction has qualmed [*sic*] my human vanity I still have enough scruple left to be worrying to death about what Mozart meant. To me it is not going at all well – I cannot find any identification to the work and have not yet been able to fathom or understand it. It is a great worry and for one or another reason I have just not done enough work on the piece – and the lousy singers don't help. How I wish and long for [a] situation where one can search into the depths for an Art instead of this prima-donna preening. I am experiencing – not only that, but conductors who think they are greater than Mozart. I hope I shall be able to sleep when this week is over. Please write soon. Much love to all at home.

Yours,

Gordon

P.S. At [the] 1st performance Freni broke into tears after "Sempre libera" when the curtain opened again. The strain must have been tremendous and taxing. The audience loved her and she was pelted with flowers – a luxury around here!

2A, Colum Road, Cardiff. Wales. Great Britain.

30 July 1967

My dear May,

I am stricken with utter and unabashed shame for not having written before now, and this sensation is only doubled when I notice that your letter is dated May 31st. If I were an ostrich and had the sand, I would surely be burying my head – but just as well I'm not or this letter won't get much beyond this preamble.

How are you? Well and making the most of things I hope. [...]

---

192   A well-known classical record store in Cape Town at the time.

Figure 2.2 Joseph Manca conducting the Eoan Group in rehearsal in the Cape Town City Hall.
Source: Cloete Breytenbach Collection, DOMUS.

I listened to the tape several times and as Mr. Manca warned me in an accompanying note, the recording [of the Eoan singers] was by no manner nor means excellent – perhaps just a bit too much treble to make the female voices sound shrill and sharp – but however, not too distressingly so. Further, I don't really know whether I should blatantly say all the things that occurred to me while listening to the tape because after all, it is much easier to sit in an arm-chair, as it were, 6,000 miles away and pass "judgement" than to get on that stage and "bark" in a sensible manner. But here goes and a request for your indulgence. Good impressions first – the Italian pleased me in nearly every single case – not impeccable by any means but comprehensible and such a joy after the excruciating pain one has to endure with the "English" Italian. Then the innate musicality of the singers – another great joy – and though not necessarily right every time in the context of the style of the aria involved – it nonetheless gave great pleasure that they felt some sort of rhythmic pulse and shape for the operatic phrases. What most appalled me was the lack of precision about what the composer wrote (unknowingly perhaps in this case).[193] Vera, sounding composed again and splendid in moments, in "Ritorna vincitor"[194] sang just that much too many notes which Verdi had not written. Something like it, but not quite. And in view of what you had written about how she had to learn the piece, her courage is admirable – but this must not be allowed because one thing leads to another and before we know where we are just anything will be accepted! God forbid that day! Though I'm not in the habit of showering you with congratulations, for the obvious reason that a word of congratulation cannot compensate your artistic worth alone, I cannot resist the urge to admire the poise, professionalism and vocal understanding. But alas, you did not convince me that you understood the meaning and drama of the aria.

193   Inaccuracies in performance were perhaps exacerbated because several of Eoan's singers could not read staff notation.
194   Aria from Verdi's *Aida*.

"Pace" is not my best piece as you well know so I'm most likely being unfair. So you have the benefit of the doubt.

Of other concern was Winnie's[195] disregard for the coloratura in "Caro nome" and the abusive chest voice. (Strange coming from me? But there's chest voice and chest voice.) If she must sing coloratura stuff she ought to do something about singing every note in those passages instead of an abysmal portamento – not her fault perhaps and I do know that she has much difficulty in this respect but this by no means means that any member of an audience has to endure it. Chest voice is out of place for Gilda who is virtuous, 15 or 16 years old – wouldn't you say? Her resort to this device was far more admirable in *Oklahoma*. Jimmy [James Momberg] makes sounds in the Italian tradition and I'm trying to work out the facial contortions you mentioned but cannot imagine what he can be doing. Just as well one cannot see on a tape. Bennie[196] sounds sonorous and in healthy voice and for improvement I give full marks. If he works in this manner – one has high hopes for something worth it.

I adored Patricia [van Graan]'s sound in *Oklahoma*, but there again I would like to see.

Well, I could have seen had I conceded to Mr. Sydow's earnest request for me to come back with them. Unfortunately, months before his discussion the [Opera] Centre [in London was] negotiating for me to play the piano for a 6 month tour of Wales and England doing "Opera for All". As I was likely to be stranded and penniless I agreed to accept if the work permit and legal side got sorted out. And as this was all going on when the Sydows arrived, I had to give them preference. This means that I will be performing in hazardous conditions – no orchestra, no chorus, but 3 operas from cover to cover with solo singers.[197] Now I'm stationed in Cardiff until mid-September – so don't wait months to write in my example. [...]

To the two records I've mentioned before you must add another – Elena Suliotis Recital. She sings arias from [Verdi's] *Macbeth*, etc. I have talked about her before – [she has a] voice of fire like Callas, but cannot act my friends tell me. [...]

Because the Opera Centre released me several weeks before the end of term, I had to forfeit my chance with Joan Sutherland – another fury to add to my standing Serafin[198] one. As compensation Mrs. Sydow and I went and stood through a performance of [Donizetti's] *Daughter of the Regiment*. We saw Sutherland before [the performance] and she posed for pictures and was, in fact, awfully sweet. Little prima donna-isms which her lesser colleagues make a habit of, but I got the impression that here was a hard-working woman staying at the top with more hard work. The performance vocally was superb and the acting a joy. Mrs. Sydow said in the interval after S[utherland] had executed a long trill on E and F (in the 4th space and 5th line) "making her voice like a bottle floating in water". This was perhaps not the most eloquent of statements, but at least S[utherland]'s art made her aware of the trill and this makes her work, for me at any rate, invaluable. [...]

I get quite excited when I think of all the things I would like to do when I get home – eventually. But as we know, there are problems and problems!

Cardiff is not exactly a beautiful place – horrid like Port Elizabeth and flat like East London. Not very congenial in any sense.

---

195   Winifried du Plessis, Eoan soprano.
196   Benjamin Arendse, Eoan baritone.
197   On this tour, Jephtas played for over 70 performances in total of Smetana's *Two Widows*, Donizetti's *Don Pasquale* and Rossini's *Cenerentola*.
198   Jephtas had wanted to study with Serafin, see his letter of 10 July 1966.

The singers are not the brightest in the world and conditions of work very far from ideal. Nonetheless, the experience may prove valuable – at least one hopes that it will.

Don't, I repeat, wait as long as I to reply – and let's know all about how the operas[199] are going. And, the best of luck to all.

All the best to your folks; kisses for Trudy and Wendy.

Yours,

Gordon.

23

2A, Colum Road, Cardiff. Wales. Great Britain.

Monday, 28 August [1967]

My dear May,

Just an hour ago at 10p.m. I got back into Cardiff after an absence of two weeks and am so moved by your letters which were waiting that I cannot resist an inner compulsion to reply immediately.

And now that I have pen and paper in hand, I hope that I will be able to spread the millions of thoughts rushing through my head out in a logical and comprehensive order. [...]

I haven't looked at a *Butterfly* score since last time and so now I'll just have to take pot luck and hope I don't make furious blunders. Better still, I shall keep this involvement general and get a score tomorrow and write details that occur to me in another letter. My only other contact with the opera was a performance at Covent Garden with Elizabeth Vaughan. But I don't remember much of it because I wasn't struck by the validity of the performance – though she walked off with 3rd prize for an international Madame Butterfly contest in Japan just recently. No accounting for tastes. No doubt, she sings well and all that but there was no "TRUTH". About the Callas recording – you don't say whether you have it or not. If *not* then it is in "my" room at [the] Sydows[200] – ask Mr. Sydow and say that I asked that he lends it to you, because if it is in the house, then it belongs to the Group, hence the "lend". (I can't remember which recording I left there!) Okay, you must get on to that immediately.

That you've read a book on Japanese art and culture and one on Puccini is wholly admirable. That you have not found much that is tangible as regards Cio-Cio-San shouldn't despair you. These things are only found by much research and what you have seeped in from these two books will be of use also subconsciously, and never wasted. If you can get a book of *Puccini's letters* and read his correspondence to family and friends at the time when he was writing *Butterfly* you will have more chance of discovering his own feelings about Cio-Cio-San and the opera. I'll see what crops up this end – Cardiff is not well equipped in these things. Cape Town is perhaps more efficient.

[*Butterfly*] at the age of 15, I cannot agree more that the love-duet should be tender – and a Japanese 15 at that. And this conception would suit your "young-voiced" tenor ideally. And all the other things you say – Yes – sincere love, teasingly, childish, innocence, etc. YES.

---

199 Preparations were underway for the Group's 7th Opera Season, to take place in September 1967.
200 Jephtas lived with Ismail and Carmen Sydow for much of the time that he was with Eoan.

The big change for me is between Act I and II – nine months later Butterfly bears Pinkerton's child, and you're a mother yourself to have 1st hand experience. From my own personal observation – once a woman has borne the first off-spring she almost immediately becomes mature by the purely maternal instincts. Whether she is Japanese, American or Italian – believe me. Therefore you must establish already from when Suzuki mutters her prayer and not later that your "pigri ed obesi son gli Dei giapponesi" that you are a mother. How? In attitude! The pain of childbirth leaves a remarkable stamp – so when the curtain goes up for that you must create in every mother in the audience the feeling inside that B[utterfly] has given birth – and this is later confirmed when you bring in the child for Sharpless's benefit. Also, 3 years have passed (Sharpless in the letter-scene reads "tre anni son passati") and in Japanese ancient feminine life this is a *long time* and you deduce from your book "she would not have been (virtuous) had she been a year older". [...]

My general observation – the great difference between Act I and what follows in Act II and III. For instance, if Act I is sung lightly and tenderly, childishly say in a white voice then the rest in fuller tones to suggest her maturity and aging (after 3 years). You have to find your own medium and I can't lay down any convictions unless I hear it which is how we are accustomed to work – on result alone. And how much I wish I were around. But, let's not bemoan the fates and search for deeper truths for an artistic performance of the highest level. [...]

I am especially pleased that you refrain from comments from you-know-who[201] to the tenor about how it was done last time[202] – I don't believe that it is the way to get a homogeneous performance – what matters is what inspiration you can evoke in the tenor and others when you are singing and when they are singing to you. With the lack of time there is hardly any for letting anybody get inhibited by his or her shortcomings. All the best of luck for making your Callas magic work.

Don't get too depressed with the irritation caused by the flu, etc. Remember that for *Tosca* Callas went on stage with a temperature of 104° and worse other ailments. And if she could, you can, should these afflictions keep up. I hope they have disappeared when you receive this epistle of mine.

My hand is aching. I hope I have given some encouragement towards "our" ideal standards, but will write even more in a few days when I have laid hands on a score.

For now, chin up – even the best have to work in hard conditions.

Until later then.

Bye.

Much love and regards and kisses for the children.

Yours,

Gordon.

I am at this address until 19 October, so do write when you have the chance.

2A, Colum Road,

Cardiff

Wales.

P.S. Hope your first orchestral rehearsal was satisfactory.

---

201 Jephtas is probably referring to the producer Alessandro Rota.
202 Eoan's 1962 performance of this opera was produced by Gregorio Fiasconaro.

2A, Colum Road, Cardiff. Wales. Great Britain. CF1. 3EG.

Sunday, 1 October [1967]

Darling May,

So many thanks for your immensely interesting correspondence of the week. I could continue reading such delightful writing all day long without the slightest hint of tiring; and these epistles have indeed become a veritable joy in my life.

Your season[203] ended yesterday, though no doubt the odd repeat performance will follow in due course; and because of your vivid description I don't feel nearly as bad for having missed witnessing the spectacle (I consciously abstain from mentioning the aspect of hearing because there might just arise the chance of hearing it on tape at some later stage.)

I've been devouring numerous newspaper clippings and feel absolutely saturated in the abundance and mass of praise. But before getting on to that, let's reply to your chronicles. […]

How touching of you to write after your 2nd performance and at such a late hour. Tears of sheer joy blinded me for several moments on reading of Fiasconaro's big hearted interest in your work – we believe in your ART and his gesture[204] is, I think, worth far more than any of the flattering newspaper critics or the judgement of other individuals, whoever they may be. Why don't you go and have a chat with him – and should you think of repercussions[205] – nobody need know what you do in your private capacity. Think about it.

Vera's Violetta … it is most pleasing that she has been so well received and I'm very glad of that because she needs just that boost especially after the recent calamities and near-catastrophes. Capetonians seem to love Violetta in any form and are not as discerning as those who know and remember La Callas. So for me, from the newspapers it is difficult to gauge any distinction because you, Ruth [Goodwin], Abeeda [Parker] and Winnie [du Plessis] have earned the same sort of reaction. Perhaps it's Verdi's genius for having written such fantastic music that one … can accept that and forget the rest. I cannot imagine that it was dramatically interesting because I remember Rota's approach.[206] But I live and hope that one day Cape Town will see an incomparable and one-whom-one-can-believe Violetta – the more I hear and see the music the greater it becomes. But I hope that this success does not go to the heads of all concerned. Please convey to her my admiration and the hope that I may hear it soon. […]

I find it particularly difficult to imagine the achievements of the new [principal singers][207] and wonder how much I would accept now and how much my ideas might have changed. Perhaps we will have the chance to see in the near future? The minor principals? … a miracle must be happening.

---

203 For their 7th Opera Season in September 1967, the Eoan Group presented Donizetti's *L'elisir d'amore*, Puccini's *Madama Butterfly* and Verdi's *La traviata* at the Cape Town City Hall.
204 It is not clear what is meant by Fiasconaro's "gesture", but it could have been singing lessons.
205 It was no secret that loyalty towards Eoan's management was required of its members. Manca tended to be an authoritarian music director, and training the singers was a tightly controlled matter. Most of them had vocal tuition from Alessandro Rota, who was also the stage director for their operas. Consulting Fiasconaro, who had directed Eoan productions between 1956 and 1962 but then parted ways with Manca, could have placed Abrahamse in an awkward position.
206 Jephtas considered Rota to be "old school" and preferred Fiasconaro as a director. Rota worked freelance, but Fiasconaro was employed full-time at the UCT Opera School.
207 After Jephtas left for Europe, new soloists joined the Group. They included Martin Johnson (tenor), Lawrence Hosain (tenor), Cecil Tobin (baritone), Freda Koopman (mezzo-soprano) and Ernest Janari (tenor).

Our operas [here in Wales] are going abominably and I would be so grateful if it could [achieve] one thousandth of a measure of artistic success. There's so much politics, daft producers and too much talk. But we'll see. I have still enough scruples to be petrified, and even more than depressed. We start [again] on 22 October, and leave Cardiff on [the] 25th for 6 months of hotels and living out of suitcases. Think of us as we bump over the musical deficiencies.

So you're all film-stars – wow![208] [...]

To the newspapers – for the large part I cannot help but feel that they are just humouring one. It is just that bit too complimentary ... and all the time. To change this is up to the Group itself ... that is, if they want.

Write soon and then perhaps [I] can reply before I leave.

Love to all,

Gordon.

25

2A, Colum Road, Cardiff. Wales. Great Britain. CF1. 3EG.

Sunday, 16 October [1967]

Darling May,

Just now I wish there [was] time to write a long and detailed reply to your letters of yesterday. But alas, this seems unlikely especially as I've a rehearsal within an hour.

And being in a particularly loquacious mood, I shall have to curb the innumerable comments flashing through "upstairs". [...]

I wondered about the Callas *Butterfly* records and am pleased that you got them and that they were of help. Thank God you didn't interpret my reference to "light voice" as being "white" – though through a roundabout fashion.

I want to delve into realms about the programme notes,[209] etc., but dare not. Excuse me!!!

These last weeks [Welsh National] Opera has been in Cardiff. The main company put on about 8 productions of which I saw *Fledermaus*, *Carmen*, [Verdi's] *Nabucco*, *Figaro* [and] *Butterfly*, but [I] rarely stayed till the end. *Butterfly* had a very good conductor and the orchestra stole the performance artistically – for me any[way]. Madama Butterfly was the conductor's wife – horrid voice and just too fat. *Fledermaus* I saw all of, if only because of the excellent Orlofsky, enhanced by the fact that I first saw her as Flora in the Visconti *Traviata* looking ravishingly beautiful and more than feminine and as Orlofsky she gave no indication that it was one of the uncomfortable trouser parts. And she looked like a 16 year old Russian prince.

But as I've no doubt bemoaned before – English singing lacks excitement and that extra something.

With the group I'm with, things are so depressing – no artistic achievement or attainment involved. Everyone is a prima donna and tries to be the star and ART goes for a holiday, or better into exile. What a hard way to learn, but that seems the price to pay at the moment. And here I worry about Rossini and Donizetti and they only about [their] ego, what a life. If La Callas has worked amongst this sort of atmosphere – no doubt, yes – then her fantastic

208 A few productions of the 1967 season were filmed, though without sound. These silent films are part of the Eoan Group Archive, held by the Documentation Centre for Music (DOMUS) at Stellenbosch University.

209 The programme of the Group's production of *Madama Butterfly*.

achievement is even more admirable because her greatness stems not only from herself but the respect she has for the composer.

But enough. To tell the truth, I hope that this will egg another reply out of you before my 6 months of hibernation and forfeiting the privilege of hearing from you …

Much love,

Gordon.

P.S. If you can get a copy of ROSSINI by STENDHAL, it is worth reading the chapter on *Giuditta Pasta*.[210]

26

2A, Colum Road, Cardiff. Wales. CF1. 3EG. Great Britain.

Monday, 23 October [1967]

My dear May,

Thanks so much for your letter which has been the most cheering thing of the day.

It is our first performance in roughly an hour and so while I'm waiting to get on, I thought of replying, and also because I'm fed-up with practising and it's so freezingly cold.

I have succumbed to the dreadful habit of only remembering to answer your questions when my reply is already in the post.

No, they don't do a concert version, nor a full-scale one because there is no chorus nor orchestra; but they have a set, furniture, masses of props, costumes, wigs and God knows what. The singers assist with the stage management and keeping costumes in trim. [...]

I'm sitting on the scaffold holding the main curtain up and [there's] not much light filtering through, so excuse the angle of my writing.

On Friday [Elena] Suliotis appeared on television for an hour singing "Madre, pietosa Vergine", the letter aria from *Macbeth*; another from *Nabucco* and finally "Casta Diva". All in costume. She has this exciting voice but cannot act … and her face doesn't even indicate any sort of emotion. She moves about, throws her arms towards the angel and now and then clutches the throat in full operatic fashion. But nothing is real … she doesn't seem to believe what she sings about. What is most to be admired is how recklessly she uses her voice … sounded like a bass on the "ma" of "conforto e calma" in *Forza*, especially in this country of dainty chirping. Maybe her histrionics will get better… one hopes anyway.

Am glad that the *Traviata* was of interest and of course, I'll tell all about it when the occasion arrives. Elizabeth Vaughan is a tiny creature – like a ballet dancer, with a booming voice which she darkens and darkens to the point of distraction. And very liberal with the chest voice – I once heard her go for a Burton[211] in "Un bel dì, vedremo" by venturing to sing the whole phrase "e poi la nave appare" low in the chest – disaster …

The stage have just told me to bail out.

So Au Revoir

and heaven knows when next I'll have the courage to write.

Much love, Gordon.

---

210 He is referring to *The Life of Rossini*, a biography of the composer by Stendhal.
211 English slang: in this case, "meet with disaster".

c/o Welsh National Opera, Central Hall, Charles Street, Cardiff, Wales. Great Britain.
[written on paper with the letterhead "The Royal Hotel Scunthorpe"]

Monday, 5 February [1968]

My dear May,

Suddenly I have the urge to write, and although I really ought to get myself prepared for the performance of later.

Suddenly, I'm filled with a heavy sadness. I've just been down to breakfast and on opening the paper learnt that Tullio Serafin has died. At the age of 89, naturally one has been expecting such to happen nearly any day, but all along I've been praying and hoping that he might last until I had had the chance of talking and learning from [him]. And I was planning to go immediately [after] this contract ends in April. And now ... How awful can fate be, and how selfish am I (that's what it boils down to!). But he was the one man whose work I've had more respect for than I would be likely to admit and I believed that he would be the only one to have answers for the problems that we encounter in this art-form of Opera.

Now I've missed the boat and can't help but feel dreadful – and cheated. But still!

Forgive me for unloading all this on you – but I have the need to share such a blow, and you are the only one who would really understand this matter, because most others are more concerned with mundane material matters.

Then, while I'm about it, I apologize for being quite such an abominable letter-writer but I guess you appreciate how little inclination one has for the physical exercise of writing when involved with continual performances – and there is still some integrity left to make the attempt to improve on each.

Last night has been snowing pretty heavily and so this morning is rather miserable – for a start it's freezing and then slipping up and down the pavement on the snow that has turned to ice.

Hardly a day for bad news.

We are touring this Northern part of England for the next 4 weeks still – all dirty industrial areas, and the population up this end have such impossible accents that I have already given up trying to understand. After this, it will be back to South Wales for six weeks. And then I shan't be sorry to say goodbye to [Donizetti's] *Don Pasquale*, *Cenerentola* and the *Two Widows*.

I've been babbling on consistently!

How are things with you?

I'm dying to know what you are doing.

All sorts of messages for Wendy and Trudy.

I must go, or be late.

For now, au Revoir,

Gordon. [...]

Welsh National Opera, Central Hall, Charles Street, Cardiff, Wales. Great Britain.

Cardiff, Wednesday, 6 March [1968]

May dearie,

Thank you so much for your very interesting letters which I've just received earlier today. We were having a break from our routine of "detouring" and have now recommenced the Rossinian roulades and out-of-tune singing routine.

But before I go off at a tangent, as is my wont, allow me to express many, many heartfelt thanks for your magnificent birthday card.[212] You are always so thoughtful and heavens, I do really appreciate it. Though I must admit that I do feel rather wistful to think that I've clocked the quarter of a century mark. Soon I shall have to consider investing in some sort of walking stick apparatus. [...]

You ask about my holidays – it seems positively ages ago. But in case you're still interested to know. Quite inadvertently, no, the word [is] unexpectedly, I got on a plane to Switzerland and made for my beloved Italy and La Scala. I saw three productions – I'm sending the latest issue of *Opera* which covers what I saw – and also to induce you to subscribe if you haven't yet. I spent Christmas with some friends outside Perugia and enjoyed all the heavenly spiced Italian home-made dishes, and, of course, drank far far too much. In Milano I saw Joseph, Mabel and their baby.[213] Joseph's working fearfully hard at his singing and I was suitably surprised at his unwavering dedication. Anyhow, he seems to have the right connections and a maestro whom he respects and understands, so pretty soon he will land some contracts and ought to do as well as he can because there is nothing to stop him. And by the time I had done this the holidays were over and 1 January is but an ordinary working day here. [...]

I still haven't quite recovered from the blow of Serafin but what can one do. Your suggestion to work with a pupil of his is an admirable idea except I don't know of any except Callas – and I can hardly see that happening. For the moment, I have just to keep on thinking. [...]

We come now to what you must have found difficult to write about.[214] I must then apologize for having made you feel that you would let me down badly by your decision. Let me say first – I think that it is a very, very wise decision and I can imagine that it must have been a very hard decision to make. Your children are of great importance and I have first-hand knowledge of a fatherless home and it isn't very pleasant in any respect for the children. And so, if even for this alone, I admire you for having made up your mind on so difficult an issue. I am naturally sad that you will not any longer be a member of the Cape Town music scene, but am greatly relieved that you are planning to keep the flag of your art flying high. And so there is no reason that we shall not have the chance of co-operating together. I hope, then, that such an occasion will make an appearance in the near and immediate future.

---

212 His 25th birthday was on 8 March.
213 Eoan's principal tenor Joseph Gabriels relocated to Milan for opera studies in the course of 1967. His wife Mabel and their daughter Vanessa joined him shortly afterwards.
214 In May 1968, Abrahamse moved to Durban with her daughters to join her husband, Jonathan Rushin, who was working there. During that time, she no longer participated formally in Eoan's productions, but was contracted by the Group in 1971 to sing the role of Nedda in Leoncavallo's *Pagliacci*. During this time the principal soprano roles were sung by Vera Gow, Patricia van Graan and Freda Koopman. Abrahamse returned to Cape Town and the Eoan Group in 1972.

I do feel grieved that the Group is to lose an artist of your integrity but we must remember that they have not always offered you a fair deal and so a break might well make them appreciate your art more for future commitments that I hope will crop up.

Under all the circumstances, it strikes me that settling down in Durban would be greatly advantageous and you must no doubt look forward to having your own home again.

Of course, we had plans and let's hope that some of these will materialize.

In the meantime, let me wish you all the very best and don't feel bad about letting me down. In fact, my own plans are so vague that I don't know when I shall reach home. If it will make you feel better, I'll tell you some of my story.

The [Eoan] Group recently offered me the post of assistant musical director on a permanent basis. Unfortunately, [neither] the conditions, nor the financial arrangement suited me, so I turned the post down and offered to come out and work for a few months towards the end of this year (after this tour) and then after having seen the situation we could talk again. Whether they will accept this, as yet I haven't had a reply.

To make matters worse, I don't know whether I can live in South Africa for any length of time without going mad. But that I can only see once [I am] there [...]

On the other hand, I want to go back to Music College and if I can settle negotiations and find the money (which is a problem) I want to go to the Santa Cecilia in Rome.[215]

Then thirdly, I am more than seriously toying with the idea of living in Zurich, (a) because I like the place and (b) the chances of finding occupation seem quite positive. If I had a choice, I'd probably opt for living in Zurich but it is not easy to make such decisions.

I feel that I need to work with the Group because of purely humanitarian reasons and because of the talent and individual people involved. Unfortunately, I have heard such disparaging reports about Cape Town and the insides of the Group. And so, I don't know whether I want to face all this. [...]

If I do come home this year, it won't be before 1 June and you will already have left; but who knows, something might well be arranged.

For now,

ALL THE VERY BEST.

Much love,

Gordon.

P.S. Excuse the scrawl – am writing on my knee. I hope I have indicated all that I meant to say. All sorts of messages for Trudy and Wendy. [...]

---

215   See his letter of 29 December 1968.

29

Eden Villa, Blomvlei Road, Landsdown, Cape Town.

Delta House[216]
Sunday, 8 September [1968]

My dear May,

Having reached what seems the end of any artistic morale, a sudden inclination to answer your most welcome letter of some weeks ago has come over me. Only to find that my pen is completely dry and there is nothing but this damned pencil in sight. But one needs to be thankful for small mercies!!

As you can have gathered from my opening gambit things down here [in Cape Town] are hardly going well in any sense. The present phase is one of despondency and a reluctant admittance to failure on my behalf. I had so hoped to raise the standards of performance just ¼", but the opposing forces are just too tremendous and the whole business is just swivelling away in typical Eoan Group fashion.

Not that anybody cares about any artistic scruples around here. A top note here and a loud blast there seem to satisfy the "discerning" directorial ears and as long as a sense of power is involved, whoever is at the head, enjoys this momentary inflation like champagne.

Art is a word that I'm sure nobody has even heard – what a lousy mess to be involved in.

Neither producer [Alessandro Rota] nor director [Joseph Manca] have any idea of what they want nor of what they hope eventually to achieve. I've been playing at odd production rehearsals and honestly I've not seen the like of it before. The singers seem left to their own resources and in most cases this is non-existent.

The singers are trying hard – but that in the end is not nearly enough.

But I suppose in the end everyone will pull through no matter how, slap each other on the back and bask in the patronizing newspaper reports.

What I can't understand is how people can have so little respect for the composers whose music they are using.

After this I think I've had enough.

But enough of all this wailing and moaning and let's answer your letter.

Down here we were rather concerned [about] you during your initial period of silence but I'm so pleased that you've settled in and that you're enjoying it. A change always does one a world of good.

Fortunately for me, the last days here have been exceedingly hot and I've at least had a taste of what summer can be like – and it will be something to recall in the snow and rain of Europe. [...]

I'm leaving Cape Town at the end of this month (Sept.) and perhaps just as well I won't be around to witness nor hear the performances. [...]

Don't thank me for the coaching – I loved every minute. It was always in search of Art, to reach those heights where everything is harmony.

---

216 The Ochberg Hall in District Six was too small to accommodate all of Eoan's activities. Delta House was an additional practice venue for the Group in Bree Street, in the city centre of Cape Town. However, Delta House was in a "whites only" area, so the Eoan Group had to obtain a permit to use it. See Roos (2018): 83.

I must admit to feeling sad that our paths lie in opposite directions as it were, but still it's not the end of the world. Go on searching for that truth in your approach to your work and that will provide at least some compensation.

For now,

au revoir.

All the best to Johnny, the children and you.

Yours,

Gordon.

Figure 2.3 Alessandro Rota, Gordon Jephtas and Joseph Manca in 1965.
Source: Cloete Breytenbach Collection, DOMUS.

30

Marplana, 1, Paseo Maritimo, 295, Castelldefels, Barcelona, España.

Monday, 29 December [1968]

My dear May,

How are you?

I have been on the very brink of writing to you countless times before now but for one very selfish reason had not completed my good intentions. I refused to risk not getting a reply – and your replies are always over eagerly awaited. And the reason for this was because I was hopping around like a yo-yo and therefore without address to collect your answer. So please forgive my selfishness. [...]

So my news first. Where to start though? What about Cape Town roundabout the time of your letter? Things with the opera season were not going well. The orchestral rehearsals came and the general rush was beginning to show up on all concerned. First was *Traviata* – a rehearsal of much out-of-tune singing from Violetta[217] and Alfredo.[218] Then *Rigoletto* – Bennie [Benjamin Arendse] had an attack of nerves and Winnie [Winifried du Plessis] sang what is supposed to be a 16-year-old virgin like a 95-year-old elephant. But mercy – next came *Barber of Seville* and Manca had not even yet rehearsed Act II with the singers before. It was frankly chaotic. Then after the 2nd rehearsal of *Rigoletto* Bennie had a chat with "us" fabulous directors to say that he couldn't see himself getting through the part. Manca wanted to know how to manipulate only 2 operas with the limited number of singers – I eagled [*sic*] for a repeat of *Butterfly*, but this got dropped. Rota aimed for cancellation. Manca in a moment of utter weakness echoed "all right cancel" and before he had time to change his mind the cancellation was official and then he couldn't retreat for his honour. The usual round of meetings followed – Manca subconsciously blames Bennie for this calamity – and in my opinion the cancellation was the worst thing for the Group's image – but it was not so. Rota wanted a complete cancellation for his own reasons. He was appallingly bad at the production plus the added responsibility of voice-training not facilitated by Manca's idea that after one session with Rota the singers should be able to have a technique better than [Enrico] Caruso and [Amelita] Galli-Curci put together. In spite of the bad reflections, deep down I was happy that the season was not going on because it was going to be really ridiculous. Rota, to cite but one instance, was going to put Jimmy in a bobbed wig (alla 1920 - long) and the chosen costume was all but enhancing Jimmy's thin physique and pencil thin legs. Can you imagine what would have emerged? Instead of a handsome, fulsome reigning Duke it would have been a titter-producing mess.

Anyway, with that over the season was to be postponed possibly until the next October (the next date with the orchestra) and Rota was to continue intense voice training, I felt that at least one good thing had come out [of] the fiasco. Every single singer needed vocal sorting out and with my innumerable sessions with Rota I was convinced that he alone could raise the standard of singing instead of the pot-luck system used up to now. But my luck did not last. Teaching is one of those things which needs preservation more from the teacher – and it is a long process if [it is] to have any success. After ten days or so Rota's enthusiasm had

---

217   Sung by Vera Gow.
218   Sung by James Momberg.

already waned and [he] announced to me his intention of starting touring concerts[219] in the country – and items from *Cavalleria* to *La sonnambula*. Dashed was my only remaining ideal. It would be the same as usual – churning out arias for personal glory for all concerned but little of that extra knowledge or technique gained. By this time I was leaving and did so with a very heavy heart because there was nothing I could or can do. And I do so much believe that with intensive training, an awareness of Art, etc., that [the] Eoan Group can become a respected thing – every singer can be one to look up to – but not without learning and a desire to perfect that Art. Alas, I feel that now it is so much a case of "the Coloured people do so well" – with that tone of condescending superiority. [...]

Anyway, on leaving S.A. I came to Italy with the intention of studying in Rome, but my spirits were exceedingly low and especially as regards my own relationship with music, and the first provocation from the Rome College lot made me leave without making too much effort to gain admission. I sauntered to Switzerland to regain some moral strength and then accepted an invitation from Mabel and Joseph and the possibility of going to the Milan Conservatoire. But in Italy it is much [a] life of knowing the right people and although Joseph most wonderfully gave me contacts, the Conservatoire would not accept me for those courses I wanted. But still I stayed on a while working with Joseph and some of his friends, but everything was accumulating and I got continually more depressed with the operatic trend in Milan – top notes – top notes – and well, never mind too much about the rest. So I had to escape – I wanted nothing more to do with music for a while. I had a plane ticket and got wind that Montserrat Caballé was singing in Barcelona and made for here, and waited for her performance in [Donizetti's] *Roberto Devereux* as Queen Anne [*recte*: Elizabeth].

I went and this time she sang. I admired her work – sincere and the next best I've seen after Callas. Quite different to her records, she doesn't use that pure beautiful sound alla Sutherland to the point of distraction all the time and no matter what the situation. She will do all the things not a single teacher would advise, but she produces theatre and a truth. She screamed in the chest when the Queen was angry, sang ravishingly beautiful high notes softly in the happiest moments – and lived the part.

The voice is not large, but she knows how to use it, hardly sings above the high D flat and has fabulous breath control. The only thing that distracted me was that whereas Callas makes everyone on stage with her work and react, Caballé was alone, living, moving around, cajoling, bellowing with laughter, while the rest of the cast was as motionless and uninvolved as a lot of Greek pillars. Anyway, after her second performance there sparked in me a desire to continue with music and I started to make inquiries here at the Liceu.[220] Now I am to do an entrance examination in a fortnight but I don't know whether things will work out. There is for instance a big language problem for me, having studied Italian half my life, now to be confronted with just that much difference with Spanish. So God knows just what will happen, and the way I feel now I don't much care because the depressions have been exceedingly great during these last 3 months. [...]

I went to see Caballé again in *Manon* (the French one by [Jules] Massenet). But a trip to the opera is an involvement. The last public transport from Barcelona is at 9.15 at night and the opera starts at 9.30. Well this little trip meant sitting in a cold station from 2 a.m. (after the opera) until 7 a.m. waiting for the 1st train. For Caballé it was, on reflection, worth it. She is a dumpy lady and a severe diet would do her well, but I was amazed at her dexterity

---

219 Eoan soloists often went on small tours, and this may have been one of them.
220 The Barcelona Opera House.

in portraying a young and flirtatious girl – and she succeeded except once when she loving-ly sat on the tenor's knee and completely obliterated him from view. The audience shrieked with audible amusement, but Caballé didn't bat a lid, and in fact remained on his knee for at least 5 interminable theatrical minutes. And also the voice she employed was no longer that of a regal, and irritable, queen in *Roberto Devereux*, but that of a young girl in love. Yes, she's good.

Callas has been [in] the news of course with Onassis and Jacqueline Kennedy marry-ing. The magazines and newspapers still carry lengthy reviews, opinions and what have-you. The one great thing is that she is going to resume work, not only in opera but apparently also venturing into films. And everybody is clamouring for her services – here in Barcelona they say she's coming to sing Medea – and in Paris she is to sing a modern opera. Meanwhile she refuses to talk to the newspapers except to say that she is practising scales every day and will let the world know which offers she will accept after she has studied them all carefully, in about a couple of months. And of course, the opera world just buzzes with "she's finished" – "she'll never sing on stage again".[221] To this she wonderfully replies that she is studying hard again and one will only be able to tell when she is on stage. But even if she has to croak her way through Musetta's Waltz Song I'm sure the whole world will now want to see the hurt and jilted heroine and unfortunately her supreme art surely warrants more. But we'll see.

My first stroke of luck for weeks: I found your letter. [...]

First, thanks for all the nice things you say – and now that I'm reading it again it makes life at least less miserable. [...]

I was much appalled with the Group in several ways and the artistic differences were great. Manca and I had several foul-ups but in the end all patched up if not neatly, at least, compromisingly. I admire Manca for what he has done, his verve and energy and he has tried hard to project the father lean-upon image and I have more than once hoped that it could have been – just to turn to somebody to ask [for] musical advice or judgement – but he has not been able to fill the part. It has, and very much is, one of my deepest regrets. Our relationship continues superficially friendly but underneath rather strained, and yet he seemed more than sincere in his parting desire that I return to work with him at the Centre.

But that Centre and myself need still much thinking. I don't have any capacity for direc-torship of any sort and I am merely interested in having music performed with respect for it itself. Where will all this lead? – I wish one could foretell. But we'll see. [...]

Spain is not all friendly and outgiving – they put on that special face for the tourists and their money – and hard for us to understand, tourism is as much an industry as clothing manufacture. And it's cold – winter is here, my second in succession and that doesn't help to keep the spirits animated either. In fact, I tend to sleep for a large part of the day and have insomnia at night and can then only practise finger exercises in the dark on the cushion or count the "imaginary" (not always) cockroaches slithering around the marble floor. So I'm in a kind of rut because the Spanish music education (if I'm fully accepted) does not promise to give me what I need from what I gather in my present studies and I only hope that I make up my mind soon and pull myself together.

I haven't heard from home since leaving except my mother and the Sydows once, so any snippets of interest you have will be enlightening.

---

221   Callas's last stage performance was on 5 July 1965 at the Royal Opera House, Covent Garden.

Please write soon, or as soon as you're able to shake off the festive spirits and inclined for pen work - anyway, I'll be here at least for the 1ˢᵗ 3 weeks of the New Year - alive I hope.

All good wishes to Johnny, the children and you.
Yours,
Gordon.
P.S. A happy, prosperous 1969.

c/o MARPLANA 1
PASEO MARITIMO 295
CASTELLDEFELS
BARCELONA
SPAIN

Please, please write soon.

3. ITALY

3.1 "SURE, I WON'T FORGET MANTOVA"

Jephtas moved to Milan in February 1969, remaining there for the next three years. His résumé thus far was in European terms unremarkable: he had trained in Cape Town then at the London Opera Centre, and had gained practical experience with both Eoan and a touring group from Welsh National Opera. But he needed real work that would bring him money, and experience of Italian opera on its home territory.

As it happens, Jephtas was not the only member of Eoan to have succeeded in reaching Europe. In 1967, the tenor Joseph Gabriels had been awarded a private scholarship to go to Milan, where he was later joined by his wife, Mabel Kester. They let Jephtas stay with them at first, and soon he started to support himself financially through language teaching at the Shenker Institute for English, where he worked until 1971. He also undertook freelance vocal coaching, accompanied singers in their lessons, and in 1971 became a regular accompanist for the students of Vladimiro Badiali. Professionally, he also profited from contact with Mercedes Llopart (1895-1970), a much sought-after singing teacher who had worked under Toscanini and later trained singers such as Elena Suliotis, Renata Scotto, Fiorenza Cossotto, Alfredo Kraus and Ivo Vinco - all of whom were coached by Jephtas himself at various opera houses in his later career. Besides improving his Italian skills and refining his craft as a vocal coach by accompanying singing lessons, Jephtas also made sure to attend opera productions at La Scala in Milan, even if it meant sitting behind a pillar in the cheapest seats. In 1970, he started taking conducting lessons with Franco Ferraris, who had worked with singers such as Maria Callas and Renata Tebaldi, and whose behind-the-scenes anecdotes Jephtas gleefully shared with Abrahamse. In a letter to Abrahamse of 3 June 1970, Jephtas claimed to have turned down an opportunity - facilitated by Ferraris - to conduct performances of *La bohème* in Milan because "the level was not going to be what I wanted". He offered no details of the dates, venue or casting, though it seems barely credible that an aspiring conductor would willingly turn down any such offer - in Milan, no less - at a time when he needed experience, money, and a proverbial foot in the door. But it was not the last time that Jephtas would claim to have turned down a conducting opportunity that was offered to him.

Jephtas continued to have financial difficulties, and in late 1971 he was apparently struggling so much to make ends meet that he would give a vocal coaching session in exchange for a plate of spaghetti.[222] Apparent prospects of a job with the New York City Opera fell through because of permit problems,[223] though in February 1972 he was able to tell Abrahamse that he had landed his very first proper contract on the European continent. There was a catch, however. The Mantua Opera House, he wrote, had wanted him as a *maestro sostituto* (répétiteur), but the labour office in Rome had denied him a permit because the opera company had reached the maximum number of foreign artists allowed. Instead, Mantua had devised a scheme whereby he would be appointed the personal assistant of the conductor Francesco Martini, but could then unofficially (i.e. illegally) perform the duties of *maestro sostituto* anyway. It was during his time in Mantua that Jephtas was able to work with singers such as the soprano Elena Suliotis and the tenor Plácido Domingo, though he complained to Abrahamse that he was being paid a pittance and that colleagues were exploiting him because they all knew he was working

---

222 See his letter of 6 June 1972.
223 See his letters of 10 October 1970 and 7 February 1972.

illegally. He was "drowned with a black depression", he wrote on 7 February 1972, and reduced to "humiliating arse crawling", but he pressed on because he wanted "the chance to work in Italian theatre". Soon, further offers of work in Italy came his way, but everything began to fall apart when the Italian immigration authorities finally realised that he was not adhering to the conditions of his (presumably tourist) visa, and issued him with a 10-day notice to leave the country. Luckily, it was soon rescinded on condition that he undertake no work, and deliverance now came in the shape of a job offer from the Zurich Opera House. Jephtas did some initial coaching there in May/June 1972 and was promptly offered an extended contract to assist the conductor Nello Santi in the Italian repertoire for the following season. At almost the exact same time, the Lisbon Opera engaged him as a vocal coach for several weeks in the spring of 1973 - a job he would be able to combine with living in Zurich. Jephtas's career was finally gaining momentum, and his talent as a vocal coach was being recognised. For the first time since leaving South Africa, he would now be working at a major house alongside a recognised master conductor, with a regular work permit, earning a regular salary.

3.2 THE LETTERS, 1969-1972

31

Via Plinio, 42, Milano, Italia.

Monday, 23 June [1969]

My dear May,

I have been on the point of writing for, oh! such a long while. My apologies because this reply must be some 6 months overdue.

As you have no doubt guessed from the outside of this letter-card, I'm back in Italy. Back to square 1, as it were, without having won a single game. It seems that I simply cannot stay away from the place.

But to cut a long story short, I've been here since mid-February and just settling down having made the decision to halt myself here for some length of time. [...]

[I]n order to keep just along the bread-line, I'm working for one of the Language Schools here.[224] Having never really worked and studied simultaneously before, the strain is enormous - and this to a large extent has been responsible for this procrastination. [...]

On first coming here I stayed with Mabel [Kester] and Joseph [Gabriels] with their Italian speaking daughter (she won't utter a word in English and often corrects her parents' Italian much to their consternation) for a few weeks and subsequently moved into what I suppose could be called a flat. [...]

Not having written any letters at all I don't know too much about Eoan Group activities except that there is to be an opera season shortly - and what operas. I believe including the last lot of 3[225] there is also *Trovatore*. Without sufficient singers for barely two, it sounds so unfeasible. I don't know but this has really put me off the Group.

---

224   The Shenker Institute of English. Jephtas worked there from 1969 until 1971. See Davids (2021): 11.
225   During 1969, Eoan's 8th Opera Season included Verdi's *Il trovatore* and *La traviata*, and Rossini's *Il barbiere di Siviglia*. See Roos (2018): 130.

And on the other hand Mr. Sydow writes fervent letters that they are expecting me back round mid '70 to be the Director of the Opera School with staff (very posh, etc) but after last year,[226] I don't want to go near such an unholy mess! I think it would be wise to stay away for 5 to 6 years and let things simmer down to a more sane level – what would you say?

I've been to the Opera as often as possible but also here has been nothing near exciting or satisfying. The Italians have lost the art of performing Italian opera and the Americans seem to be showing them how to do it. The most successful production was the one [with] nearly all American singers and conductor. The soprano was fabulous – her work really made a big impression on me. I'll send you the programme. [...]

Love to the children and Johnny.

Yours,

Gordon.

32

Via Plinio, 42, Milano, Italia.

Saturday, 30 August 1969

My dear May,

Thanks over and over again for your oh, so welcome letter of a month ago. [...]

Joseph [Gabriels] is still here in Milan and trying to get into an opera house. The going is very hard; just now the Italians have promoted a law against having foreigners sing in Italian houses with the exception of the instrumental artists, etc. Now he has just got through to the Verdi Voice competition[227] at Busseto (the old man's birthplace) and consequently is now in the heats of another [competition] in Parma - and this, if he acquits himself well, is most likely to procure him some contracts because the publishing house of Sonzogno are interested in him to perform the works like *Pagliacci* [and] *Cavalleria* for which they have the rights. But it is difficult – the mentality is completely different because they particularly adopt the system of oiling the palms of the influential people. A corruption of which we know little – but here it is common knowledge the amount of money singers have paid to agents (for instance Callas to Serafin) in order to make their debuts.

[Joseph and I] have been working together – he has voice and voice [*sic*] and a certain musicality but little sense for artistic finesse or dramatic application – but once he gets a break, on the grounds of voice, he should procure much work, and then it would merely depend on his performance and public opinion. [...]

The Eoan Group operas – what can one say? I don't have much news from that direction, in fact, none at all. For myself, I cannot help but feel that if they could not even really accommodate the 3 operas of last year, how can they have the audacity to include further a *Trovatore*? Many of the names you mention I don't know, like de Long & Bernie.[228] I heard further that Yvonne[229] pulled out of *Rigoletto*. What makes me really sad is this path of

226 Jephtas spent part of 1968 with Eoan, training and preparing the singers for the 8th Opera Season. However, one week before the season was due to start, the executive committee cancelled it. See Jephtas's letter of 29 December 1968 for his explanation, and also Roos (2018): 129.
227 Gabriels won this competition. Roos (2018): 141.
228 Eoan singers: Charles de Long (baritone) and Jacobus Erasmus (tenor).
229 Yvonne Jansen, Eoan soprano.

continually lowering and lowering standards. No artistic good can come out of any such action and now I hear that for [the] next season both *Aida* and *Ballo in maschera*[230] are being negotiated. Doesn't it seem that somewhere along the line are people intent on self-destruction? Such a thought, let alone the evidence of it, is very, very sad indeed. [...]

All the best for you, Johnny and the children.

Yours,

Gordon.

33

Via Plinio, 42, Milano, Italia.

Monday, 23 February [1970]

My dear May,

Having become a most atrocious letter-writer (the setting in of middle-age),[231] I must confess that I am utterly ashamed of my negligence. But honestly, the words "write to May" have been in the "dominant" column of my daily diary for weeks and weeks, but for all this procrastination. [...]

I'm more than thrilled that you are moving back to Cape Town, if for nothing other, but to continue your artistic development and [escape] the bad artistic blow Durban offered you. The fact that you had some lessons with [Olga] Magnoni was another joy – and it is more than true that the first thing that is lost when not singing is the "breath" control. And now that you have discovered this, for heaven's sake, my sake, or anybody's sake, please keep working on it because it was amongst your greatest assets.

By the way, do you have a cassette-tape-recorder, or do you have access to one? If so, do let me know because there are some things I want to send for you to hear. Okay? Also, because one of the recording companies has issued a record called "Conversations with Callas" which I plan to get – unfortunately it is issued only in stereo and I don't have a stereo-record-player. You ask about Callas. Yes, she made the film *Medea*[232] which I saw here, and it will undoubt-edly go to S.A. She plays a straight actress, that is, the film is a re-write of the original play by Euripides (or whoever it might be) and not the opera of Cherubini which according to many was among her best interpretations. Seeing the film gives one an idea of what Callas's stage art must have been like, but fortunately, or unfortunately, she (and her producer) is much too intelligent to have merely rehashed her theatrical success. In the film she starts from an entire-ly different basis: that is, everything, every movement is much more interior and within herself (probably [because] in a film to flick a mere eyelid is more appropriate than a long gesture that must also be seen by the spectator in the last row of the Opera House). Thus I found myself in conflict – it was not Callas of the operatic stage, but Callas as an actress, without the music for her to interpret – and that as we know is her forte. There were memorable scenes and I remem-ber one where she leaps through a mass of burning flaming grass and screams and growls – and apparently she did this scene herself refusing to have the usual stand-in.

---

230 Although these operas may have been planned by Eoan, they were never performed by the Group. Their 9th Opera Season included Verdi's *La traviata* and *Rigoletto*, Mascagni's *Cavalleria rusticana* and Leoncavallo's *Pagliacci*.
231 Jephtas was 26 years old when he wrote this letter.
232 *Medea*, a film starring Callas, directed in 1969 by Pier Paolo Pasolini.

But the film deals largely with the psychological and underlying effects of the complicated aspects of Medea's character – whereas the opera relies on the more practical and theatrical sides. For instance, the scene where she kills her children when Jason (the husband) decides to marry another – in the opera her anger and vehemence is clear – in the film one sees her mental processes and then a dagger covered with blood after the killing. But I want you to see this film and then we can compare notes.

Roundabout the time the film was launched there was much talk about her returning to the opera stage and in fact, the Scala tried to interest her and [Franco] Corelli to do *Werther* (Massenet) but this fell through. Right now all is quiet, and some people say that her ten-year absence has been too long a gap to want to re-start; others say that her present jet-set life of very late nights will prevent her vocal resources to reach even the worst of her peak years – and then, they say, she lives a very rigid life of the singer – that is, early to bed, etc. etc. But whether she will return or not, one thing for sure is that she has become a monument, and can never present anything less than her own phenomenal standards.

I don't know whether I told you that I'm studying with a conductor Ferraris[233] who worked at La Scala during the Callas years and consequently knew and worked with her. As we are studying *Norma* together, the discussion frequently reverts to Callas. He cannot sufficiently emphasize the joy and admiration for her musicianship which in singers is nearly always a big void – and often he says she was the only singer who could get that rhythm correctly as written, etc. According to him she was unsurpassable in the lighter roles – *Lucia, Sonnambula, Puritani* (and from the *Tosca* I saw, her voice is not naturally voluptuous and huge – like for instance Birgit Nilsson or even Gwyneth Jones) and in fact, in *Norma* her voice was too small for an *Italian ear* (note!), but who could make the character anywhere nearly as alive?

I'm learning much from him and all the little Scala secrets and details. How Tebaldi had difficulties with a mere B flat – (she just never could sing it in tune) – how when she sang *Traviata* the aria was transposed from "Che spero or più? Che far degg'io" (and still she had problems). She has been engaged to sing *Manon Lescaut* at the open-air theatre of Verona this July and it would be a treat to hear it even if she sings badly (which they say she is doing). About my studies, with this man I'm doing conducting and finding out just how little I know of that complicated subject.

While on the subject of opera over here, I might just as well continue with all I'm thinking to say.

This season I saw a good *Manon* with Mirella Freni. She has a beautiful instrument – and in all I must have seen 8 or 9 of these performances. But it remains beautiful all the time and that in itself became a bore. Then there was [Saint-Saëns's] *Samson and Delilah* with the negress[234] Shirley Verrett.[235] She had a phenomenal success and the Callas fans I spoke to afterwards said that she indicated just a touch of that Callas fire on the stage. I personally found her style of singing good but the role lies low all the time, and although she was always busy with histrionic moves, the voice didn't match nor come near to enhancing this. Maybe I should see her in something else. She is coming back to do Eboli in *Don Carlos*. The next few weeks promise to be alive. Tomorrow evening Montserrat Caballé opens in *Lucrezia Borgia* and the following week Beverly Sills[236] is to sing Lucia. Similar singers and the same kind of

---

233 Franco Ferraris (1922–1994), Italian conductor.
234 See the section "Editorial approach and terminology" above regarding Jephtas's vocabulary.
235 Shirley Verrett (1931–2010), African-American mezzo-soprano who later became a soprano.
236 Beverly Sills (1929–2007), American soprano.

opera, and both are excellent singers, will provide much speculation, fighting and arguing in the audience. And [about] time too, because since the Scala opened in December things have been rather dull.

Yesterday I went to Bologna to see a performance of *La forza del destino*. Apart from the fact that in order to get in – it was sold out ... I had a pillar (beautiful though it was) half blocking my view, it was an interesting performance. One really needs to go into the provinces to appreciate just what a high standard there is at La Scala. For example, for each performance at the latter, there are ten assistant conductors on stage apart from the prompt – giving cues, conducting, etc. In fact, nothing is left to chance. And I really like this thoroughness. But back to *Forza*. Seeing the opera in performance I realized how unfeasible the plot is – and it is interminably long – nearly 4 hours. All the business with Leonora knocks at the convent in man's clothes rings false when the priest doesn't recognize the voice of a woman while just a few scenes later, after hearing the voice, the tenor says "heavens, it is a woman". But there is some glorious singing and music and it really needs voice, voice and voice as Verdi himself said.

About your meeting with Eoan. Incidentally, is Mr. Tobin[237] in an administrative [or] artistic capacity? I can't figure why he was present. Frankly, I know nothing about the Group's additions, etc. Your feelings about Violetta [in Verdi's *La traviata*] are admirable – I couldn't agree more. If it means that it will be prepared in the same wishy-washy fashion like instant puddings with the hope that re-costuming will do the trick, then that is a hopeless beginning, and now you are ready to do an excellent Violetta but with care and people who understand and who want to present something that is really good.[238]

It is indeed a great pity that things should be this way. But whatever your ultimate decision, don't do anything that you are not happy about – your main concern should be artistic success. For the life of me, I cannot see your point about first opera, first singer, first night, etc. In my view, you are above this sort of rationalization – it is not of any importance whether on any night, etc., but that whatever or whenever, it *must* be done with care, dedication and truth. Don't you think? Though I clearly see your view about undercurrents as the situation stands. If only those bastards could see the possibilities of producing great theatre with you which would elevate the appalling standards. I have always believed in your work, your intelligent approach and your attitude forever searching [for] improvement. [...] If I ever come back and reach any dictatorial position I would fight for such a realization. The more I think about it, the more convinced I am that something of a higher artistic standard would be reached. But all the surrounding factors and sanctions must be right.

To me, it is quite obvious that Rota would not be interested in producing new works. He is not that kind of man. New works mean more work, more use of one's energy, etc. and he for sure is not going to risk nor break his neck for anybody, except for himself! And competition is the last thing they want to be involved with. In fact, just today I had a letter from Manca. Only the second since I left C[ape] T[own]. A rift had been created between the two of us and hence relationships have been cool – and consequently I left the first move up to him – and with time he bit at the bait. Up to [now] everything [went] via a 3rd person. So about 3 weeks ago arrives this letter ostensibly with the pretext of sending me some useless income tax receipt and I presumed also to fix some idea about me returning.

237 Cecil Tobin, Eoan baritone.
238 In 1970, Eoan only performed the musical *Carmen Jones* by Hammerstein to music by Bizet. It is unclear what performance is being discussed here.

As it was too evasive a letter I wrote back, asking him to state his point of view and then I would decide from there. And this was [in] the second letter of yesterday [that] I [was] particularly struck by one sentence: "Obviously you are better off in Europe, but although you may make a success of your career, you will be involved in the most competitive fields of employment" – and in fact, *this* in itself is just what is attracting me to the European field – competition is what I want. And this is just to illustrate the conception in the Eoan Group – and [the] thing I dislike most.

iiiIt was to be expected before the outset that the Centre was to be no more than a 2nd class building for 2nd class citizens!!!^{239}

About the singing lessons when you are in Cape Town. My advice is that you join Rota's class. As you have the brain to watch, listen and absorb you will learn infinitely more about Italian things regarding opera from him. And this will be of great use to you. I am not forgetting the fact that Mrs Magnoni has helped you tremendously but I think you have already absorbed 90% of what she has to offer. So now take from Rota what you can. Therefore, I suggest that you join his school,^{240} but yet not abandon Magnoni – go to her occasionally for any other clarification – like once a month or 6 weeks. Mrs Magnoni is English and doesn't know those fine details which Rota as ex-performer has up his sleeve – and believe me, now that I myself am working at this – there are millions of things not written but passed on from one to another only. Think hard about this. I must admit that I have gone off Mrs Magnoni because she behaved most ungraciously at the time when Rota started teaching singing in the Group – artistic ideas were never considered – and that for me is unforgivable!!!!!!

It is now Wednesday, and I just cannot promise when this letter will reach you or even be completed if I write all that I have in mind. I went to the opening night of *Lucrezia Borgia* last night which was halfway between a great success and a big joke. A phenomenal success for Caballé who got a Callas-like ovation and reception but a laugh because the rest of the cast including the conductor could not match up. The trouble started when Raimondi,^{241} the tenor contracted to sing, got indisposed and the understudy had to step in. Well, by Eoan Group standards he would be a great new discovery but at La Scala he was ridiculed. Not that he was a hopeless singer but he had problems on the bridge and every single [time] after he had hit an F or G which would incline to be throaty, the audience would descend on him with hissing (the Italian signal for disapproval), whistling and shouted comments. In fact, it got so bad that after one painful and uncomfortable phrase, a female voice boomed from the gallery "Try it again, it *might* be better next time"; and further on, just before the end of the opera he dies. In what should have been a touching scene he says "madre addio" [goodbye, mother] on some more (for him) uncomfortable sounds when another voice from the audience, saturated with annoyance at having to listen to this, shouted – "well then, go home to your mother where you will be better off". But what I found so comical was that immediately after a bad hissing for the tenor, Caballé would open her mouth with a beautiful angelical pianissimo [on a] high B flat which would enchant the audience until the next tenor entry. Personally I found her to have less refinement and histrionic attempt than in Barcelona, but then one has to consider

---

239 This is a reference to the Eoan Group Cultural Centre, "consisting of the Joseph Stone Auditorium ... several ballet studios, practice rooms, and office space for administration". The building was inaugurated on 21 November 1969. See Roos (2018): 136. Jephtas's Spanish exclamation marks are original.

240 In the course of 1970, Eoan renewed its efforts to train its singers through formal singing lessons. This initiative was led by Alessandro Rota. Roos (2018): 148.

241 Gianni Raimondi (1923–2008), Italian tenor.

that it was her first time here[242] and the importance of it all. I must get to see the other performances. What really bowled the Milanese audience over was her breath control. In the 1st act finale with chorus she hit an A flat pianissimo, held it like that for 16 bars (4 beats in a bar, the chorus singing under her) and after beat 64, she swelled into a magnificent fortissimo and down to a low F – well, she must have the best control in the world. We were spell-bound by the mere technical achievement apart from the sheer beauty of the sound. The main difference between the better singers and the others is that they make the observer believe that they are singing with utmost ease. The conductor was in bad favour because he just didn't seem to understand the music too well, and seemed intent on covering the vocal line with orchestral sound – and unfortunately, there are 2 young conductors here ([Claudio] Abbado and the American [Thomas] Schippers) who certainly make orchestral noise (and how), but never losing sight of the vocal sound. And in 18th Century Italian Opera, it is always "voice first" in double-sized capitals.

Now, where was I before this gigantic digression? I think I've commented on most of your latest letter, and with a crimson face I notice I have 2 others to answer as well. Oh yes, thanks for your family picture – you all look so healthy and colourful compared to us sallow-looking ones in the winter here. I'm now on your letter of November 11th. [...]

Letter no. 3 of October 13th – more apologies!!!

About Leonie Gordon.[243] Yes of course I know her and it is a case I feel badly about. When in Cape Town I saw and heard her as well. But to start the story: several years ago (I can't remember how many) I knew Leonie, was most impressed with the "kaffir" quality of her voice,[244] and appreciated her strong views, whether through outside influence or not, about not joining the Group. I suggested she have regular singing lessons. [The] College of Music seemed the reasonable choice and hence [she took lessons with] Madame Armhold.[245] I really expected a development vocally and artistically – then she was younger and more humble. The voice was raw but [had] immense possibilities. Well, Armhold did nothing for that voice. Last year, after 8 years (I think that's what it is), she was still singing the same *Madama Butterfly* arias with the same appalling Italian and less voice. The only thing Armhold gave her were 4 notes from top G to top C sounding like Leontyne Price with no centre and generally badly placed. Her repertoire was enhanced with "Oh my beloved Father" and further songs like "Butterflies and Springtime Breezes". I did not object to the songs if they were meant [to] improve the voice. But worse still, after all those years she had had too easy success because of those few glorious notes, lost her humility, and backed by the firm fixation that she is South Africa's Leontyne Price – no doubt the opinion of her fans. I was deeply disappointed and must confess that all the blame does not necessarily lie with her. She told me of her plans to go to England and study at the Royal Academy or something. My honest opinion, having worked in the English opera scene, is that she will get nowhere over there, unless she has a sudden and drastic vocal change and a different attitude towards her music. But how could I tell her all this and discourage the glitter of overseas fame in her eyes? She will learn when here, which is probably what is happening right now. Maybe I sound on the hard side but I have no

---

242 This was Montserrat Caballé's debut performance at La Scala.
243 Leonie Gordon, South African singer.
244 While "kaffir" is a derogatory term denoting black South Africans (see the section "Editorial approach and terminology" above), it is not known whether Leonie Gordon was classified "coloured" or "black" under apartheid laws.
245 Adelheid Armhold (1900-1992), Dutch-South African singing teacher at UCT who trained prominent South African singers including the soprano Nellie du Toit (1929-2018), the tenor Gé Korsten (1927-1999) and the soprano Désirée Talbot (1926-2020).

compassion for people who have lost their humility towards their music – and this is another factor that distressed me amongst the Eoan Group's singers – the same powerful tendency increased by the idea that they are little Gods themselves, when in the world scene they don't even count for a grain of sand.

About Callas again – answers to your questions. The new record was supposed to be *Traviata* with Giulini conducting, and for this de Hidalgo[246] worked with her. But the recording was dropped – the reason is not known. How awful to be a celebrity you say. In fact, a journalist wrote that her position is like that of the Queen of England – she can do nothing without everyone else knowing. The film producer was the one of *Medea*, but immediately after [that] there were pictures of Onassis entering her flat, stories of a dinner party of reconciliation without Jacqueline Kennedy, and heaven knows what all. [...]

About my own intentions. I have made no definite plans. As I've said before, the Sydows are passing through here and according to Manca they have much to tell me – I'm sure – so I'm not making any pre-conceptions till I've heard their case and if they have a sufficiently strong or convincing one, I might be back in S.A. before you know. Manca's letter indicates that my expected arrival is May – but I won't make it for several months after that – and I just hate others making my personal decisions for me, so even if I were free to go, then I would not on pure principle.

Of one thing I'm pretty sure. If I do go back I want to conduct – and this for my own personal callous interests. Very clearly in between the lines Manca has indicated that he is not keen to have competition on the conductor's podium with cryptic phrases like "in the future taking the baton in your hands". Well, we'll see what will happen – but I strongly do not want to return home merely to do his groundwork for him and then still to entertain all the back-biting and aggravation that goes with it. They are offering me the chance of the Opera School, whatever that might mean! I feel badly, and have always felt so, about myself regarding the conducting – Manca has always said "in the future" without presenting an opportunity for me to try my skill at this, for example, a mere matinee during one of those interminable long tours which would have provided me with some basis, but obviously he was never interested in sharing his glory – and glory is the very last thing in the list of things I want. And so, if they really want me, compromises or rather certain beginnings will have to be made, if not, I'm much happier staying here.

My "job" continues – I make money but spend it all as soon as I get it. I enjoy the teaching inasmuch as it takes me into the countryside – I do most of it outside of Milan. So I drive out at 7 a.m. and get back at midday – have four hours to study and then out again until 8 p.m. And then if there's a performance or something goes from 9 p.m.-1 a.m. – no wonder I never get around to writing. Musically I'm studying with this Maestro [Franco Ferraris], had a successful concert with 4 American singers as a result of which I've been asked to conduct some performances of *Bohème* later this year.[247] Friday afternoons I accompany for one of the singing teachers when she teaches and this is very interesting except she has many French students and the lessons are then in French and I don't know a word in that language. Apart from this there is the possibility of taking a job in Kiel (Germany) as repetiteur and assistant conductor – and how much better for getting the experience I now want so badly.

---

246 Elvira de Hidalgo (1891-1980), Spanish coloratura soprano who taught Callas at the Athens Conservatoire.
247 Jephtas later declined this opportunity to conduct *La bohème*. See his letter of 3 June 1970.

This last paragraph read like an America publicity hand-out. I didn't mean it to.

So whether I will come home will depend much on what the Eoan Group are prepared to offer me apart from the finances.

From my scrawl it is easy to see that I haven't written for ages - and forgive the uncertainty in the English. I'm like confused between English and Italian - and master of neither.

It seems I've written a book. If you've got this far - congratulations.

Please write soon rather than follow my example.

All good wishes to Johnny, the be-spectacled Wendy and Trudy.

Arrivederci.

Gordon.

34

Via Plinio, 42, Milano, Italia.

Monday, 20 April [1970]

My dear May,

Well, well, well! How are things with you? As you seem hesitant to answer my last letter I have just decided to pester you until you do. Though, I must admit that pestering act number one has been prompted by quite another reason - more of which within a few lines. [...]

Mr. [Cecil] and Mrs. Tobin have appeared on the scene passing through to London. Last night we saw *Don Carlos* together at the Scala and they realized just what a crisis the Eoan Group music is in. I wish the whole Group would come and perhaps the mere shock alone would raise the standard. Also Tobin has been trying furiously to propagate my own return to their aggravations but somehow has never got past the opening gambit - and I am not likely to offer any cues. [...]

But I'm not letting any cats out of any bags until your reply, as I said before.

More news next time. Whenever I write you I have at least a million and one things to want to write about.

Keep well.

All the best for Johnny, Wendy and Trudy.

Gordon.

35

Via Plinio, 42, Milano. Italia.

Wednesday, 3 June [1970]

My dear May,

Thanks a million for your letter of April 25ᵗʰ [...]

You ask who sang the Leonora in *Forza* at Bologna - it was Rita Orlandi-Malaspina[248] - the leading Italian Verdian dramatic voice today. I don't know that she has made any records as yet - it is a big, rich voice (much like Vera [Gow] in quality), and it certainly is beautiful, but she has the minimum of artistry - she is very good, but has no exceptional class. I've heard her in several things - *Trovatore*, *Ernani*, *Aida* and also *Don Carlos* - and each opera and performance is the same as the other - nothing exceptionally interesting. While listening one is pleased, but the moment the performance is over one has already forgotten it. One doesn't arrive home still feeling moved or remembering certain touching moments of greater artists.

Sure the whole opera performance set up here is quite different. I [saw] a performance of *Don Carlos* this season with [Ayşe] Leyla Gencer. She is a Turk in the decline of her vocal powers, but who for a long while was the Callas understudy here and consequently sang the Callas operas when she was someplace else. Well, she learnt much from Callas - that is colouring words, etc. and being more involved in the role than most. Anyway, to cut a long story short, she has a great following. So came her "Tu che le vanità"[249] while the vocal powers were lacking but she did a few exciting things and her sheer artistry made it possible to sing the whole unaccompanied first part pianissimo because she simply had no voice to do otherwise. Well the reception after the long scena lasted about 10 minutes and went something [like] this - the first 3 minutes spontaneous applause from everyone who liked that performance - the next 3 minutes of applause continued by her devoted fans who no doubt were remembering her glorious past with exclamations of "you are great" - "wonderful interpretation" being shouted simultaneously. Until an irritable voice from the other side of the gallery screamed "enough now, you are exaggerating". To this the fans replied - "you seem to know very little about Art". The anti-Gencer voice retorted - "and how much did she have to pay you for your applause" - the fans reply - "we are not the claque" (the officially paid applauding body of the Scala), "we recognize an artist". At this La Gencer strode straight down-stage and openly faced the complete public - a bouquet of roses (or carnations, I couldn't tell which) descended upon her from the Gallery - another round of applause from the whole audience, and eventually the conductor picked up the stick for the last 20 minutes of the performance. I personally preferred this uneven performance - she grovelled in the chest, had to make an octave jump for each pianissimo attack above high F - but the whole thing meant something rather than a night of pleasant, beautiful [singing] [...]

Thanks for sounding so enthusiastic about my small "successes" - did I really overblow them that much? I turned down the *Bohème* because the level was not going to be what I wanted [for] myself - and as it was to be in Milan I didn't feel confident enough to take that much of a risk. You ask "what about us". You know how I feel deep down about that and I would indeed want to do all in my power to put the Group on the "map of music" - it is an

---

248 Rita Orlandi-Malaspina (1937-2017), Italian soprano.
249 Aria from Verdi's *Don Carlos*.

ambition that is always hankering after me – and, at the expense of sounding very immod-est – I'm sure I could do so, though only with an element like you and all-round participation. In fact, at one stage during the last months, I was completely convinced and decided to return and do something, being more than largely (now I'm free to admit it) attached by the idea of working with you and preparing for your next Cape Town appearance. [...]

But to get back to where I was ... Still being very attached to working with such a tremen-dous artistic element as you, I just cannot bring myself to fight the Macbethian ambitions of nearly everyone else down there, especially as these ambitions appear to me to have nothing to do with the will to improve or create and understand Art. So consequently I've decided it would be best to stay clear. And quite frankly, I have never been all that interested in making a career abroad – maybe because chances [are] not easily [available] and I know even more my shortcomings – but now I've decided to take the plunge with more determination. Up to now I've been more happy to learn more for the sake of using it in raising Eoan's artistic ideals. But who knows what will be, though I cannot help but feel a heavy weight of despond-ency about the Eoan affair.

Anyway, let me know what's happening your way. [...]
Closing time.
Regards to Johnny and all kinds of messages for the children.
Yours,
Gordon.

P.S. My grammar is up the pole. I hope you have understood everything in spite of it.

36

Opernhaus, Zurich, Schweiz
[This letter was written in the USA and later posted from Switzerland.]

Barton, Vermont [USA]
6 September [1970]

My dear May,
I hope my initiation into a typing career does not offend you. Type-written scripts always are so impersonal but believe me that this letter is not meant to bear any such thing.

I had planned to open this with some obnoxious remark like "Hello there from America" – not being able to restrain my gypsy, or better, nomadic talents! [...]

I'm so happy that you got a thrill out of listening to the Callas interview. It was originally an American Radio broadcast of '68 and subsequently issued on record as a bonus disc along with a two-record recital of previously recorded arias. By now I hope you have been able to listen to it a few more times and maybe next time we can talk about what she says. Okay? The tape, of course, is yours. While on the subject of tapes, I can hardly wait to hear your tape in spite of your approaching negative feelings. So no "buts". [...]

Thanks more than a million for the programmes and all the amusing anecdotes of your concerts. It sure was a long programme, the likes of which I have not seen since the Eoan Group days - you forgot to include your "Sunshine and Butterflies". But joking apart, I wish I could have been there. [...]

Now to why I am here. I had always had the intention of coming to America out of curiosity, and so when I was invited to attend an Opera Workshop Program[250] as a coach and pianist I accepted without asking too many questions. The workshop was run by Boris Goldovsky,[251] the Mr. Opera of America, and for three weeks I worked coaching and preparing the young singers in the music and Italian [language] (there were other coaches for the things in English). Goldovsky's primary concern is stagecraft and very meticulous at that. I was pleased to see this approach which no doubt ought to produce a richer whole in Opera but [I] was [a] little disappointed that musical values were not exploited in the same way. Anyway, he has also written a book[252] on his views, which I plan to send on to you for scrutiny. The singers by and large had good voices and I was particularly impressed by a Negress mezzo who made a superb Eboli in *Don Carlos*. Americans work very hard at their music and strive for a technical perfection and they have a big capacity for work and never lose sight of the ultimate goal. It was a good experience to see that. So it was a very interesting three weeks.

Afterwards I spent some time in New York and besides the general sight-seeing also did many auditions, including [at] the Metropolitan which started badly, but fortunately did not end as bad because I managed to leave with the invitation to come back when the present management changes hands. But why am I telling you about the bad ones? The New York City Opera made me a good offer and I am keen to accept this because they perform in the original language and being an assistant conductor will be most invaluable. The offer is for next year[253] so now I'm going back to Milan and study like mad.

At present I am spending some time with friends who have a summer house about twenty miles from the Canadian border, in fact [I am] kicking my heels for time. The day after tomorrow I have an audition with a New York agent before leaving the States. Unfortunately I could not see any performances because everything is shut for the summer, but maybe I will get into a *Lucia* tomorrow, at the City Opera.

I've blabbed too, too much about myself, so perhaps I had better shut down.
Please write soon and remember I'm waiting for the tape.
Much love to you, Johnny, Wendy and Trudy.
Yours,
Gordon. [...]

---

250 From 3 to 24 August 1970, Jephtas attended the 18th annual Opera Workshop hosted by the Oglebay Institute, a non-profit arts and cultural organisation in Wheeling, West Virginia, USA. See Anon. (1970).
251 Boris Goldovsky (1908-2001), Russian-born conductor and broadcaster active in the USA.
252 *Bringing Opera to Life: Operatic Acting and Stage Direction* (New York: Appleton-Century-Crofts, 1968).
253 In his letter of 17 October 1971, Jephtas stated that he had decided to defer this offer. When he finally began negotiations for the job, work permit problems prevented him from accepting it. See his letter of 7 February 1972.

37

Via Plinio, 42, Milano. Italy.

Saturday, 10 October [1970]

My dear May,

I just know that this letter threatens to look an absolute mess, because I'm writing on my knee – because I couldn't be bothered to sit down at a table in the other room. So have my apologies in advance! [...]

[B]efore I get around to answering your letters, let me see what it is that I want to say. Firstly, as you know, I accidentally bumped into Doc Robertson,[254] his wife and a friend [...].

Well, while talking with the Robertsons over tea (sounds posh – in fact the place was a dump – tea sloshed all over the saucers and both Mac [Robertson] and I got more milk on the table than down our throats) the idea of having a concert with you in Durban came to me. This is my idea: you give a solo recital and I will come and be the accompanist. I have great ideas about a programme – in the first half: you start with this fabulous Mozart "Et in carnatus est" – it is originally from a Mass – the music is really beautiful and bel canto – I mean beautiful singing piece. This I visualize as being performed absolutely vocally and musically (not dramatically), no movements, nothing extraneous. This to be followed by 3 or 4 groups of songs – vocally not taxing but with vocal acting – still no movement. I think for instance, 3 English songs ... then in another group of 3 or so Italian arie antiche ..., another 4 negro spirituals ... then a pot-pourri group of things .... I haven't yet thought how to end this half on a high note – I've many ideas but can't yet decide.

The second half would be devoted to opera – vocal acting, gesturing – each aria to have its own gestures to suit the style, the character, the music (I sound like Callas – I don't mean to). In this half I really want to emphasize your operatic stature – it is now at its peak and it must be used to every advantage, though without abusing it. I'm thinking of starting with "Casta Diva"[255] – just the prayer not the "Ah bello a me ritorni"; this to show you off as a Greek goddess, regal, proud, powerful, etc.; the mad scene from *Puritani* – as I remember how well we worked on that ... . This to show this pure puritanical madness of this simple, rather plain but shaken girl; an aria from Bellini's *Romeo and Juliet* (called *I Capuleti e i Montecchi*) to be sung with all the youthfulness of a 15 year old Juliet ... ; then "O mio babbino caro"[256] – to show off this coquettish little monstress (and here I feel the need to couple with another lively aria which hasn't yet occurred to me): A Verdi aria – but this I want to decide after hearing you on tape because I've several in mind – our famous "una macchia"[257], one from [Verdi's] *Aroldo* or from *Traviata*; I have in mind also an aria from Spontini's *Vestale*. The final and big piece would be either the final aria of *Anna Bolena* – such a different madness from *Puritani*, a mature woman, powerful acting, or the final aria from *Roberto Devereux* – the Queen Elizabeth I in her last frantic moment; or the final aria from [Donizetti's] *Belisario* – a wife who has condemned her husband, and when she repents, she finds him dead – a very emotional scene and fantastic scope for all sorts of gestures. All these last 3 operas are Donizetti.

---

254 Mac and Barbara Robertson, mutual friends who were living in Durban at the time. The couple were instrumental in organising the recital by Abrahamse and Jephtas that took place a year later.
255 Aria from Bellini's *Norma*.
256 Aria from Puccini's *Gianni Schicchi*.
257 Aria from Verdi's *Macbeth*.

The second half would have to be thinned down as I have too many ideas and we must establish which of these will come off best artistically; also because I want each half to last not more than 1 hour. [...]

Besides the reason that I want to do this for you, it would also allow me an occasion to go home. I've decided to hell with the Eoan Group for the moment, having got tired of playing their infantile games, and have decided to accept the New York City Opera offer [that] would most certainly entail staying in the States for the next years. The other reason is that if this concert in Durban comes off, I would try to sell it off to the Eoan Group (one recital) in order to show them your worth - why show them your worth? - because through unofficial sources (I can't remember who or which) I've heard that they plan to offer you "Santuzza".[258] Fine, but they can do better than that. So, [if] you could prove your worth in repertoire other than Manca's big box-office operas, it might open their eyes and ears and realize that there are other works within the ability of their material, which could be done well, and at any rate better than the current *Trovatores* and stuff. Consequently, they might offer you something more substantial and it might mark a healthy change. The latter I can perhaps only hope for!

I can't tell you how anxious I am to do this [recital] with you, because I respect your value as an artist so much.

These last pages have read like an "order". Forgive me.

I have to ask you: do you want to do this [recital]; would you like to? If yes, what ideas have you, etc. etc. Please talk with whoever might help or be of use, and let's have all your opinions soon. Promise. Now I hope I've got everything down I wanted so far. [...]

[Mercedes] Llopart, the teacher of the "greats", as you say, has just died. I was kinda sad because I had come to like her very much[259] and usually I don't get along with people past 70. She was, I believe, touching 80. [...]

Yea[h], I get around in compensation for my frustrations with the Eoan Group. I've said before that I will accept the [New York] City Centre proposition. My audition with the agent went extremely well, they want to find me work as concert accompanist because of my brilliance, blah, blah, blah. All very flattering though I honestly don't believe I'm that good to have had all those sorts of epithets. In the end, I decided that it just has to be the American way of being friendly. But I have to work hard, the harder I work, the less I know and so it goes on. I'm flattered that all sorts of people call me up, wanting to work with me; fancy coming all the way to Milan to work with a pip-squeak South African. I double my prices merely because I don't want to be bothered because most just want to show off their beautiful voices and not caring about much else. So, if they're fools or rich enough to want to pay that, I stomach it, but usually it scares them away. Maybe this is a bad tactic. But with all this, I'm painfully aware of my shortcomings and really want to concentrate on them now, at least to improve them or find out why they are so bad. But I sound like Manca, singing my praises - the only person I believe to have a right to do so is Callas. [...]

Yes, it is true that the Met has signed Joseph [Gabriels] for a performance of Canio.[260] Let me explain. In Opera Houses there are 2 systems generally used. One is the "stagione"

---

258 Santuzza is a character from Pietro Mascagni's *Cavalleria rusticana*. In Eoan's 1971 and 1972 productions of the double bill *Cavalleria rusticana* and Leoncavallo's *Pagliacci*, Abrahamse did not sing the role of Santuzza, but rather the role of Nedda in *Pagliacci*. Roos (2018): 149.

259 Jephtas had contact with Llopart because he accompanied her students during their singing lessons. Davids (2021): 12.

260 Joseph Gabriels, formerly of Eoan, made his debut at the Metropolitan Opera on 5 February 1971 in the role of Canio in Leoncavallo's *Pagliacci*. He was the first South African opera singer to perform at the Met. Roos (2018): 140.

system which is at the Scala [and] Covent Garden. That is, a production is rehearsed, from 5 days to 3 weeks and then presented for 6 or so consecutive performances allowing singers a few days rest in between. After these performances that opera is generally not performed during the existing season again. The other system is the "repertory" one, used by most, or rather all German houses. That is every night a different opera is performed and quite likely the opening opera might still feature at the end of the season 6 or 9 months later. The Met uses this system, but because they use mostly international singers, casts in the same operas change very frequently and are in fact planned so. So what happens for example, they engage Callas to sing *Tosca* on June 23rd and maybe the 30th (or more likely those are the two dates she has free) - maybe on the 18th of June, Birgit Nilsson sang it, but on the 23rd Callas just walks on and does her performance. This means that rehearsal is [at] a bare minimum. I know for a fact that for her last *Tosca* at the Met, she had only one piano rehearsal, and not even on the stage (and in the latter part of her career elsewhere when she was famous, she always had all her rehearsals from the production moment to the performance on the actual stage with the sets and props - like for the London performances I saw). So this is how the Met runs. So they discovered they haven't a tenor to sing *Pagliacci* on February 5th - so they engaged Joseph - the next performance Richard Tucker[261] sings, etc. etc. [Rudolph] Bing[262] had already met Joseph before, he had sung to him with a cold, but Bing liked the voice but recommended that Jo[seph] sing in two European Opera Houses before the Met would consider him.[263] This he tried to do, he nearly did *Manon Lescaut* in Switzerland, last season the Scala was interested in him for *Pagliacci* (he had originally studied the role for that purpose) etc., but all these things fell through for one or another reason and he wasn't seeming to get anywhere ... Opera house administrators appeared interested but made no offers. Meanwhile in the international circuit there is a great lack of tenors in the lirico/spinto range and the Met was especially in need. [Franco] Corelli was singing all the time, so was the new Placido Domingo[264] (with a voice that seems too small for the repertoire he is doing), the others, [Carlo] Bergonzi, [Giuseppe] Campore[265], etc. were having vocal troubles. So there is a need for tenors. Consequently, Bing when hearing Jo[seph] the last time was sufficiently impressed to make him an offer[266] - and believe [me] such a contract is one of which each of the at least 10 thousand singing students in Milan alone are more than envious. This performance will act as a trial because they've offered him [Giordano's] *Andrea Chénier*, *Carmen* and the Kaiser in *Die Frau ohne Schatten* (Strauss), possibly for the 71-72 season.[267] But these contracts will only appear if he gets through the *Pagliacci* reasonably well. If it goes very well, he would immediately launch into [an] international career because the Scala has an eye on him, but [is] not willing to take the first chance.

261   Richard Tucker (1913-1975), American tenor.
262   Rudolph Bing (1902-1997), Austrian-born, British opera impresario who was the general manager of the Metropolitan Opera House from 1950 to 1972.
263   According to the South African soprano Emma Renzi, Gabriels was given this opportunity via the South African consul in Milan, Malcolm Smith, whose Italian wife Elda Ribetti (herself a singer) knew Rudolph Bing. Roos (2018): 141.
264   Plácido Domingo (*1941), Spanish tenor.
265   *Recte* Giuseppe Campora (1923-2004), Italian tenor.
266   Emma Renzi has explained that she had advised the Smiths to help Gabriels gain sufficient experience elsewhere before sending him off to the Met, as he lacked the necessary experience; an unsuccessful debut there might be highly detrimental to his career. In her view, letting Gabriels sing at the Met was primarily a means of making a political statement by promoting a disenfranchised coloured singer from apartheid South Africa on one of the world's most prestigious stages. Emma Renzi, Interview with Eoan History Project (2009). Eoan Group Archive: uncatalogued.
267   After his debut performance at the Metropolitan Opera, Joseph Gabriels never sang at the Met again. Roos (2018): 142.

The strain will be great, because at most he will have 2 or 3 rehearsals – possibly none with orchestra and none on stage. That means he has to be able to cope with that side too. This contract has given his confidence a tremendous boost and his singing has profited by this confidence and is more sure. Vocally, during the last years he has had many phases – mostly bad ones, trying to fix a vocal technique after all that Eoan Group battering around. He hasn't solved all the vocal problems, but at least the top notes are now secure and sure and this is the 1ˢᵗ requisite of the international tenor. I must say that he is approaching the matter intelligently. Never having performed the opera, he is working with a producer to fix a production set of rules for him, in case he doesn't have a production rehearsal. What happens in this case is that just before curtain time the stage director would point out which areas to keep clear of because of chorus or prop obstructions. The rest would be up to him. The chances are also that he might not sing with his colleagues until the actual performance. Fortunately for Canio there is no ensemble singing, not even a duet, so this already helps.

You might wonder why the Met works like this – well people who sing at the Met are expected to know their jobs. And Joseph is aware of this, and I'm healthily happy that he is trying hard to create a character rather than just vocalizing and moving about, and so we are working at it. One just hopes he will not abuse the success, once having got through this performance. Yea, he is still fat – but apparently dieting. Most singers (specially the men) are big tending towards fat – but they're tall – 6 footers. [...]

My last word – asking for 5 more years of singing is *not* asking too much, and I want to help. So let's see what can be done about "our recital".

It's 3a.m. We'll talk more if you answer soon.

Much love to Johnny, the children.

Yours,

Gordon.

38

Via Plinio, 42, Milano. Italy.

[5 December 1970]

My dear May,

I have some hours free and have the inclination to write you – but I've not pen nor paper – so forgive this unkempt letter.[268]

Thanks more than a million for your letter and subsequent tape. [...] A reason for not having made any attempt to reply sooner has been that I have been listening very attentively to your work as often as possible, and with my severest critical cap on, I admit that I can find nothing terribly wrong vocally and frankly can only think of good things to say... and as a result I don't know whether to tell you what I hear... the good things, I did expect to hear, though your pessimistic build-up beforehand frankly did make me wonder just what it would really be like.

At the outset, let's eliminate the accompanist for whom you did apologize and after all she was nearly sight-reading – but it wasn't nearly good enough, at least for the standard of singing you were producing. [...] [Your] voice sounds much more mellow and well-placed than

---

268 This letter is written in pencil on the back of a report form of "The Shenker Institute of English".

I can remember without any signs of the technical work and the vowel sounds are excellently moderated to make it sound like one voice ... I admired the ease of delivery in the middle voice – but you were working too hard on the high notes – the relaxation had gone and so also the intensity of these notes (you did talk about this yourself). You think your "e" sounds too English – I don't get that impression – in many cases on the tape it sounded to me more Italian than many Italian singers can make it – some of your pronunciation was suspicious – like you'd say "diiiiio" and then "mioooo" and all the double consonants were messy. Next [time] you listen to a Callas aria, follow it with the score and listen carefully how she treats double consonants and also single consonants like "vo-ce", and not "vo-cccce". It is an education.

Interpretation-wise the most convincing on the whole tape was "Altro di me non le saprei narrare, sono la sua vicina",[269] etc. It was alive – maybe because you didn't have to worry about the accompaniment at that point. Also the "Summertime"[270] sounds most idiomatic and you capture a good atmosphere. In the rest, there were only minute moments of histrionic interest – you could thank the fact that you can at least keep things alive vocally all the time – but that's your job, isn't it? What a mess the *Traviata* duet turned into – I feel real sorry – you don't deserve that! [...]

Having heard your work, I want all the more to do a concert with you.[271] I've made up my mind and [am] determined to do so.

From the outset you have misunderstood one thing – possibly through my unclear explanation. I did talk with [Mac] Robertson[272] about this concert, but with no idea that he personally should finance any part of it. I gathered that you all do welfare work and giving concerts for this or that charity – and I figured that if you had some cause, it might be possible to arrange a concert and the profits could go to the charity. I've looked into expenses – and they are enormous, that is, just considering mine. So why don't I meet half-way? I want to come home before leaving for the States because it seems that I will not go home for several years after that. So instead of your concert paying me a fee, could my one-way fare be arranged? I will write again to Robertson and if some such organization can be arranged, all the better. What ideas have you? I am not too clear, but I hope you understand what I mean to say.

Whichever way, I *do* mean to have this concert with you because after hearing the tape I admire your work even more, and so much so, that I've already decided the second half of the programme from what I've heard you do. So just hold tight, because here it comes: –

"Casta Diva" (*Norma*); "Ecco: respino appena" (*Adriana Lecouvreur*); "O mio babbino caro" (*Gianni Schicchi*) [by Puccini]; "O nume tutelar" (*La vestale*); "Una macchia è qui tuttora" (*Macbeth*) – I had to get this in!! – and "Vivi, ingrate" (*Roberto Devereux*).

What do you think – the *Vestale*, which is short, and the *Devereux* (which is long) would be new for you.

Now, having said all I have to say, let's hear all your arguments. But remember, we have to decide quickly because the only free time I have is in *April*. [...]

Next week the Scala season opens with *Vespri siciliani* with Renata Scotto[273] (you make your "e" sounds like her). She is possibly the most accomplished Italian soprano today – shrills on anything above high C, but knows how to shape a phrase and can sing remarkably "piano"

---

269 Aria from Puccini's *La bohème*.
270 Aria from Gershwin's *Porgy and Bess*.
271 This concert was given on 7 August 1971 in Durban, South Africa at the "Indian Cane-Grower's Hall at the M.L. Sultan's College".
272 The organiser of the concert.
273 Renata Scotto (*1934), Italian soprano and opera director.

and has a magnificent line. So I wonder what this will be like. Not so long ago, I heard her in *Traviata* – and the "Dite alla giovine" was just breathtakingly soft and intense.

I must close – forgive this mess of a letter. All the best, and I do so hope you will approve and be able to arrange our concert.

Much love to Trudy, Wendy & Johnny.

Yours,

Gordon. [...]

39

[Via Plinio, 42], [Milano.], [Italy.]

Monday, 15 February [1971]

My dear May,

Thanks a million for your letter of this afternoon; I'm replying immediately also because I do have every intention of mailing a letter off to you today. [...]

Joe's [Joseph Gabriels] debut at [the] Met on the 5th was successful; the *New York Times* gave him a good review[274] and I heard some of the performance tape and he seemed to credit himself well enough after ballsing [messing up] only the very first attack. But that's what he needed and provided he doesn't go off his head with the ego, he will get a lot of work, and probably good work too. They are still in the States and expected back within the next few days, so next time I ought to have some inside or rather behind the scene stories. About [you singing] *Pagliacci* – well, why not? It is not the ideal role for you at this stage, but vocally and musically it is far more attractive than Santuzza, because Nedda is a bitchy role with some glorious moments in the music. If you have accepted[275] – I hope you have – start learning it slowly. The idiom is different from the other composers and if you know your way about the notes in June, we can talk about it then too. [...]

P.S. Thanks a million for the cutting. It is good to see what the SA press has to say, good to know that they have something to say. No, I do not work with Emma [Renzi],[276] only that once and I remember we did *Ballo in maschera*.

Thanks again.

Ciao for now.

Gordon.

---

274 "Mr. Gabriels is not a Caruso. His voice is actually on the smallish side, although it carries easily because it is well fo-cussed. In other respects, he gave a creditable performance. He phrased musically, carrying some phrases through where other tenors have to make a break. He did not overact, so that his round face and portly figure acquired a feeling of pathos". Ericson (1971)

275 Abrahamse sang the role of Nedda in *Pagliacci* during Eoan's 9th Opera Season in October 1971.

276 Emma Renzi (*1926), South African soprano.

Via Plinio, 42, Milano, Italia
[The envelope, stamped 28 June 1971, contains this letter as well as the following letter, dated 20 June 1971.]

Wednesday, 5 May 1971

Dear May,

How are things your way? I'm okay – the bronchitis has finally given up the battle – and what a battle it's been.

The wretched Italian post has been on strike again – this place is going through a heavy period of strikes. If it's not the telephone company, it's the bread-shops or restaurants, and so on! As a result your tape did not reach me till yesterday. Thanks a million and right away I must say how thrilled I am with your progress – I've listened to it all only once and I'm not going to waste too much time telling you about the things that are excellent – they are supposed to be so! What struck me enormously, is the fact that throughout your vocal placing is much, much better than on the last tape and so I assume that this venture into the bel canto repertoire is doing your voice good – right or wrong? Continue along this road – and it seems that right now you are your best teacher. The sounds are more collected and even through the whole range. [...] There are so many good things about your delivery which makes me feel confident that you will be ready for the whole challenge of it.

I realize that it is hard for you to make a tape a week with teaching, etc.[277] so let me make a concession. Send me a tape of the complete concert every 2 weeks. When recording try and do everything at one go like it would be in performance and then we can also judge the strength needed. How's that?

Also, yesterday I got Mac [Robertson]'s letter with details that the Bruins[278] are taking over [the arrangements] as you said, etc. In order to stay 19 days I'll have to change dates again. The only time I can is between *July 23rd and August 11th* (it makes 20 days in fact) – is that any good? Is it inconvenient with your Eoan Group booking?[279] I've been trying to rearrange things – but try and fix anything with an Italian agent – it's murder just because of the disorganization. One advantage of the new dates is it gives us more time, which we can always do with. [...]

By the way, did you get my diagrams of the "operatic" dress and Callas cuttings? What do you think? [...]

The day before yesterday [I] saw [Giuseppe] di Stefano in *Bohème* – he hadn't sung at the Scala in 7 years – so he has little voice left – but it sure made me realize the difference there is between "great" and others. But this gives us another aspect to talk about when we meet.

Thanks ten million for your much appreciated hard work.

Love to the kids.

Regards to Johnny.

Yours,

Gordon. [...]

---

277 Abrahamse was probably teaching at a school during this time.
278 The "Bruins" ("The Browns") were a coloured cultural organisation based in Durban; they helped to organise Jephtas and Abrahamse's Durban recital of 7 August 1971.
279 Jephtas means Abrahamse's engagement to sing Nedda in *Pagliacci* (see above).

Via Plinio, 42, Milano. Italy.

Lago di Garda.[280] Wednesday, 8 July [1971]

Hi there May,

How are things with you? Thanks a lot for your 2 tapes which I got on Monday. I had to leave Milan on Monday to do a job here for my English School and so barely had time to listen, but not enough to make a reply tape, and as I don't expect to be back in Milan for a while, I'll have to content myself with writing …[281]

The first thing that I have on [my] mind is that your effort to keep the voice in place (after all my cajoling) is remarkable and admirable. The result is audible, but I need to make additions - it needs to be without losing your own vocal colour - that is, in the process you whiten the sound considerably, which in listening is equally unsatisfactory as over-darkening and rounding - now you need to find a road in between; because *the aim of singing in one place is to enhance the natural vocal sound*. Does that make sense? The other and more important point is that if in any of these processes it affects the throat, then that method you employ is wrong, and you must stop and try another approach, as you already have indicated. [...]

By and large I was wholly satisfied with what you did - and also the *Pagliacci* sounds more part of you. Now, we know the music, and so we must study the words and their meanings. I want you to study the translation over and over again, until you can translate any line, and until you can feel the meaning of every word - then when you sing to try to understand every word as you sing it - until you can reach the stage that the words are your own thoughts, rather than read from paper and written by [Salvadore] Cammarano, or whoever the librettist is. I realize this is a marathon job, but it is our responsibility.

For this I'm especially happy that we will have 15 days of rehearsal - believe me! Talking about this! As far as possible, I would prefer not to rehearse in a house - as you know that by nature, I cannot (like you) work with the idea of people around unless absolutely necessary. Ideally, if at all feasible, I would like to do as many rehearsals (or better still, all) and workouts in the actual hall of the concert as possible, so that we do not have to spend hours and anxiety adjusting to new acoustics and surroundings. We will spend as much time together working as your domestic commitments will allow, but outside of this would I be able to find a piano for private practise at hours when singing is unfeasible like 7.30a.m. etc.? To tell you the truth, I need to put in many hours of work - and we must be better than good. Am I making things complicated? If so, forgive me. [...]

I'm enclosing a dress-design[282] which I've just come across, and if you have not settled on anything yet (1st half), it might appeal to you. I don't even object to the colour - perhaps it might be softer (the colour). The head-gear here worn by Aretha Franklin[283] is what I had in mind - still [for the] 1st half - look at it and we can discuss it when we see each other.

---

280 This letter bears Jephtas's Milan address on the envelope, but was posted from Verona and written by Lake Garda. Since Callas and her first husband had owned a villa in Sirmione on the banks of Lake Garda, perhaps Jephtas was on a form of pilgrimage.

281 Jephtas and Abrahamse regularly communicated by recording their "letters" on tape - especially about matters of vocal coaching.

282 This addendum is lost.

283 It is unclear why Jephtas recommended the American soul artist Aretha Franklin (1942-2018) as inspiration for wearing a hat. No photos exist of Abrahamse wearing a hat during this recital.

This year sure is mine for car accidents – on Monday morning I had a spectacular crash – a Fiat 124 came out of a side street without stopping – hit me and I overturned twice and landed on the driver's side with wheels in the air, and the car on my leg – but, I'm still alive, though right now my knee and leg's in a mess; and apart from bruises all over, I should be lucky to be alive. That's life, isn't it. Anyway, the car is irreparable and at least it's got rid of that.

I wanna get this off to you. So, au revoir for now – till later –

Gordon.

42

[Via Plinio, 42], [Milano], [Italy]

Sunday, 22 August [1971]

Hi there May,

I figure that right this minute you are already in your mother's house – my clock reads five after seven p.m. Well, how are you and have you recovered from the hecticism [*sic*] of the last few weeks?[284]

I got back to Milan only last night having spent the days before in Rome catching the sun and just generally having a rest, and now I'm left with the hollow feeling one is left with after [a concert] – you know better that kind of feeling I figure.

This is not a letter to say thank you or one that is expecting thanks from you. We don't have to say thanks because I think that we have both tried to express ourselves to humanity through art. This is not [a] time to praise ourselves on artistic success, and how do we really within ourselves know whether it in fact was that – what is more important is that we have tried as sincerely as we could and the general reaction alone should make us happy that we have at least aroused more feeling for this music and art. I must add that I have come out of this venture admiring even more your stamina, fortitude and artistic ability, not mentioning any of the other attributes of which [we] are aware of.

Now I hope that this experience will for you produce good results in the role of Nedda. As soon as you can, send me a rehearsal tape – I want to help as much as I can without making things too harassing for you or the company, and it would be stupid for me to think that Cape Town will see things the same as I. They have their own prerogatives, but I still believe that you as the artist deserve higher ideals, and so you need to make the very best and exploit every artistic avenue of your next project.

In one way I feel kinda sad having left home escaping from our problems as people and on a selfish route of proving myself to myself, rather than to stay there and present my bit in our fight to achieve our ideals – a difficult conflict.

Our recital has been an important thing for me too, and though I feel bad that we could not also show Cape Town our intentions ... one cannot have everything – let's start thinking when we can have another and remember I am always open to be asked.

---

284 Jephtas had returned to South Africa to give a recital with Abrahamse in Durban for the "Bruins" in the Indian Cane-Grower's Hall at the M. L. Sultan's College on 7 August 1971. He returned shortly afterwards to Italy.

There are a hundred and one things that I want to say, but with two fingers on the type-writer my concentration has left me.

Give my best wishes to everybody and for now have a great time.

Ciao.

Gordon.

[P.S.] I thought I had your Cape Town address but be damned if I can find it now.[285]

Via Plinio, 42, Milano, Italy.

Wednesday, 15 September [1971]

Hi there May,

Thanks billions for both your letters and before I go off at a massive tangent about my comings and goings, let me first reply to yours.

Having said all the thank-you's that were necessary to each other, we now cannot rest on the old laurels but must forge ahead for a next time and the future - right? That you show little emotion off-stage is perhaps a tremendous asset because just talking for myself alone - there is little worse than someone who is always gushing around profusely, and in any case I did nothing to deserve and merit any such thing - I was merely doing what I believed in and in any case, I don't have to do anything I don't want to do. Not so?

I am still more than overwhelmed with the Bruins as a group[286] - or more exactly, with the ones with whom I had contact - that any group of people could get together and give so much of themselves for so little, if any, personal gain was for me a tremendous lesson in humanity. You know I've lived for so long in a world of brutalities and realities where the most important concern is survival, that I had really forgotten any such sentiments and really one need look no further than Cape Town for nothing-for-nothing conditions![287] - and here, that is a principal regulation of living. Thinking about it now, I can't remember just how long it took me to accept such conditions, but having conditioned myself by now, it makes me appreciate the Bruins even more - you (or much rather, we) were lucky to have such a group behind [us]. I have been meaning to write to each of them but apart from the fact that writing is kinda difficult for me, I just am not able to express what I really have in mind to say to them - so I'll send cards as usual!! [...]

Oh, what did I say about Charles de Long's voice - I can't remember anyway, having got yourself a pre-set reputation is good because it will make you produce even better work, don't you think! How is the *Pagliacci* going? Now that you've studied [it] for nearly a month you should have it under control - you're dead right about the details you mention - sexy movement of the arms on the chords before "o che bel sole", and the duet scenes - remember the movements must be "young" and arrogant - that is quick movements with the head for example, and Nedda listens a great deal and must re-act to whatever she hears and how she hears it - she is

---

285 The letter was sent to the Eoan Group instead of to Abrahamse's home address.
286 The proceeds of the Jephtas-Abrahamse recital for the "Bruins" in Durban went to the Durban and District Community Chest, which was used to fund "any undertaking that will benefit the less privileged". See www.communitychest.co.za/, accessed 17 October 2022
287 He is probably referring to the Eoan Group.

not sophisticated nor even elegant - remember I told [you that] Callas's Violetta was a whore and though Nedda is not exactly that, she is not Tosca nor Leonora [from *Il trovatore*]. Okay. Have you been able to do anything about Nedda's face? You must - that's as important - and the words - check yourself on pronunciation - double consonants! Single vowels all long - and understand every word - the sense is not enough - yours and your colleagues'. Maybe then you can pull up the others when they realize your detail and precision - it is a responsibility but you can do it and only you because the directorial staff there care about so little! [...]

Yea[h], I saw Mr. Sydow and as long as things stayed at the platonic "family-affair" level, it was excellent; but to talk business under such terms was not easy. He did not convince me about coming back, maybe because he must realize that to do anything like that at this stage would be impossible and unhealthy for all, so he merely made his proposition which deep down I cannot completely ignore because I am concerned about cultural values down there. My main obstacle into saying "yes, I'll come tomorrow", is whether I care more to better and satisfy myself or go out there and help others with little chance of bettering my own personal needs. I cannot make up my mind and so right now I've settled for the first choice and given Mr. Sydow the answer that I would consider such an offer after 2 more years, after having also to go back there in the meantime for a short period to see the whole mechanization of the company at close quarters; and furnished him with a list of possible conditions within my own interests. More than that I could not offer and it would be up to them to accept or reject as [much] as it would be up to me - but 2 years is a long time and as yet I'm not committed to anything. That is how we left things and I don't know how much of this he would want everybody to know, or what he might report back as the results of his trip - I would of course be interested to know, so if I'm not delving too much on your integrity, do let me know what is made public and known in this direction. In any case, contrary to their thinking, I do not feel ready to accept such a job and they are not very precise about what exactly they are offering me and so they play cagey about whether I would be artistically subordinate to Manca or not - and that I would not be able to accept; so it seems that they need to sort themselves out more - and then from what I understand, the position is mainly a teaching one. Apart from the fact that my interest is more towards performing, I really don't know whether I could teach any of the people there (as I saw it in August) because they have been too spoilt by their glory and past the point of learning - if only just 30% of what there is, had your kind of approach and ideals the picture would already be quite different: but regrettably that is not so. [...]

While in London, I saw a film of Callas's 2nd Act Tosca at an exhibition and was astonished that at close proximity she has the same nervous tensions as you, which don't pass the footlights. That was quite something and a compliment for you or her - depending how you look at it!

For now arrivederci and let's hear how the Nedda is going.

All sorts of messages for everybody.

Bye for now,

Gordon.

44

Via Plinio, 42, Milano. Italy.

Friday, 24 September [1971]

Hi there May,

Thanks millions for your utterly welcome letter of the day before yesterday. [...]

I'm sorry that things have not been going all that well with Manca being ill and all that – yea, he did talk much of his health to me and though some of it did hit a true note, a lot of it I thought was just the old hypochondriac that he always was; but as you say he is an old man and that I did notice. It would be nice if they did ask me to do this season, but it would have to stop there because though it would be great, I could not take a chance on *Pagliacci* because to my mind the opera is a beast for the conductor and certainly not one that I really want to conduct. Of the operas they are projecting the only one that would interest me personally would be *Traviata*, but then the singers are not what I would want in that opera and rehearsals to get it going my way would mean a cancellation until god alone knows when. But as you say, I also figure they will not permit me the joy of saying "no". [...]

I'm also sorry that Magnoni was of little joy, but I hope that you can get some vocal work done with her. I think I know exactly how you feel – kinda out of place with everyone else with a teacher and you around with nobody – they probably figure you don't need much which would be typical of their way of thinking. I would just love to help you with the production also, more so as you are not getting any direction. Well, we cannot have any of the sophisticated things of [*Roberto*] *Devereux*, so keep the movements of Nedda natural but enlarged for the operatic purposes – also I think she moves quickly, defiantly and her love duets need to look voluptuous – think how tall you think she is, what her face is like – and question, what do you have for hair? Long, short, your own? Then in the play scene her movements along with the shrill voice are clumsy and stilted because she is a bad actress. Write and tell me what you are doing and maybe we can make some ideas, okay?

Great, so the S.A.B.C. have made an offer[288] – I am really pleased. Now that they want you, my first reaction is to ask for a change of date. Tell them that you are already engaged for that period, and that is true anyway, and ask for a date in '72. My reason for this is that you would have been doing too much in these last few months and you will be tired physically and vocally, so I think you need a break to collect yourself together and why do everything at once and possibly nothing all next year. ... About what to sing? I agree about offering something that we have done in Durban which would mean not having to start something from scratch, and from what I remember, Cree[289] is not the most sympathetic nor sensitive of conductors and so from that point of view also something like the *Devereux* is out. What about "Casta Diva", *Adriana Lecouvreur*, *Gianni Schicchi* and I would say both the Afrikaans things, if they are orchestrated.[290] I am not suggesting anything out of the way because obviously the rehearsing will be a bare minimum and for the audience it would be more of a pop type, because to make the *Devereux* really work one needs a lot of working together as we

---

288 The South African Broadcasting Corporation (SABC) had engaged Abrahamse to record a number of arias with the National Symphony Orchestra. This did not come about until 1974.
289 The Englishman Edgar Cree (1914-2002) had emigrated to South Africa in 1946 and served as conductor at the SABC Orchestra from 1946 to 1978.
290 Jephtas might be referring to "Heimwee" and "Mali die Slaaf se Lied" by the South African composer S. Le Roux Marais.

discovered; hence I think that if you work along these lines you would be able to make a happy collaboration with the conductor and at the same time be doing your own thing with the artistry, etc. You get me? [...]

All the best and good wishes to everybody.

Ciao for now,

Gordon.

45

Via Plinio, 42, Milano. Italy.

Thursday, 7 October [1971]

Hi there May,

I was so thrilled to get your letter today, and I'm so eager to know all about your Nedda [...]

I have a death of a cold and in fact there is rumour that Italy is to have an Asiatic flu attack, and I've been on vitamin C's and all that mess for god knows how long already, but it obviously hasn't helped, and then worse, I have a concert in Brussels next Thursday. Nothing terribly exciting nor what I would have really liked. It is with two singers and the whole first half is all Monteverdi which means it [is] a completely different idiom and then the second half is mostly Mozart and Italian verismo meaning [the composers Alfredo] Catalani and [Amilcare] Ponchielli, and I've been feeling so bad with a snotty runny nose it has been just too much of an effort to exert myself to really study all that music; but I must. [...] New York[291] right [now] at this moment seems out of the question and so I'm waiting around a few more months to see how things turn themselves out. No, this year I'm not teaching music because I wanna be free to follow up any leads in Europe, and although there are some things in the air it is better not to talk about them until a contract has been signed or until after, otherwise it means bad luck, which to my thinking has had a lot to do with my American fiasco,[292] that is, too much talk beforehand and then the people around one who, although they mean well, tend to ruin things. But that is enough of me for now. [...]

About the make-up and Nedda's face: I would say that as they have a make-up man, use him rather than try to fathom out a solution as you have enough other things that only you can think and sort out. Discuss the problem with the man, tell him that according to you (as he doesn't know me) your own face is not exactly right for Nedda because of the hollows in the cheekbones and that the mouth is too small, could he make suggestions how to eliminate that because she has to look sexy and voluptuous and young; and then the eyes might need long lashes, etc. Talk to him and pose him your views of the character as you see her and I'm sure if he is reasonable as a person he will try to make suggestions and as he has the practical experience (I hope) he could put some thing together within the framework of your conception and he might easily be thrilled to have a challenge of this kind. Okay? [...]

Ciao for now and let's hear how everything's going.

Ciao, ciao,

Gordon.

---

291 Jephtas is referring to the offer made to him in 1970 by the New York City Opera. See letter of 6 September 1970.
292 The nature of this "fiasco" is unclear.

P.S. About the blond wig. In all the different performances I've seen I don't remember that, and I always remember black hair, but in Rota's time it seems to me that obviously she would have been blonde to single her out as an outsider to the people of Calabria who are basically dark haired. She was blonde because her behaviour at that time would have been very unlike the women from those parts, so you could probably use this way of thinking into the frame-work of your character – the average woman from those parts plays a very subservient role to their male partners whereas Nedda does have more of a streak of rebellion which is foreign to those people. Modern producers put her in black hair to conjure up the atmosphere of that area, that is dark tanned skins and dark hair.

46

Via Plinio, 42, Milano. Italy.

Sunday, 17 October [1971]

Hi there May,
   I just got back from Brussels this afternoon earlier and I figure that I might just as well answer your letter which I picked up on my way out last week. The concert went okay, or rather as okay as one could expect, and then also it is so difficult to make an affirmation if oneself has been involved, mainly because one does not hear things like others do; but still, if relying [on] and believing what others have said afterwards, then it was a good success and more so for me. [...]
   On reading your letter, you have everything to moan about – many things appear to be a real mess down there. By the time you get this the first ... performances will already have been,[293] for better or for worse; that you would have gone on with just one orchestral rehears-al does amplify the sad state of things because no matter with all the good blessings of god or whoever it might be, it simply is not good enough. I hoped that I'd find a tape waiting on my return, but that not being so I guess that rehearsals have not been that forthcoming and so I figure I'll hear the performances, right?
   About the SABC contract, I'm real glad that you agree to postpone until next year, after all it would be within your interests and as far as possible one wants to avoid the standards of Cape Town. It is with great pleasure that I see that Francesco Mander[294] is to conduct, and that is every bit to your advantage because he is Italian (I had no idea he is working out there) and I remember meeting him in Rome some eight years ago. So at last you will have the sup-port behind you of someone who understands what your art is all about rather than some affected Anglo-Saxon [Edgar] Cree who frankly is not that much of a musician as a position of that calibre demands, if he were he would be doing better things and so it seems to me all the better that you are dealing with Mander. [...]
   You ask whether the operas in London are performed in English; at the Sadler's Wells yes, because they work on the format that the public must understand what is being sung, and in some cases this is absolutely true especially in Mozart etc., of which they do a tremendous amount and also in operas where there is spoken dialogue, like is the vogue in *Carmen* these

---

293   Jephtas means Abrahamse's performance of Nedda in *Pagliacci* in October 1971.
294   Francesco Mander (1915–2004) was chief conductor of the SABC Orchestra between 1969 and 1976.

days, though on the other hand, in the Italian works like *Traviata* and *Ballo*, say, it is unfeasible to really believe that the audience do understand every word, because one doesn't, not even in Italian. Secondly, the language is so antiquated in English that one wants to laugh in the most touching moment (in Italian it doesn't ring a humorous note because they are more attuned to that kind of repetitious emotion which happens all the time in opera), and then another factor which to my mind is so important is that the English have such dreadful foreign accents because they turn every single pure Italian vowel sound into a whining diphthong; and so the solution at the Wells, although far from happy, is better. At Covent Garden the story is the opposite because they deal mainly with international stars, and unless they want dual language performances like I have heard in Germany, they do everything in the original language, though problems arise when *Boris Godunov* is written in Russian, but it cannot be expected that people like [Birgit] Nilsson learn *Elektra* in English or La Callas to sing *Norma* in English; apart from anything else they don't have the time. Though I must say that I much prefer to hear things in the original language. [...]

For now, all the best with the performances, and let me hear all you think good or bad because one way or another, your comments will make me understand better the conditions down there and so when I eventually decide a "yes" or "no" about coming there, I will have something to base my views upon and nobody else is going to give me any honest and frank views.

Love to all.
Yours,
Gordon. [...]

Via Plinio, 42, Milano. Italy.

Wednesday, 24 November [1971]

Hi there May,
Finally here I am – also to prove that I have *not* forgotten how to write. But reasons and motives later. [...]

First of all, since I last made contact, I've been going through a black, black period without work and with agents and people who just continuously led me up the garden path with the usual lies and what have you. To cut a laborious story short, I was in no frame of mind to concentrate on writing, nor did I want to labour you or anyone else with a problem that you would no doubt have worried about .... Right now things are better – I am coaching a soprano [Ángeles] Gulín[295] in [Alfredo Catalani's] *La Wally* (to be sung in Venice) and *Lucrezia Borgia* for Genoa; and the wife[296] of my maestro [Franco] Ferraris in [Amilcare Ponchielli's] *Gioconda* – at least I'm doing something, but I must find something better – I have been trying hard to get into an opera house – I need that experience so badly right now – but the doors seem slammed shut and obviously I've not yet found the right channels. Anyway, I'm trying and I must at the price of the depressions and frustration that the last weeks have cost me.

---

295 Ángeles Gulín (1939-2002), Spanish soprano, known for her Verdi roles.
296 Lucy Kelston Ferraris (1923-2010), American soprano.

Many a time I was about to pick up the phone and call home to say that I would be on the next plane out - but on reflection then, that would not have solved "my" problem by any means - and the work that I might do out there would not be good if it is affected by my personal frustrations. I've tried to explain my silence hoping that you've understood - and every now and then I would feel bad thinking that after you had gone to all the trouble of sending me tapes and waiting for a comment - you were having none! Do forgive me! [...]

Let's talk about the tapes - the rehearsal with piano and Manca I found hard to listen to because I kept getting annoyed at his inane comments - like not even knowing that you were continuously getting the wrong notes on "sei lá" - and even worse, the tenor sang at least 1/3 of the opera a semitone too high - all those "vile, vile, t'ascondi" - I read F sharp in the score and he was singing Gs. So I was angry that Manca really hadn't studied the work nor taken the trouble to even learn the tune. Under all those circumstances you were doing well and like I said before, it sounded and seemed professional. [...]

For the rest, I don't know how or what to say - I found Gilda[297] the most acceptable in that she sounded so [much] more accomplished than her colleagues and the vocal placement is even - I cried on hearing that beautiful voice of Sophia[298] going through such torment - and I was not displeased with Pat's[299] sound, though I can imagine how constricted she may have looked. The others have something, there's no doubt, some with more natural endowments than others, but talking from the vocal point alone - as I didn't see any of it, and we know the opera is not only vocalizing - one just has to work with good guidance to obtain even a reasonable result, and work a lot more. It makes me really wonder if I really would be able to do any good by being there, and then during listening to the tapes I was continuously faced with the desire to go and try and save the situation. Maybe I will be out there sooner than we think - there is just no knowing, is there? [...]

The Scala opens next week with [Verdi's] *Simon Boccanegra* with [Mirella] Freni, [Gianni] Raimondi, [Piero] Cappuccilli and [Nicolai] Ghiaurov - so it ought to be good. Followed by [*Madama*] *Butterfly* - who exactly is singing I don't know - the tenor is [Giacomo] Aragall[300] I know.

Write me, that will cheer me up.
Sorry for having been so bad at answering.
Love to all.
Yours, Gordon.

---

297 The main female character in Verdi's *Rigoletto*, sung by Eoan soprano Freda Koopman.
298 Sophia Andrews sang the role of Maddalena in *Rigoletto*.
299 Patricia van Graan also sang the role of Nedda in *Pagliacci* during the 1971 opera season.
300 Giacomo Aragall (*1939), Spanish tenor.

48

[No return address provided.]

Mantova[301]
Monday, 7 February [1972]

My dear May,

How are things with you?

I received also your latest letter which was waiting when I was called to Milan on Friday - thank you so very much, and as you write "al help dit nie, troos dit"[302] - and it did "troos"[303] as I will tell you later. [...]

Where shall I begin - I don't know where the beginning of this episode might be. The two singers I worked with have gone and sung, and the woman, Angeles Gulín, was so enthusiastic about the work we did on *La Wally* that she immediately asked me to work with her on *Lucrezia Borgia* with her later this season and there was much talk about going to Madrid this summer.

In the meantime the Mantova and Cremona seasons sprang up, both of whom were interested to have me as maestro sustituto which in effect is some sort of glorified repetiteur and assistant conductor job - well that was [what] I wanted; and with the American [job][304] lost because of the immigration mess - and believe me I suffered a great deal because of that loss, but still had the strength to face such a defeat and force myself to forge ahead and break through elsewhere. Well, the amount of arse licking and shit I had to go through to establish either of these two seasons is just horrific and too cumbersome to relate - but I remember there were moments that I myself when alone would vomit in disgust at the whole mess. And the more I wanted the job, the more the pressure from all sides became. When eventually, Mantova decided that they wanted and needed me and made me the contract (even at a cut-rate, but to me that did not matter, I just wanted to work), I heaved a sigh of relief and thought, thank God, now I can get down and work with music. But no, the Labour Office in Rome refused to give me permission to work in [the] capacity of maestro sustituto - the number of foreign artists engaged in a season is controlled - Milan gave a right of way, but Rome headquarters would not budge which meant the existing contract was not valid. Well, at this stage Mantova needed me as much as I them, but the impresario, clever and able businesswoman that she is, immediately offered me the possibility to be her son's assistant - the conductor Martini[305] - the same duties - but not under contract to the theatre, but his private help at a price nearly half the previous. At this stage I didn't care anymore, and the fee, barely [covering] expenses, was of relative importance - I wanted the experience and the chance to work in Italian theatre. And so after all that humiliating arse crawling and having to accept what was being offered, I eventually found myself in Mantova for the first rehearsal - I remember well, at 6 p.m. on Jan 15th - the opera, *Anna Bolena*.

I knew the opera as well as can be, because as you know, it is one that has interested me for some time - anyway, there was Martini - the kind of musical director of the season - and

301 Jephtas consistently uses the Italian name for the city of Mantua in northern Italy.
302 Afrikaans for "although it does not help, it consoles".
303 "console".
304 The position of assistant conductor at the New York City Opera that was thwarted by work permit issues. See his letters of 6 September and 10 October 1970.
305 Francesco Maria Martini, Italian conductor active in the 1970s, no further information available.

me, and by 6.15 the whole company of principal singers were there and after having said all the hello's and long-time-no-see's, but the contracted conductor was still missing (there were rumours that he was sick and not coming, but he had not informed the theatre). At 6.30 [Elena] Suliotis walks in - the diva - she has no airs - but everybody else cringes - and Martini decides to take over the rehearsal and bluffs his way through because he does not know the opera from Adam and tells the signora (Suliotis) not to sing unless she wants, but she is professional and marks through the ensembles with the others - we get to Act III to the duet with her and the mezzo - and she opens up and in the notes lower than A she sounds twice the mezzo and she has the Callas facility to alternate between chest and head notes - well, everybody looks up in amazement at this sound she puts out and with no problem and no fatigue. The rehearsal goes through to the end and all go to supper. Two days later the conductor had still not arrived and Martini had all his hopes to conduct the opening night - and with clever manoeuvring he succeeded and did well enough. [...]

The other operas followed [along] less dramatic and traumatic lines - generally with only one production rehearsal - a couple of music rehearsals with the conductor in question and then dress rehearsal. The conductor Gavarini[306] didn't like me and showed it - I think mainly because I refused to bow the knee every time I saw him - and he played the big diva scene - but still, I played that *Ballo in maschera* love-duet like my whole life depended on it, and both he and [Plácido] Domingo (who was extremely kind to me) came to me after to say how well I had played and what have you - but that didn't change our relationship because in the *Manon Lescaut* rehearsals he was even more piggish - but while I was at the piano I could still win, but in other circumstances of course I was helpless.

All these millions of little things to diminish my force - just to be protested [at] shortly after my arrival by the chorus - that is, as a foreigner along with the 2 only other foreigners in the company I was redundant and exceeded the official % of foreigners [allowed]. All those little old ladies wanted me out - nothing personal I understood, but syndicate rights - nevertheless the blow was there all the same to be taken - and not even the thunderous applause the chorus gave me after the 1st rehearsal of the [Verdi] Requiem could wipe away that initial sting. And then last night at the official cock-tail party this very old woman who wanted me out came up to say that she is sure that I will be great, blah, blah, blah, and at that time I must not forget Mantova. Sure, I won't forget Mantova.

Then again a week later I was protested [at] again - this time by the inspector from the Union - big scenes again - and although I played it brave and hard in the theatre once alone in my room, time and time [again] I would break down just out of nervous exhaustion - and drink myself to sleep, and eat - at least I have 10 extra pounds to my bones - and now I know what a depressive eater is.

By the 3rd week I was winning more - people were sitting up and listening - Genova [opera house] approached me for an immediate contract from March through May - Treviso [opera house] asked about my availability in August - Martini asked me to come and be his assistant for May - and there was even talk of La Scala - I was furiously unhappy, but I thought, at least I will work - but no, I get called to the Home Office in Milan on Friday and issued with the ultimatum [that] the Foreign Ministry has given me 10 days to leave Italy because I had no right to work under the conditions of my visa to the country. Just the kind of wonderful news for extra cheer.

---

306   Loris Gavarini (1925–1983), Italian conductor active in Italy, Argentina and elsewhere in the 1960s and '70s.

So I'm drowned with a black depression and continuously ask myself – but hell, haven't I suffered enough already – I can't tell you how tired I am of the whisky, the sleeping tablets, the crying and having to force myself to work and smile outside. Maybe I should be grateful that I've had the strength till now – this evening is the Requiem. What will happen tomorrow doesn't matter – but shit it does.

Anyway, everybody has promised to do something about this exit visa, from Rossi Lemeni[307] who will call on the Ministry in Rome to the impresaria – but I've learnt not to depend on words and so expect the worst.

Man, I feel so alone and desolate – and do I really deserve this – what have I done to merit all this mess when all I want to do is make good music – and at this price is it really worth it? I'm in a trap like some animal and I turn from wall to wall but can find no [way] out – but I figure it's up to me to make things work.

Forgive me if I don't answer your queries now but I [will] wait until I am more settled about my immediate future – don't worry, I'll be okay – "'n Kaffir is mos hard gebak".[308]

Love to all. Gordon.

49

Via Plinio 42, Milano, Italia

Saturday, 26 February [1972]

Hi there May,

At long last I'm getting down to answering your letter of more than a month ago – and before I digress madly let me tackle replying first. […]

Glad – very glad, that you have restarted vocalizing – That's a medicine one cannot do without. You ask about finding a teacher. I am in doubt, and as you say, *who* is there and if you choose from what is available you would most probably be wasting your money because you can teach them![309] But this does not mean that you must not study. I suggest that you know what you want and what is necessary, that you do scales every day, taping them and afterwards listen to the tape with a critical ear, keep the good and work on the bad. Consequently you will also learn to listen to yourself even more carefully than you already do. Some things to remember – keep the throat open and as relaxed as possible at all times – in the effort to sing in the mask, make sure the sound is free.[310] In your case, it is not so much the sound which is not in the mask, but rather the vowel formation which is improper. You see, for the blessed English language we speak, we speak in the mouth so to say and naturally form our vowels there. (N.B) = listen to Renata Scotto = her vowels are excellently forward – try and imitate her and listen what you sound like on tape. A speaking Italian naturally makes his vowels in the mask. Now our problem is to learn to make those vowels in the mask – and so, "ah"

---

307 Nicola Rossi-Lemeni (1920–1991), Italian-Russian bass who had recorded with Maria Callas, Carlo Maria Giulini, Leopold Stokowski and others in the 1950s.
308 Afrikaans for: "A kaffir is baked hard," an idiom similar to the English "tough as nails". "Kaffir" was a derogatory term for black South Africans during apartheid; see "Editorial approach and terminology" at the beginning of this book.
309 Finding a good teacher was indeed a problem for Abrahamse, not just because of apartheid restrictions, but because the pool of potential singing teachers was already small in Cape Town.
310 This sentence was underlined by Abrahamse.

is most likely to be the worst in our case because our language habits immediately shove it half-way down the throat and further from the resonating chambers of the mask. [...]

By the way, what has happened about that S.A.B.C. engagement?[311] Let me know! [...]

I wrote you from Mantova but it seems that none of the letters I sent ever got to their destinations. Anyway, things are better for me – no, not really, but I feel better about them because I've had time to sit back and just reflect.

The Foreign Ministry ruling to leave Italy was appealed and annulled through fortunate contacts, but on condition that I do not work. I looked around England but cannot get myself to work there and so I've decided to go back to Italy and see what happens – shit alone knows what I will do when money runs out; but that's a bridge to cross when it is reached. Right now the prospects seem bleak and I'm really tired of the phony side of the business – I am much too subservient by nature and that throws me every single time a situation calling for extreme arrogance arises. I was looking around at the people in Mantova – the widowed mother whose almost pathological love for her only son was pushing and engineering her son's conducting career;[312] the famous soprano, [Elena Suliotis][313] ostensibly successful and wealthy, but going through a heap of problems and wanting to die on-stage; the cock-sure (but no-good) producer who strutted around after Act II proclaiming what a superb production (it) his was – (and worse, all the hangers-on agreed); and so on and so on ... The whole scene did make my stomach turn and turn and the thought that shit, I have to go through all the phony, bluff business too, is very nearly too much. Well, I thought at one stage, – "if you don't like it, leave it, kill yourself or something" – and maybe I would have if it were not [for] one ambition – and that is to do *Anna Bolena* with you as Anna. – Forgive me, I don't mean to alarm you and really I have no right – in a weak moment I confessed an inner truth!

– Another day has passed – it's already March 1st – this has become one of my soap-box opera instalments. I'm back here in this apartment [in Milan] where I started from and shit, I'm so sad. Everything I think about or look at wants to make me cry – and then I think that I used to be so exemplary at fighting back tears and facing whatever the situation was – but it seems that I've been fighting for God knows how long, with so very little result and now my resistance is just bone low. There are strong moments when I talk to myself and decide, well, I have talent and so I must pull myself together – but when the real situation appears I chicken out. Man, I seem to have been running – and running – from something inexplicable that bugs me but cannot shake it off – and as the thirty-years age blinks in the near future (I'll be 29 next week), the thought that I should really already have reached someplace – but this subservient, yes-boss, coloured nature that I was born with and lived with for 28 years isn't that easy to shake off.

I really should not be writing in this vein to anybody [any]more, especially in the direction of home, because we exiles always need to pretend so much how wonderful things are, but believe me, May, and I cannot be more truthful, things are shit; and so maybe I appear extensively foolish – forgive me! And my egoistic self forgets that also you have your own problems to cope with. But I'm not asking for sympathy nor help – I really am the only one to help myself – after all I'm doing what I am out of choice and nobody forced me to do so.

---

311 Abrahamse eventually did record with the SABC National Symphony Orchestra in 1974 when she sang five works conducted by Anton Hartman. These included arias from operas by Verdi and Puccini as well as the song "Heimwee" by the South African composer S. le Roux Marais. The recording is available at the SABC Sound Archives, catalogue No. TM 19760810.

312 Jephtas is referring to Francesco Martini. See his letter of 7 February 1972.

313 See his letter of 7 February 1972.

But you know how it is – when the going's well one is surrounded by people who suck the reflected glory and when the going is bad, well, you're all on your own – and even with some sincere people like Didi, Mabel, Joseph, etc – the right solutions do not cough up because after all they have their worries too!

Forgive me for talking so pessimistically – don't worry, I'll be okay – it's just a matter of time I suppose!

Do write soon. Much regards and love to Johnnie, Wendy and Trudy.

Ciao.

Gordon.

Figure 4.1 The Zurich Opera House.
Source: ETH-Bibliothek Zürich, Bildarchiv / Photographer: Comet Photo AG (Zürich) / Com_BC24-8001-003-008 / CC BY-SA 4.0.

4. ZURICH

4.1 "NELLO SANTI ... KNOWS HIS STUFF"

Gordon Jephtas first mentioned the possibility of moving to Switzerland in his letter of 5 March 1968, written from the Welsh National Opera in Cardiff: "I am more than seriously toying with the idea of living in Zurich, (a) because I like the place and (b) the chances of finding occupation seem quite positive". It is unclear who might have provided his first contact with the city, but since Zurich had for several years been one of the standard venues on the international opera scene, Jephtas will surely have met people who had worked there while he was studying and working in England and Wales. The Zurich Opera had also been running its own training programme since 1961 – the International Opera Studio, whose graduates already included singers such as Gwyneth Jones, and which also offered opportunities for singing coaches. Zurich is a pretty city, so it was hardly surprising that Jephtas "like[d] the place", and the Swiss franc was already an attractive currency (this despite an exchange rate of roughly five francs to one South African rand until the end of Bretton Woods in 1973). But the "chances of finding occupation" there were hardly as straightforward as he suggested in 1968. Getting a work permit was exceedingly difficult unless one was either a manual labourer or possessed of high-end skills that were in such short supply that a potential employer was willing to petition the city authorities on one's behalf. A singing coach did not naturally figure in either of those categories. Perhaps this was why all mention of Zurich then disappeared from Jephtas's correspondence for over two years.

A letter exists from Jephtas to May Abrahamse of 6 September 1970 that he wrote in the USA, though he only posted it later, from the Zurich Opera House. Regrettably, he makes no mention of why he was in Zurich, and he was in any case back in Milan just a couple of weeks later. He finally got an engagement at the Zurich Opera House in the late spring of 1972, as he confirmed in his letter to Abrahamse of 6 June 1972. He certainly needed it. His letters of 7 and 26 February 1972 from Mantua make no bones about his current problems – no proper working permit for Italy, an imminent lack of income, and major depression ("whisky, the sleeping tablets, the crying"). The job in Zurich would soon provide him with the regular income and the private and professional stability that seem to have been lacking in his life until now. Jephtas's letter of 6 June 1972 was written from the Hotel Conti, which was situated just behind the Opera House (whose management had presumably housed him there). He told Abrahamse that he had a proper contract with the Opera House as of the following August, but was already spending two weeks coaching the singers for a new production of Verdi's *Un ballo in maschera*. The opening night of this production took place on 9 September 1972, conducted by Nello Santi, and it was an especially prestigious occasion because it was the first performance of the new season.

Santi is first mentioned by Jephtas in his letter of 16 September 1972. It is, he says, "the first time that I'm working with a conductor of his stature and he knows his stuff". Santi did indeed. He was born in Adria in Veneto in 1931, studied in Padua, made his Zurich debut with *La forza del destino* in 1958, and was thereafter appointed the Music Director of the Zurich Opera. He gave his debut at the New York Met with *Un ballo in maschera* in 1962. He relinquished his post in Zurich in 1969, though he remained resident there and continued to work at the Opera House as a permanent guest conductor for the Italian repertoire for the next fifty years. He only gave his final performance there – with Donizetti's *Lucia di Lammermoor* – in 2019, the year before his death. In the year that Jephtas began working with him,

Figure 4.2 The conductor Nello Santi. Photo: Niklaus Stauss, Zurich.

Santi released a recording of Leoncavallo's *Pagliacci* with Plácido Domingo and Montserrat Caballé on the RCA Red Seal label (this LP was advertised in the *Neue Zürcher Zeitung* on 18 June 1972 to coincide with Santi's being awarded the Hans Georg Nägeli Medal, the highest music prize of the city of Zurich).[314] Jephtas had already worked with Domingo in Mantua earlier in the year, and he would later work with Caballé too. We can probably assume that it was Santi who hired Jephtas, and that he had heard of him through mutual contacts in Milan, Mantua or New York. Either way, Santi was just the kind of man influential enough to be able to convince the Zurich authorities to give Jephtas a work permit on account of his possessing skills essential for the Opera House.

Being engaged by Nello Santi specifically to coach the Italian repertoire in Zurich is a remarkable testament to Jephtas's abilities. There was no dearth of potential répétiteurs in Europe, not least because getting such a post at a major theatre was considered a major step on the ladder for aspiring conductors. So for Santi to engage a coloured, Afrikaans-speaking pianist to coach the repertoire in which he, Santi, was a recognised master (the repertoire that was in Santi's own mother tongue, no less) is little short of astonishing. On at least one occasion – so Jephtas once admitted in conversation – Santi invited him to conduct at the Opera House.[315] It is unclear whether this was for a house production or for a production at the Opera Studio – which would have been a more obvious venue for a conducting newcomer to start. But Jephtas declined, feeling not yet confident enough (so he said) to stand before an orchestra. The two men nevertheless remained close, with Jephtas often being invited to dine with the Santi family. It was also common for Santi to ring Jephtas at home to discuss

314   See the advertisement in *Neue Zürcher Zeitung* 193/279, *Sonntagsausgabe*, 18 June 1979, 16.
315   Information kindly provided by Johannes Lüthi.

matters pertaining to the opera schedule. He clearly became a kind of father figure to Jephtas, perhaps not unlike the latter's early mentor Joseph Manca. But the contrast between them must have seemed vast: where Manca was an amateur aspiring to a career that his modest gifts would never let him attain, Santi was a world star, respected by all the great singers whom Jephtas revered, and possessed of a photographic memory that allowed him to conduct every performance without a score.

Jephtas's fortnight in Zurich from late May to early June 1972 must have been on something of an ad hoc basis, for he is first registered as being officially resident in the city as of 16 August 1972. His address is given as Delphinstrasse 19 – presumably an apartment procured for him by the Opera House, as it is just a five-minute walk away. Jephtas apparently remained there until August 1973, when he took up residence in an apartment at Klosbachstrasse 83 in the leafy suburb of Hottingen, still less than a mile by foot from the Opera House or a direct tram ride of five or six minutes. He moved again in January 1974, this time to an apartment at Bäckerstrasse 19 in a less salubrious area on the other side of town, a two-minute walk from the Langstrasse – at the time one of the city's few red-light districts – and in a part of the city known by the derogatory name of "Kreis Cheib" (derived from the word for animal carcasses, which were in earlier times disposed of there). But he was still only a 20-minute walk from the Opera House. Jephtas's initial contracts for Zurich have not survived; the first we have is dated 23 January 1974 – just when he moved to the Bäckerstrasse – and is only for the following season (1974/75). Since it specifically refers back to a contract for the 72/73 season, we can probably assume that its conditions were similar.[316] He was engaged for a total of 6½ months during the season in question at a monthly salary of CHF 3,000 (just for the months when he was actively employed, of course). His duties are as solo répétiteur for the Italian repertoire, plus playing the piano and celeste when the orchestration of a work requires either (such as in Puccini's *Gianni Schicchi*, a production that he mentions specifically in his letter to May of 6 March 1973, and for which we may assume that he was drafted in to play the celeste).

These meandering moves across Zurich on Jephtas's part came to an end in June 1974.[317] A relatively new member of the Opera House administration, Johannes Lüthi – a few years younger than Jephtas – was looking for an affordable apartment in the city. Jephtas was apparently also keen to move again, and Lüthi suspects that Santi's wife suggested behind the scenes that it might be an idea for Jephtas to enter into a flat-share. So when Lüthi signed a contract for a three-and-a-half-room apartment at Schaufelbergerstrasse 44 in June 1974, Jephtas moved in too. They each had their own bedroom (Jephtas's being the slightly smaller one), but otherwise had joint use of the facilities. They led largely separate lives, with Jephtas often out until the early hours after performances, but they regularly ate together, and Sunday brunch would often be a communal affair when they were joined by Lüthi's girlfriend and whoever happened to be Jephtas's boyfriend at the time (Jephtas's bed was a single mattress that could fold out into a double when required). Perhaps the Santis felt that the stability of a such a domestic arrangement might do Jephtas good, though we have no proof of it. The rent for the apartment was CHF 800.- per month, of which Jephtas apparently paid less than half, given that he had the smaller bedroom. It was farther away from the city centre than his previous apartments – about three miles on foot – but close to a tramline that could get him to the Opera House in about half an hour.

---

316 The personnel dossier for Gordon Jephtas from the Zurich Opera House is today held by the Stadtarchiv Zurich.
317 Our information on Jephtas's private life in this chapter has kindly been provided by his Zurich friends Heinz Fischer, Roland Jung and Johannes Lüthi.

In his next contract with the Opera House, dated 5 May 1975, Jephtas was engaged for four months for the following season (1975/76) for a total of CHF 17,000, and seven months for the season thereafter (1976/77) for CHF 28'000 (which was upped to CHF 30,000 later that same month after Jephtas discussed his contract with the opera authorities – presumably because 28,000 would have meant a slight reduction in his monthly wage). His salary in each case was to be paid out in equal instalments over the whole calendar year. A copy of a letter from the Opera House to Jephtas dated 10 November 1975 confirms that he would in fact be working an additional six weeks in late spring 1976. His next extant contract, dated 19 August 1976 and for the 1976/77 season, engages him for nine months at CHF 4,500 per month. A separate agreement dated 30 August 1976 – just three weeks later – also engaged Jephtas for fifty hours of teaching at the International Opera Studio, apparently as Nello Santi's assistant, at a total of CHF 2,500 (thus CHF 50 per hour). Jephtas had thus increased his monthly salary by 50% over the space of just two years, and was now earning CHF 43'000 per annum, equivalent at the time to an annual salary back in South Africa of just over ZAR 15,000 – a considerable sum, and a clear sign that his abilities were appreciated in Zurich.

Jephtas was also still free to take on other work, as is obvious from the assorted commitments he mentions in his letters home. He made the occasional trip to the USA – as a postcard to Abrahamse from San Francisco dated 4 August 1976 confirms – and from 1974 to 1978 he spent some six or seven weeks every year[318] at the opera house in Lisbon, staying each time at the Hotel Borges. In Lisbon he worked with yet more of the big names, from the tenor Franco Corelli (whom Jephtas had admired since the early 1960s) to the baritone Piero Cappuccilli and the bass Boris Christoff, all of whom enjoyed major international careers. Jephtas clearly made an impression in Lisbon, too. Within half a year of meeting Corelli there for the first time, he was engaged to accompany him and Renata Tebaldi in a recital they gave at the Royal Albert Hall in London on 9 October 1973 and five days later, on 14 October, in the Musikverein in Vienna.[319] His description of his first musical encounter with Tebaldi (written on 14 September 1973) is one of the most vivid passages in all his letters. The Vienna concert was recorded, and offers one of the few extant audio documents of Jephtas as a pianist. Jephtas later mentioned to his friend Johann Lüthi that Tebaldi was keen to further his career. But when Tebaldi and Corelli gave another recital in Vienna some nine months later, it was with a different accompanist, one Eugene Kohn.[320]

On 30 August 1976, Jephtas was given another contract at the Zurich Opera House, again for two seasons (1976/77 and 77/78), at CHF 43,200 for nine months' work (plus, it stipulated, any statutory raise that might be granted to all personnel, which in previous years had been up to 5% per annum). He was thus earning CHF 4'800 per month. He was also coaching singers privately from the Opera House and the Opera Studio, which brought in extra cash. During the time that he shared his apartment with Johannes Lüthi, the rent Jephtas paid was less than ten percent of his gross salary. What's more, when he left Zurich for several weeks at a time to work in Lisbon and elsewhere, he would ask Lüthi to be excused his share of the rent. As it was easy to let out Jephtas's room to other temporary guests from the Opera House,

---

318   Since our efforts to find out more about his Lisbon activities have been unsuccessful, we cannot be sure exactly how long Jephtas stayed there; but in his letter to Abrahamse of 11 February 1974, he wrote that "Am in 'Hotel Borges,' Lisbon as from March 1st until April 20th", and it seems likely – given his contract in Zurich – that a similar pattern was repeated in each of the years he spent time in Lisbon.
319   See www.musikverein.at/konzert/eventid/15705, accessed 9 November 2022.
320   This concert took place on 28 June 1974. See www.musikverein.at/konzert/eventid/15537, accessed 9 November 2022.

Figure 4.3 Lochergut in Zurich, where Jephtas lived in a flat formerly the home of the writer Max Frisch.
Source: Baugeschichtliches Archiv der Stadt Zürich, BAZ_160347.

this seems not to have been a problem. By any standards, Jephtas was earning very well in Zurich. Much of his income went on international phone calls, however, for his bills regularly exceeded CHF 1,000 each month, especially after his travels abroad.

At roughly the same time that Jephtas was given his renewed contract in 1976, Johannes Lüthi's lease for their joint apartment was annulled (it seems that the landlords had finally decided they wanted quieter, less active tenants). Lüthi decided to return to his hometown of Wohlen in Canton Aargau. It lies just 12 miles from Zurich, but is situated at some distance from the intercity train lines. That makes the journey to the city rather circuitous, taking over half an hour each way by whatever means of transport one chooses. Nevertheless, Jephtas decided to move to Wohlen too, and even bought a car to make commuting easier – after all, travelling by car from Wohlen to the Opera House need not have taken him much longer than the tram ride from the Schaufelbergerstrasse. Jephtas accordingly ended his official period of residence in the city of Zurich on 30 September 1976. But he left Wohlen after just a couple of nights, sold his few items of furniture to Lüthi, and moved back to Zurich. Since he would usually stay out late after performances, drinking with colleagues, perhaps he realised that driving home in the early hours in an inebriated state was simply not a sensible option (though it's not clear why he hadn't thought of that beforehand). Jephtas's precise movements thereafter are difficult to determine, but he apparently moved into a spare room in an apartment in the high-rise block called "Lochergut" that his artist friend Roland Jung was using as a studio. As it happens, the very same apartment had been home to the writer Max Frisch just a decade earlier, who had apparently imagined, in vain, that this futuristic edifice would offer something of a big-city ambiance à la New York. Nor was this Jephtas's first chance brush with the local literati; during his six months on the Klosbachstrasse he had lived opposite Elias Canetti, and had presumably bumped into him on the street or in the nearby café on the corner of Römerhof where Canetti liked to spend his time. Jephtas's last apartment in Zurich seems to have been on the Weinplatz in the middle of the old town, opposite the venerable Hotel Storchen where numerous artistic luminaries had stayed in earlier times and where even the young Mozart had once dined.

At some point after his abortive move to Wohlen, Jephtas decided that his time in Zurich should come to an end. His decision was confirmed in a letter sent to him by the Opera House on 19 February 1977:

> The following was agreed with Mr GORDON JEPHTAS today:
>
> At his request, his contract for the 1977/78 and 1978/79 season is annulled. M Jephtas is leaving Zurich at the end of the present season in order to assume a new position in South Africa. This contract is being dissolved by mutual consent.[321]

Just what that "position" was remains unclear. Jephtas had hoped to be appointed the music director of Eoan back in the Cape, though they had already rejected him by this time, as he explains bitterly and at length in a taped "letter" to Abrahamse of 20 February 1977. He also tells her that he had been made a concrete though "unofficial" offer to conduct Donizetti's opera *L'elisir d'amore* for the Cape Performing Arts Board (CAPAB) at the Nico Malan Theatre in Cape Town, though it is clear that nothing came of that either (he seems to have assumed that the then music director at CAPAB, David Tidboald, was intriguing against him). Jephtas also explains that he had recently visited New York, where he had attended a performance at the Met of *Tosca* under Nello Santi. The latter had afterwards introduced Jephtas to the powers-that-be at the Met, who accordingly gave him (thus he claimed) the red-carpet treatment. Jephtas claims that they had asked him to work for them, but adds: "I don't feel that I am ready to go to the Metropolitan right yet". To turn down an offer from Santi to conduct in Zurich seems unfortunate, but then to turn down an apparent offer from the Met too seems simply self-destructive. Or was Jephtas exaggerating to impress Abrahamse? Either way, cancelling his Zurich contract without a commitment from any other house seems at best an act of pique. Or perhaps it was done in one of his recurring bouts of depression; we cannot rule out the possibility that the strangely abrupt end of his platonic cohabitation with Johannes Lüthi had somehow unsettled him (why on earth did he even leave his furniture behind?). He tells Abrahamse in his taped letter that the management of the Zurich Opera had changed (though it hadn't) and that he had told Santi in a long conversation that he was tired of the "amateurism" in Zurich. This beggars belief, given his borderline delusional efforts to get a job back in South Africa, which was now – a few months after the Soweto Uprising had begun – being boycotted by most of the world. The Nico Malan Theatre had meanwhile ceased to be a whites-only institution, but in name only, as it was being boycotted by the coloured population at the Cape.[322]

Jephtas's last comments in his taped letter are particularly revealing: "I'm gonna emigrate to the United States, I cannot deal with living in Europe anymore. I've had enough of seeing white people, I can't bear to see all these pale, pale people – I wanna vomit". But he immediately

---

321   Original in German. Held by the Stadtarchiv Zürich, like all the other contracts mentioned here.
322   See e.g. Mike van Graan (2015).

qualifies this by adding that he "will com[e] to South Africa every now and then, if this whole thing works out with CAPAB". From our perspective there is little logic to this. There is nothing unusual about Jephtas's desire to live in a more multicultural environment, and we have some proof of his interest in black American culture in the form of a subscription to *Ebony* magazine from the 1970s[323] (even his accent on his tape to Abrahamse is oddly Americanised, though the nasal vowels and slang - "gonna"/"wanna" etc. - are countered by frequent South African inflections). But apart from the obvious fact that most people in opera management in the USA at the time were also white, the "white people" "in Europe" who made him "wanna vomit" were the very people - like Santi - who had actually taken him seriously as a musician and furthered his career. Returning to CAPAB would also have meant working for and alongside "white people" - but they were whites who through apartheid had steadfastly refused to recognise him as an equal human being, let alone as a fine musician. And it would have meant ignoring the general coloured boycott of CAPAB, potentially making Jephtas a pariah among his own people. Or was this the point? Did Jephtas imagine returning home in some kind of triumph after his European and American accomplishments, thinking: "I'll show them"? Did he really believe that his hitherto successes - working with the finest singers in the world, performing at the Vienna Musikverein and hobnobbing with the best at the Met - would truly be able to trump his skin colour in a country where the latter trumped absolutely *everything*? Did he even think he might be reassigned "white" or afforded "honorary white" status? In light of his later attempts to forge a career back in South Africa, it would indeed seem that he was convinced he might somehow overcome the laws of apartheid where millions before him had failed (as would he, too). But homesickness can negate logic, and Jephtas was obviously torn between his longings for home and his desire for an international career. In October 1977, several weeks after having left Zurich, he wrote to Abrahamse to complain that "I cannot tell you how very tired I am of all this hassle I have [had] to go through by not having the birthright to work in any country and the only place I have that right, denies me any possibility". This tiredness clearly didn't stop him trying - though when he finally was indeed offered "honorary white" status there, several years later, he proved unable to cope, and would flee the country yet again.[324]

It is ironic that it was just two days after his resignation from the Zurich Opera House in early 1977 that Jephtas received what appears to have been his first-ever mention in a Zurich opera review. On 21 February 1977, the local composer and leading critic Rolf Urs Ringger wrote a glowing report for the *Neue Zürcher Zeitung* of a revival of Verdi's *Nabucco* conducted by Nello Santi. At the close, Ringger added: "The rehearsals for this 'Nabucco', which has clearly benefitted from a new influx of musical inspiration, were directed by Gordon Jephtas".[325] It is highly unusual for anyone not directly involved in a performance to be singled out for special praise. This suggests that Ringger might have had some connection to Jephtas, though we have no proof of it (Ringger was a prominent member of the Zurich music scene, was flamboyant about his homosexuality,[326] and had much direct contact with the Opera House - his first ballet, *Narziss*, would be performed there in 1980).

323 Proof of subscription in Jephtas's archives at the University of Stellenbosch. The *Ebony* website explains itself thus: "Since 1945, EBONY magazine has shined a spotlight on the worlds of Black people in America and worldwide. Our commitment to showcasing the best and brightest as well as highlighting disparities in Black life has been, and will always be, cornerstone to EBONY". www.ebony.com/, accessed 9 November 2022.
324 See Chapter 5 below.
325 "Die musikalische Einstudierung dieses offenbar musikalisch neu inspirierten 'Nabucco' lag bei Gordon Jephtas". Rolf Urs Ringger (1977).
326 Anyone active on the Zurich music scene in the 1980s and 1990s - gay or straight - knew who Ringger was. See also the interview with him about the Zurich gay scene in Moser (2007): 65-68.

We have no idea what Nello Santi thought of Jephtas's decision to abandon Zurich, as he is named no more in the correspondence with Abrahamse, though Jephtas's mention of a long phone conversation suggests that Santi had tried to convince him to stay. Perhaps Santi's absence in subsequent letters is a sign that things had gone awry. Perhaps Jephtas had tired of being dependent on yet another white, Italian, surrogate father after Joseph Manca, or had even begun to resent Santi's power to provide him with so many opportunities. Or perhaps all was in fact well, and Santi was actually helping Jephtas with his next career move, given his own extensive contacts in the USA. All this remains supposition. We know only that by the autumn of 1977 Jephtas was in America, and that it remained the focus of his career for the rest of his life (barring two brief South African interludes, each in its own way disastrous). According to Roland Jung, Jephtas's move to Chicago late that year was facilitated by his acquaintance with a singing coach resident there who worked for Leontyne Price. But details are lacking – not least because Price does not seem to have visited Zurich at this time.

There had been many good reasons for Jephtas to make Zurich his base in the 1970s. Superficially, Zurich was a conservative, highly Protestant city that had never ceased to uphold the moral principles of the Zwinglian church – thus it was only in 1972 that the canton finally lifted its ban on (heterosexual) couples living together before marriage (the Swiss term for which – "Konkubinat", "concubinage" – itself smacks of Old Testament lust). But in most respects, Zurich was surprisingly liberal. Switzerland had decriminalised homosexuality back in 1942 (a full 25 years before the United Kingdom), and from 1943 to 1967 Zurich was home to one of the most important gay journals in Europe, *Der Kreis*.[327] Decriminalisation naturally did not result in immediate destigmatisation, and sexual equality was still a long way off. In 1957, for example, one of Zurich's most prominent composers and music administrators, Robert Oboussier, was murdered by a young male prostitute he had taken home with him. Not even Oboussier's closest friends had known he was gay, and the newspapers were soon full of lurid, moralistic reports about him.[328] But a more or less open gay scene nevertheless became established in the later 1950s and '60s, with gay bars initially clustered around the red-light districts such as that of "Kreis Cheib",[329] near Jephtas's sometime apartment on the Bäckerstrasse (perhaps that was one reason why he moved there; we shall naturally never know for sure). By contrast, homosexuality in apartheid South Africa was still an offence punishable by prison throughout the 1960s and '70s, and it was considered so subversive that the military ran brutal "conversion" programmes to "cure" it.[330] It is true that attitudes to gays on the South African music scene were more nuanced. The aforementioned David Tidboald lived openly with his male partner,[331] and there are well-documented cases of predatory male music staff at universities, both gay and straight, having been protected or reassigned by university management during the apartheid era.[332] But those people were all white; Jephtas was unlikely to be given such leeway back home. So for a coloured gay man like him, Zurich must have seemed an island of sexual freedom and normality (which also makes his repeated attempts to return to South Africa all the more perplexing). We have no

---

327 Today available online at www.e-periodica.ch/digbib/volumes?UID=kre-003, accessed July 2022.
328 See Brunner (1997): 102-103.
329 See also Moser (2007): 65-68.
330 See Kaplan (2004).
331 Tidboald is open about his relationship throughout his (post-apartheid-era) memoir, which is also dedicated to his partner. See Tidboald (2008).
332 Names withheld here for legal reasons.

precise information about his partners during his Zurich years, except that they indeed existed; he did not enter into any long-term, permanent relationship while living in Switzerland.

Jephtas does not seem to have become fluent in German, though this was probably no hindrance to his career in Zurich, where the local dialect is in any case far removed from High German. He probably spoke Italian with Nello Santi, while English will have otherwise served him well at the cosmopolitan Opera House and in the rest of the city (Jephtas's boss at the Opera Studio, for example, Marc Belfort, was an American who still spoke German with a heavy New-York accent and occasionally ad-hoc grammar a decade later). But any linguistic limitations on Jephtas's part did not prevent him from enjoying the convivial aspects of life in Zurich. He was a keen visitor to the bars around the Opera House after performances, was a relatively heavy smoker, and his liking for red wine could at times verge on the excessive. For the moment, however, these were apparently his only stimulants. To be sure, Zurich was becoming increasingly notorious as a centre of drug consumption – in fact, the illegal dealing scene was for a while centred on Bellevue and Stadelhofen, both sites a two-minute walk from the Opera House[333] – but Jephtas's friends of the time are convinced that he did not take any hard drugs during his years in Zurich. They only seem to have become a problem for him after he became a freelance singing coach in New York in the 1980s. Perhaps having a steady work routine and a heavy workload in Zurich helped Jephtas to establish an equilibrium in his private life that proved impossible to maintain when he ceased working regular hours at an official institution.

A delight in conviviality did not mean that Jephtas easily let his guard down, however. His friends recall his being highly reluctant to share any details of either his personal or professional life with others. They claim that he spoke little about his work and almost nothing about the young singers he was coaching. Whenever he was faced with potential interpersonal conflict, he would react by simply withdrawing. This makes his letters to May Abrahamse all the more remarkable, for they reveal not merely a willingness to communicate on his part, but almost a compulsion to do so. It is noteworthy that Jephtas also told his friends in Zurich very little about his feelings towards South Africa – and in fact just about the only story he told them about his youth back in South Africa seems to have had little basis in fact. He claimed that he had been made to sit on the floor for his classes at the College of Music in Cape Town because the chairs were reserved for white students. But the Head of the Music Department at the time was Erik Chisholm, a man with communist leanings who was no friend of apartheid, and whose office was on at least one occasion raided by the police. It is highly unlikely that he would have tolerated any such treatment of a student unless it somehow happened completely without his being informed (which also seems unlikely).

Jephtas did not demonstrate any real interest in any field except his own while in Zurich. He was not much of a reader – unless the topic was music – nor was he a movie-goer or interested in art. Oddly, Johannes Lüthi never even heard him "practise" the piano in his room – he would play slowly and softly through passages of music that were presumably important for his work at the Opera House, but little else (perhaps he felt uncomfortable playing in an apartment where others were bound to hear him, and so preferred using the pianos in the rehearsal rooms at the Opera House for practice purposes). It is also remarkable just how few people remember him in Zurich, with the exception of those whose hospitality he enjoyed. Regrettably, Nello Santi died before we were able to consult him, but enquiries among other former personnel in the upper echelons of the Zurich Opera House resulted in next to no information.

---

333 For information on the Zurich drug scene at this time, see e.g. Kieser (no date).

Figure 4.4 Weinplatz, Zurich, presumably 1970s, with the church of St Peter in the background. Jephtas apparently lived in a small furnished flat in the building marked "Kurt Stäheli & Co". This was his last address in Zurich.
Source: Baugeschichtliches Archiv der Stadt Zürich, BAZ_077069.

It is impossible to tell whether Jephtas experienced any racism in Zurich, as there is no mention of it in his letters, nor do his friends recall anything. Zurich was at the time still a predominantly "white" city, and was presumably no less immune to occasional racist incidents than was any other Western European city. There were indeed regular racist incidents after the influx of Tamil refugees to Zurich in the early 1980s. But it seems unlikely that Jephtas would have experienced overt racism at the Opera House (unless this is sheer naiveté on our part). His close working relationship with Nello Santi would surely have afforded him a certain elevated status, and it was not unusual for singers of colour to perform there (in 1977, for example, the year that Jephtas left Zurich, Grace Bumbry gave a concert of arias with Nello Santi at the Opera House, and Simon Estes, later a Zurich resident and a regular at the House, gave his debut there in the role of Gershwin's Porgy). Although one former member of the Opera House recalled Jephtas, oddly, with the remark "He was really very black" ("Er war schon sehr schwarz"),[334] his skin colour was probably not much different from that of the Latin Americans or southern Europeans who lived in the city at the time. And the impression given by those who do recall him is of a man who was generally at ease with his surroundings, in demand at work, and highly respected. But Jephtas's background had left

---

334 Telephone conversation; name withheld here. We should mention here that this interview partner clearly did not intend his remark to be derogatory; Jephtas's skin colour, for whatever reason, was simply what this person remembered best about him.

him with many chips on his shoulder, and if he were at any point made to feel that his defining characteristic was his skin colour rather than his talent, however innocent the intentions behind the words, it will hardly have enamoured him to his situation. If there was a hurdle to his advancement in Zurich, however, it probably lay more with Jephtas himself than with others. He had given his accompanying debut at the Musikverein in Vienna – surely just about the most prestigious concert venue in the music world – but that event had essentially also marked the end of his career as a public accompanist. His real ambition was to conduct; and yet when offered the chance in Zurich, he refused it. Perhaps he was suffering from a case of what is today generally accorded the name "imposter syndrome".

The work of a répétiteur is by definition a backroom activity, conducted one-to-one with a singer, where the répétiteur's authority depends on his or her knowledge of the work and their ability to help a singer to learn a role and interpret it in a manner stylistically appropriate (with some singers, even professionals, coaching can even involve sheer note-bashing). This is also probably one of the reasons why so few people remember Jephtas: unless they actually worked directly with him, they might not even have been aware of his presence in the Opera House. As already mentioned above, working as a répétiteur has historically often been a prelude to a conducting career. But wielding a baton before an orchestra requires a different set of skills from coaching a singer in the privacy of a rehearsal room. Did Jephtas fear that by standing in front of an orchestra in one of the leading European houses he might reveal few of his strengths while exposing all his weaknesses (whether real or imagined)? Or did the knowledge of his impoverished, racially disadvantaged origins, in a society that from the outset had always told him he was "second-best", weigh too heavily on him, especially when working in a profession that is notoriously replete with over-healthy egos? We shall never know now. What is clear is that Jephtas's years in Zurich were crucial to his career. For the first time in his life he had been able to work at an internationally acclaimed house in close cooperation with a master in Italian opera who treated him with professional respect – Nello Santi. His foreign engagements in Portugal and the USA, plus his ever-rising salary in Zurich, ought to have convinced him that he was valued and appreciated. But for reasons that remain unknown, Jephtas left Zurich, his colleagues and his friends behind him in the summer of 1977. Before leaving, he packed assorted scores, cassettes and other belongings in suitcases and deposited them with at least two friends – which in retrospect is oddly reminiscent of how he had abandoned several belongings when he quit Johannes Lüthi's apartment in Wohlen. Leaving items behind when one departs one place for another is often a sign that one desires to retain a connection, even implying that one hopes or intends to return. But Jephtas never came back.

50

Hotel Conti, Dufour Street 3, 8008 Zurich [Switzerland]

Tuesday, 6 June [1972]

Hi there May,

[...] As you no doubt have gathered I have been in the "can't-get-down-to-writing" phase, largely because I felt so ashamed for having lost so much self-control – my Christian-English upbringing certainly did not come to [the] rescue. Anyhow, it was a hurdle to cross and whether it has done good or bad one cannot tell, but I do now realize that I had no right to perplex you all so much and in fact, it was a very outspoken and angry letter from Mac [Robertson] that really made me reflect and I thought "well, baby, you got yourself in the mess and now haul your arse out" and so I sat around for months without work and somehow managed like giving a coaching in exchange for a plate of spaghetti and so on, but more important, I had rejoined the fight. Then I got signed for the '73 Lisbon season as assistant conductor and Zurich made me an offer for a year starting August and in fact this is the last of my two weeks up here coaching *Ballo in maschera* which opens their season in September and I remain appalled that these singers are not keen on being exact, or rather, on singing how the composer wrote and let's not even mention the Italian. For the whole of last week I had one battle after another – you know the attitude – "well, I've always had great success doing it the way I do" – but fortunately for me I was unable to distinguish the "stars" and so I insisted on every detail – that accent, the staccato and repeat a phrase 20 times to get the pronunciation right – well they hated me but now respect me I figure, but either way it's no water off my back. And so whether I want to sit around here for a year depends on whether I get a work permit to accept a job for the Treviso [opera] season which runs from September – December and the operas are more appealing – *Andrea Chénier*, *Medea*, *Ballo in maschera* – I'm particularly anxious to work on *Medea*. Heaven knows what'll be.

I worked with the tenor who was to sing *Anna Bolena* in Rome, but after a week's rehearsal in the theatre, the project was abandoned because Caballé is not well. Also worked with Angeles Gulín on *Lucrezia* – she's said to have the biggest soprano voice of this day – the divas of today don't have too much to throw away.

Joseph [Gabriels] has sung one *Don Carlos* in Düsseldorf and returns for two more mid-May – he says it went well – but like we both have discovered, the Germans have their own way of wanting it.

[...] Here are some pictures to look and maybe smile at.[335] Do write.

Love to all.

Yours,

Gordon.

P.S. send me a tape of your vocalising immediately. I haven't made any tapes because I have been without a machine, but plan to buy one with my pay cheque from here. – What happened about the S.A.B.C. concert?

---

335 No longer extant.

51

Opernhaus, Zurich, Switzerland

Friday, 16 September [1972]

Hullo there May,

Man (shit I should have said "Lady") was I glad to have your mail.[336]

You know I had thought – well, my "fall"[337] and therefore bad behaviour had lost and cost me a friend and though after a while and through the conditioning of my nomadic existence of the last years of making, losing, forgetting friends, I could adapt myself to such a situation with time (and time is a wonderful cure) but man I was sad to think that I had lost [you] the artist and those one don't meet every day. [...]

So, I am relieved to know that the delay in hearing from you was all purely circumstantial.

I'm back in Zurich on the first part of my contract as Nello Santi's[338] assistant which goes until February 15th. I have been back since mid-August and rehearsed *Ballo in maschera* which opened the season last Saturday. The cast [is] made up of house-singers except for the tenor, Barry Morell[339] from the Metropolitan. I didn't end up having much admiration for any of them, except Morell who first of all is completely professional - the rest they sing well enough and all that, but they say nothing - the soprano[340] for example could be singing "I love you" or "Get away" or "oh, what horror" and it comes out all the same. I spent so much time just insisting on singing nearly what Verdi wrote and correcting the atrocious Italian that I figured, they are professionals so the expression or details thereof they will find themselves - but not so!!!! But I have learnt that here one cares only to do your own job well, let the others care about theirs and so I endeavoured to do my best and Santi was pleased with my work and in fact was very complimentary and we get on well because I'm prepared, and he's making me work from memory which is something for lazy me.

It is the first time that I'm working with a conductor of his stature and he knows his stuff, and supports a very healthy tenor voice and does everything from memory[341] and I am watching and learning - and sometimes I get real depressed to think where I need yet to arrive - but I'll get there somehow and sometime. [...]

It's October 16th and a month since I started this epistle - born a snail and stay a snail - so I figure I ought to let you have it as soon as possible so that you don't begin to think I'm lost.

I'm working my guts out with all the ups and downs that go with it. Since last I had to put together a *Traviata* and *Nabucco* and for Wed[nesday] there is *Tosca* - this place is like a factory - one is expected to churn out things like a computer and I don't like that approach much. There is never enough rehearsal [time] - but two things keep me interested, one is Maestro Santi and Antigone Sgourda[342] who sings *Traviata* - a type like you, interested in searching and finding a truth in the music rather than just rehash notes and sound -

---

336 Jephtas sent Abrahamse a brief postcard from Milan dated 24 July 1972, saying he would write properly later; Abrahamse wrote on it "answered 8/8/72"; this was presumably the letter to which Jephtas refers here.

337 Jephtas is referring to his "black depression" that lasted from late 1971 until mid-1972.

338 Nello Santi (1931–2020), Italian conductor, renowned especially for the Italian repertoire. Attached to the Zurich Opera House for over 50 years; its music director in the 1960s.

339 Barry Morell (1927–2003), American tenor.

340 Eva Illes (1929–2020), Hungarian soprano, a member of the Zurich Opera from 1971 to 1975.

341 Santi was himself renowned for conducting everything from memory.

342 Antigone Sgourda (*1938), Greek soprano.

we have been studying *Ballo* together and in all the weeks I've been here it has been the most rewarding singer.

I heard from home that Alie [Sydow] died suddenly & that cut me up a bit, but what is there to do?

I have a tape for you have finished and maybe I will finish this letter on tape.

Love to all

Gordon.

52

Hotel Borges, Rua Garrett, 108, Lisboa - 2, Portugal

Tuesday, 6 March [1973]

Hi there May! -

It is something like 2.45 in the wee hours of the morning and I've just got in from rehearsal and eating. We had an evening call - 9-12.30 p.m. - with full company and orchestra for *Carmen* which opens on Thursday. The mezzo [Viorica] Cortez[343] is extremely good in the role. She is probably about your age - the voice is not exactly extraordinary, but she does wonders with the character and all the notes - the high and low are there! I saw her do it at La Scala last year with [Giuseppe] di Stefano and it was her victory - and since then she has moved into *the* top bracket of mezzos. The tenor is [Franco] Corelli - when he arrived yesterday - already from the wings he looks impressive, and famous[ly] handsome but I was amazed that from near he looks all of his 52 and no doubt the nervous worry that goes with being a star. Up to now, he has not sung a note in voice - all down an octave in a goat-like drawl and just pacing his moves. He is not likely to sing out until [the] performance. The others sing some phrases - generally most of their parts except for some high notes. It will be interesting to hear Corelli from close by in performance - and man, you can see he is a star - billed here as the greatest tenor in the world. After that comes *Tosca* still with him and Sesto Bruscantini[344] and a woman I don't know; then *Trovatore* with Fiorenza Cossotto, her husband [Ivo] Vinco[345] and [Piero] Cappuccilli who is the finest baritone, I would say singer, I've heard in the theatre - at La Scala that is. I am enjoying working with the conductors Oliviero De Fabritiis[346] - very exacting, old and what experience. For the *Trovatore* there will [be] [Nicola] Rescigno[347] - he made that famous *Macbeth* record with Callas - so I'm looking forward to him.

But of all this I will talk later.

The real reason for writing is about your proposed *Barber of Seville*.[348]

To tell the truth my first reaction was negative. I thought - May has a voice with dramatic accent and *Barber* demands a voice with coloratura accent - which is the *whole Rossini style*. Now Donizetti for example also writes coloratura passages but the accent is towards

343 Viorica Cortez (*1935), Romanian-born mezzo-soprano.
344 Sesto Bruscantini (1919-2003), Italian baritone.
345 Ivo Vinco (1927-2014), Italian bass.
346 Oliviero De Fabritiis (1902-1982), Italian conductor.
347 Nicola Rescigno (1916-2008), American conductor, especially prominent in Chicago and Dallas. Rescigno apparently made Jephtas a job offer in Dallas. See his letter of 4 April 1973.
348 In Eoan's 10th (and penultimate) Opera Season in March 1974, Abrahamse sang the role of Rosina in Rossini's *Il barbiere di Siviglia*.

Figure 4.5 The Lisbon Opera House.
Source: Jasper Walgrave.

the expression, that is the drama – remember *Roberto Devereux*.[349] And as we both know coloratura has never been your thing if merely for the simple reason that you have never been exposed to it – if for example you started [your] career along with *Traviata*, also Gilda [from Verdi's *Rigoletto*] rather than *Cav[alleria]*.

So, I thought, why can't they have an opera which will show your good things? But then I thought, goddamn, why can't she sing Rosina! The result is, according to me – only provided you have enough time to prepare the opera well – at least 6 months – why not? When I get back to Milan on April 4th I'll immediately make a tape and send you the score I used for the Cape Town production.[350] [...]

Remember one important thing – not to whiten your voice excessively to sing the coloratura. *Sing always with your voice.* [...]

Now, I will be more than happy to help you with the role ... Right now, it seems May 1974 is when I'll be free to come, and I'm very much in favour of this slow 15 month preparation period so that all that music can mature within us. [...]

I'm fine – I signed with Zurich for 73/74 season, a periodic contract to prepare *Ernani*, then later *Gianni Schicchi/Tabarro* which Tito Gobbi is directing and still later *Otello* – and May 74 is free. If you like to write here please do – am here until April 3 – in Milano Apr. 4-13th – then Zurich until June 30th. [...]

P.S. Balls, it's now 3.45 [a.m.] – and I planned to be in [the] theatre at 8 a.m. to study – wonder if I'll make it??

Regards
Ciao to your Mother, Father, Wendy and Trudy.
[Gordon.]

---

349 Eoan never performed this opera by Donizetti, but Abrahamse and Jephtas included arias from it in their 1971 recital in Durban.

350 Eoan first staged this opera in 1969. During his visit to Cape Town in 1968, Jephtas worked with Patricia van Graan on the role of Rosina.

Figure 4.6 The Hotel Borges, where Jephtas stayed when working in Lisbon.
Source: Jasper Walgrave.

53

Hotel Borges, Rua Garrett, 108, Lisboa - 2, Portugal

9 March [1973] - 5.25 a.m.

Hi there!

I've become a nocturnal writer.

Well, here I am and tonight (last night?) was the first *Carmen* and I'm in a mood to write my thoughts and what happened, etc. And who other than you, artist that you are to be comprehend[ing] even if I write a load of shit, but at least you'd understand and I would not go completely misunderstood or misinterpreted.

I remember how many times I have written home,[351] maybe enclosing a couple of photos to whoever, only to get a completely misunderstood answer of, for example, "Cut your hair, it's too long" or "You're too thin" - or "who's those strange people with you". Naturally, one thinks, "well, fuck it!" Don't you agree!

Anyway, all this comes because, tonight for the 1st time I heard and saw & heard [Franco] Corelli from close - apart from rehearsals (he didn't appear for the dress rehearsal last night!) - and man, like I understood with [Elena] Suliotis last year in [*Anna*] *Bolena* - I understood why he is dared to be called "the best tenor of the world". Man, that guy opens up and lets off high G's, A flats and B flats that make your mouth stay open and your skin become gooseflesh. One realizes what singing is about - and at one moment in Act III when he hit a good note and stayed - my mind went back to what must be 10 years [ago] to a statement Manca made about Vera [Gow] - "in 5 years she'll be better than Callas" - to think how stupid one is to know [so] little.

---

351   Presumably to his family; according to his Zurich flat-share colleague Johannes Lüthi, Jephtas rarely received letters from South Africa during the years that they lived alongside each other, with the exception of the letters from May Abrahamse.

Tonight I understood why Corelli is Corelli – and he deserves it – he is something, and we, even though we can discuss until next year, are nothing in comparison – but we can learn. The man has a lot of natural things in his favour as I noticed in rehearsal – when he opens his mouth, his lower jaw seems to have nothing to do with the rest of his face, leaving an immense cavity for the waves of air coming from the vocal cords to vibrate.

He is boyish and shit-scared of the arias. In *Carmen* he is nervous behind stage for the Act II aria from the start of the opera like nobody's business – and walks around with a bottle of water. Anyway, we arrive at his first entrance, and he arrives out of breath with the producer, and I am there to give him the cue when to enter (already prearranged by the producer and passed to me) – so arrives the moment and I give him the cue, and he leaves at the end of the line of soldiers, but on the way before he hits the stage, he finds something wrong with his belt and misses the entrance – fortunately he doesn't have to sing immediately, but someone else has to sing to him. He turns to me and says (translation) "shit, I missed the entrance – what do I do now?" – and God knows how many *Carmen*s he has sung ... So, I suggest "go on the other side of the stage and just walk on when the other singer speaks to you". He arrives on the other side, panics, and they have to push him on – and once on – everything's fine. Friends have told me the same of Callas, who used to cry much before saying I can't, and they'd have to push her on stage, but once there the demon broke loose. So Act I finishes without much ado – the mezzo arrives, sings her two arias – sure of herself and really very good. Act 2 – before his entrance Corelli has to sing 16 bars off-stage – my responsibility. I have to be there with blow-pipe for pitch for he doesn't trust his judgement. This time he's there long before but nervous, in fact, shit scared, bottle of water in hand and sits on a stool, waiting, muttering "mamma mia, help me tonight" – the aria comes soon after his entrance. Then he spills half the water all over him – nothing – time to sing the off-stage thing – here we go – I give the note, he sings and he indicates every time he wants a pitch correction – and finally he's on! Comes the aria – he sings in Italian – the opera was performed in French – but at rehearsal he asked the conductor if he could do the aria in Italian – for several reasons, "no go", so it was agreed that he would change the vowel on certain notes so as not to ruin his vocal position – obviously too nervous, he broke loose in Italian [...]

In Act III he spend[s] most time off stage, drinking water when he should be on – but after, when he begins to plead with Carmen, the intervention of Micaela – he began to deliver some voice, notes and dramatic intention – that I began to say to myself, "shit me, this guy's good".

Act IV – the entrance is sudden – and so I have to be there. He's nervous – and says, "when do I go?", "do you have a score" – so we both follow the music before, he pointing to each bar as the orchestra plays – I say, "Go" – and in a moment he wraps the cloak around him and becomes the desperate José in search of Carmen and he's on. [In] this act the character, the desperation, the vocalism, the acting is sublime – twice he has to say "più non m'ama il tuo cor" (I don't know the French too good), 1st [time] piano, 2nd [time] fortissimo – so he does the first [time] [with his] back to [the] audience, and the second [time] desperate and full to [the] audience & Carmen to enhance [the] fortissimo – the pathos was tremendous – and when he draws the knife – she answers "I love Escamillo" – and he shouts full of anguish "No" (not in Bizet's score) – one sees the artist – and also when he has stabbed her he breaks down in tears in remorse realizing just what he has done before the curtain comes down – makes gooseflesh come!

[…] Sat[urday] - March 10th

Hi May,

I'm here, again, on the next instalment - Man, oh man! what a world! Am I sad? If I could only tell you what it needs to make a career! Here I am in Portugal, and what might sound like heaven knows what in South Africa. Here I am at the bottom, but the very, very bottom of the ladder. - Sure I prepared myself for these operas - I played very few of the piano or "sala" rehearsals as they are called here, and found myself relegated to office-boy duties because my colleague is none other than the one who finally conducted *Anna Bolena* in Mantova last year,[352] that is, the son of the impresaria [in Mantua] - and although he plays the piano like shit, I stepped down, because after all, he is a "maestro" - even if everybody else, including Corelli, calls me by that name - in fact, he [Corelli] did take the trouble to come over and say, "Maestro, congratulations" when he learnt it was my birthday on the 8th (what more does one want!) - [Oliviero] De Fabritiis (the conductor) and Maestro [Pino] Donati[353] have asked (Donati is Artistic Director at Chicago) that I play all rehearsals for *Tosca* because they want to engage a maestro sostituto for Chicago.[354] The Impresario has already talked to me about that a year ago - and I have the advantage of being able to speak English for the Americans! - what an advantage!!! I tell you!!!!!!!!

Now I'm nervous - to win over a major conductor is a problem - At Zurich I have already won over [Nello] Santi - and that done - I'm no longer interested in working there - you know, the whole business of pride, etc. - but now I've another battle - and god knows if I'll win or even come by. The other political situations are even too difficult to explain to you as I'm such a bad narrator and writer - but we'll see when next I write. Ciao!

Tues[day] 13/3 […]

Eating is a disaster - not so much that the food is bad, but even though the basic ingredients are always what we use, the taste is foreign. So I skipped dinner this evening - no rehearsals - and I'm having a rest from music - Not eating, of course, does not help my gain-weight-programme - but what can you do.

My pianistic encounter with [De] Fabritiis and the Tosca went well. The maestro was ecstatic with my efforts - can't tell you how I had to concentrate and *Tosca* is not [a] score that I play readily because it is too difficult for me. At the second afternoon rehearsal I even surprised myself when I *did* get over certain technical impossibilities - and with these great maestri one has to play more than the notes printed in the vocal score - they expect to hear a flute entrance - or the chord in the trombones.

Anyway, everyone was there, the impresario, Ansalone,[355] who signed me for here; Maestro Donati (artistic director for Chicago also) and obviously [De] Fabritiis must be conducting many of the operas there. He asked about my availability afterwards - and though the agent already started negotiations with me a year ago - and negotiations is not yet a contract - the period in question was October to December so consequently I signed with Zurich from August 15 - October 6th to prepare *Ernani*. Now, they need someone in Chicago already early [in] September. So it seems my dates don't work out. My usual bad luck - What will be,

---

352 Jephtas is referring to the conductor Francesco Martini. In 1972, the Mantua Opera had wanted to engage Jephtas but could not legally appoint him. See Chapter 3.1 above and Jephtas's letter of 7 February 1972.

353 Pino Donati (1907-1975), Italian composer and long-time Artistic Director of the Chicago Lyric Opera.

354 Jephtas indeed got a job at the Chicago Lyric Opera some five years later.

355 Jephtas mentions this name frequently in his correspondence, though with no first name. We have no further information on him.

will be. I don't know why, but I'm keen to work in the U.S.A - and this is the 3rd of 4 chances down the drain - first New York, then last year I couldn't accept Dallas, now this! Well, pazienza [be patient], and in the meantime I need to worry & study *Trovatore* for when [Nicola] Rescigno comes next week. Sure, I know the opera, but to have it at [your] fingertips and ready is quite another thing - so one has to keep studying and whipping oneself to do better. And it is when I begin a 3 or 4-hour study session at the piano [that] for the first 45 mins I hate myself for having chosen music and would rather be pushing a pen in an office or sweeping streets, but after [a while] as the concentration increases and the involvement of getting the music right, one has the joy of making a new discovery in a phrase, or harmony, or what have you.

I'm tired of writing even though I could continue talking. [...]

[Saturday 17 March]

The weather here is much like that you are having. Lisbon is much like Durban - millions of people in [the] streets - double-decker busses and not particularly hygienic down-town. You know how on a wet day one avoids being splashed by cars - here one has to avoid being spat on by pedestrians.

Why couldn't you do that *Butterfly* if they must have someone who's done it? I remember Gudrun - we were at [the] College [of Music] together.[356]

Mimi Coertse - yes, apparently she is very down to earth - in fact, in Zurich I met a black mezzo who happens to be the teacher of a black soprano friend - and she, Lucretia,[357] asked if I knew Mimi - and she remembered how upset and mixed-up Mimi was at the beginning when people would pointedly ask her if it bothered [her] singing with blacks - they made many records together.

Fred [Martin][358] I saw at La Scala one night when I was down to see *Ballo* - we just barely had time to say "hello" and he was off [on] his way - and I [on] mine - but apart from that nothing - so if you've heard, then they're O.K.

I have to go - Act II *Tosca* rehearsal to solve some of the problems in ½ hour - this morning I already had a call with the soprano & conductor [Oliviero] De Fabritiis. He wasn't at all pleased with last night and said to her "Signora, if I didn't happen to know your work from the past, I would have asked that you be replaced immediately" - she complained of just having come from the States and the time-change (a 6-hour difference) was affecting her very much. So we'll see - but these big conductors break no bones - In *Carmen* rehearsal he says to [the character] Micaela, "Lady, your high notes are good, but most of this part is in the lower range. I can't hear you and you don't make any sense with the words - what are we going to do when in the theatre and [with] orch[estra]?" - well, someone else sang (and to think, she has 3 times the voice of Pat who sang it for Eoan - just to give an idea). To [the character] Frasquita in the Toreador's song - at the end she has a high C - "if that is your high 'C' it will not do" - and under normal circumstances it was O.K.

Must dash - ciao!

---

356 This "Gudrun" presumably studied music alongside Jephtas between 1960 and 1963 at the University of Cape Town; we have no further information on her.

357 Presumably the black American contralto Lucretia West, whose recordings include Mahler's Second Symphony under Hermann Scherchen, with Mimi Coertse singing the soprano solo.

358 Fred Martin, Eoan tenor.

Monday, March 19th 1.55 a.m.

How nice to get your two airmail letters this afternoon - it just came in time to lift me out of a black depression. I had had a 1st rehearsal of *Trovatore* [with conductor Nicola] Rescigno this morning and I fucked it [up] by just simply playing bad - a lot due to the fact that I was nervous and trying so hard to do my best because I admire his work so much. As a person he's really nice, no airs, which is a sign of greatness - except he did wince a couple of times when my clumsy paws hit some wrong notes - a liberty I can permit myself very rarely now, and my pride won't take it! - but too much a gentleman he didn't say anything and after all he was listening to the tenor - here, the 1st piano rehearsal has to be sung in voice so the conductor can decide whether you know the role, or whether he wants someone else, etc. - but all the time I knew he was also very aware of what [my fingers] were doing, or meant to be doing. Well, they just didn't function. Fortunately I have a few more rehearsals to redeem myself.

Anyway, after this evening's stage rehearsal we were all at dinner together and he talked freely and of course the subject of Callas came up. Inadvertently, because he was talking of the orchestration in *Butterfly*, [where] Puccini very often writes *ppp* - but has every instrument in the orchestra playing. And to add to this, he added that in all his dealings with Callas, there never ever was a discussion about a tempo or interpretation being wrong or not liked - except in *Butterfly*. She was singing it for the 1st and last time in Chicago and he was conducting. After the 1st rehearsals he began to feel a certain strange atmosphere from Callas and so eventually he called her and asked, "Now, Maria, what is this anti-Rescigno act all about", to which she replied, "not anti-Rescigno, but anti-forte". She wanted to make certain phrases ring true of the 15-year-old geisha, but couldn't because of the fanfare in the orchestra. So he took her into the pit, opened the score, saying "now maybe you've never had occasion to look at the orchestra score, and rightfully as you believe there are 3 p[iano]s - but look who's playing". She understood and admitted that when she made the recording, which was before, she could make all those effects with microphones nearly up her nostrils, but if Puccini wrote it that way in the orchestra, then those ideas for the theatre were not logical. So for a while Callas remained [the] topic of conversation - and knowing my admiration for the woman - you can imagine how I sat open mouthed taking everything in - from somebody sitting across me at dinner table - who is as friendly artistically with the great diva as you and I are! Many anecdotes followed - Callas said to him "Well, I'm not singing now, but if I were, the only soprano who [would] be competition for me would be [Elena] Suliotis" - and I felt that when I heard the woman last - and then, they say, it was far from her best. He told hundreds of stories of *Traviata* and *Medea* at Dallas, *Sonnambula*, the recording sessions - how they would repeat one bar and interpose it afterwards - how the great [Victor] de Sabata³⁵⁹ refused to release the Verdi Requiem because Schwarzkopf's high pianissimo B flat was awful - and then only agreed after the technicians had taken a high B flat from an earlier Schwarzkopf recording and put it in. But the greatest thing that rests in my mind is what he said of Callas and Magda Olivero (a singer you don't know much about because she is not big in the recording business, but I have mentioned) is, you tell them 90 things in a rehearsal and next rehearsal they remember 90 things - not 89, but 90. And that reminded me - you have much the same quality which makes it worth the trouble working. Shit, I've no more paper. I've forgotten I can write so much. [...]
Ciao.

---

359   Victor de Sabata (1892-1967), Italian conductor and composer.

Hotel Borges, Rua Garrett, 108, Lisboa – 2, Portugal

Saturday, 31 March [1973]

Hi there May,

Here I am again – between the procrastination and my not too fondness of the actual act of writing (which you well enough [know] about) – I've been busy.

Trovatore went on the night before the last – a great success with the public. [Fiorenza] Cossotto starred along with [Piero] Cappuccilli – Imagine, they all live here – and Miss Cossotto calls me "maestro" – so you can imagine this coloured-ass was like walking on cloud 9 thinking, I wish those white bastards back home could see us now. She is friendly, talkative, very sure on stage but shit-scared off [stage] – that is before [going on] – the price for being a star. She is very serious about her work. Before the performance she sings the whole role through – then during the interval she's again singing (in full voice) the next act – she tapes it, listens, sings, retapes. From close it is a voice – rather like a large column of air hitting your ears – round and extra lush.

I remember, I give her [her] Act III entrance, so we were back there waiting, she says "Maestro, what a performance worth only 2 pennies I'm giving tonight" – so I say, don't worry, [be] calm, take it easy – imagine me advising the great-diva. At the end of the act the audience are out there stamping and yelling for her. I see her next just before her Act IV entrance – "Hell, maestro, and now I get my period – it could have waited till tomorrow – how am I going to sing". ... Cappuccilli is a gentleman in every respect. He's no taller than me – and wears like 6" wedges on stage – he hates to stay in his dressing room and sits in a dark corner on stage during the performances – every now and then gets up to say something to one of us – now he has what is called a big voice in Italian opera – I remember him last year in *Boccanegra* at the Scala he let off some sound. From close it sound kinda woolly and thick – but when you go into the theatre it sounds round, warm and mighty good.

Yesterday I played piano rehearsals with Boris Christoff[360] and [a] Portuguese conductor, [Silva] Pereira.[361] Christoff has 3 operatic recitals with orch[estra] next week – mostly Russian music – *Boris Godunov*, etc. Maybe you remember I wrote when I saw him in *Don Carlos* how much I admired his work – well, for one thing he doesn't look like what I figured – a tall, sluggish grey-haired [man] of round 58 and not at all distinguished and he's kinda unpleasant because he is completely full of himself. That kinda disillusioned me, though I must admit he was nice to me – I worried before because I was warned that he never gets along with whoever is playing – you know, "not like that", "too loud", "too soft" – well, I missed that treatment – so that's already something! [...]

I've since delighted in getting your 2 air letters of last week – and this morning I got one labelled no. 2 – so I figure another will arrive soon. Thanks. [...]

Ciao for now

Gordon

---

360 Boris Christoff (1914–1993), Bulgarian bass.
361 Presumably the Portuguese conductor Silva Pereira (1912–1992).

Hotel Borges, Rua Garrett, 108, Lisboa - 2, Portugal

Wed. 4 April [1973]

Hi May,

It's just gone 10.30 a.m. and your letter got brought to my room - that is the first - the second reached me last Sat[urday] already.

We were real late last night - 2 a.m. the last *Trovatore* finished at 2 a.m. Well, the opera at 1.40 [a.m.] - but the audience was still howling, stamping and clapping at 2 [a.m.]. Then, by the time we ate it was 4 [a.m.]. [After that] back to the hotel, the goodbyes - [when] I got up here, it was 4.30 [a.m.].

Everybody leaves today except me. I'm to stay for the preparation work of the 3 [Boris] Christoff concerts and will leave Sunday.

Last night was a triumph for [Fiorenza] Cossotto - you know, after everybody's had the curtain calls, etc., and the audience is chorusing together - Cossotto, Cossotto - of course, I have heard this from the audience once when [Giuseppe] di Stefano sang - they were shouting in chorus & unison "Pippo" - the Italian abbreviation for Giuseppe; and another time, "Montsy" for Caballé. Before her [Cossotto's] third act entrance, she was saying [to me] - "am I singing decently? Applause doesn't always evaluate how well it is vocally -" I understood that she meant "well" from her point of view. Then she continued, "And you know, maestro, I'm so dumb - there had been a mix up of dates, and now tomorrow I have a dress rehearsal of *Aida* in Paris, and the performance the next day. Please say a prayer for me!"

[Piero] Cappuccilli is coming to Zurich for one performance of *Rigoletto* - "be sure to remember to buy me a drink when I come" (he paid for mine last night). In Zurich the 1st week in June is [a] festival with all International singers - and all the house singers sit around, listen and say "he, or she's good, but ..." - the world is the same all over. [...]

I made you a tape - one side a part rehearsal - tenor [Giuseppe] Giacomini[362] and the soprano [Ljiljana] Molnar[-Talajić][363] (she's Yugoslav - fat and dumpy) - the voice is more than good and we will no doubt hear lots more of her. I'd like you, after the initial shock, to learn what imperfections exist - these imperfections never exist on commercial records and so sometimes one thinks that is how opera is overseas. But, alas, every artist has one defect or another. But in the theatre, things can be different, and are. The other side's me!!! - take your pick - I'd opt for both. But shit, my tape recorder will no longer move. I put it on - nothing happens - no playback - no record. So I'm sending what was possible.

Later: I want to tell you something that will be of cheer. Said [Nicola] Rescigno (I'm beginning to sound like the Monday washerwoman - "so he said, so she said ..."). He was conductting *Medea* with Callas in Dallas and in Act 2 she has many words. "Now Callas never left out a note", he says "and never came a note late, but she could forget words!" Early in the scene, she somehow got mixed up and the prompt ([Vasco] Naldini[364] - the best Italian in the business, in fact [Herbert] von Karajan[365] will not conduct an Italian opera without him), do what he may, couldn't get her on the right track. So she sang the whole scene on what to

362 Giuseppe Giacomini (1940-2021), Italian tenor.
363 Ljiljana Molnar-Talajić (1938-2007), Yugoslav soprano.
364 Vasco Naldini, Italian prompter at La Scala, Milan.
365 Herbert von Karajan (1908-1989), Austrian conductor.

him sounded like u-i-ah with consonants every now & then; but not missing a single expression, rhythm or attack. At the end of the scene Medea throws herself on the ground. And he remembers that [at] that moment he caught her eye, she winked – [as if] to say "well, I got to the end of that!" He was telling how important it is not to lose control of oneself on stage, no matter what! Another incident, still *Medea*, after weeks of rehearsal, the bass at the 1st performance got in [at] the wrong place, in fact exactly where Callas had with detail planned to sing her aria. Well, she improvised the whole thing around the bass – and to those watching it seemed like she had always, but always done it that way! [...]

To your letter – sorry you can't be the flea in my ear – but on the other hand, I'd like to be the flea in your ear around Eoan.

Too bad about Chicago. Rescigno talked about [getting me to] Dallas – but I didn't want to pump anything. It's got to come from them – I'm very interested in their '74 season – *Lucrezia Borgia* (Donizetti) with Beverly Sills. This season they do *Coq d'or* (Rimsky-Korsakov), *Marriage of Figaro* (with [Victoria] de los Ángeles) and *Andrea Chénier* – none of which particularly interests me – just look at me! – can't escape my origins, climb one step on the ladder and think I'm higher than God himself – coloured, coloured!! I try so hard – and worse! counting those chickens as soon as the egg has been laid. Anyway, I do have another chicken – the agent, Ansalone, has re-signed me for next year's Lisbon season. The operas he will tell me in Milan – just my luck! – I don't like Lisbon. I can hear you thinking – "Never happy! us humans" (no, I forget, we are not human, we're coloured, not even black – and after all, only "black is beautiful").

Honey! don't believe it – me in demand – listen I'm not even in demand in Eoan, not to mention my country – so what chance do I stand in the world?

Can't stand bread and cheese – but am still alive – on malt and milk – but those added pounds are gone! [...]

Am looking forward to hear the concert tapes and your *Barber* [*of Seville*]. I wanted to say before –

It just dawned on me how to fix my recorder – the rest comes in real live spoken voice.

It worked – the tape – so "pazienza" – until you get it. It's sounds like "Here's Washington" = (broadcasting) at the races.

Ciao

56

[Return address not provided, and stamps have been removed from the envelope]

15 April [1973]

Hi there May,

How are things with you?

I'm on the train from Milan to Zurich (2½ hours more to go). This is a fast train and takes 4 hours instead of the normal 6 or 7. But I'm a bad traveller and after 3 hours I've already had more than enough. [...]

Got back to Milano late Monday – some friends from Zurich [visited] so that meant entertaining and running around for the first few days. Then followed days of tribulation about [a contract in] Valencia – at first it wasn't sure [whether] the [Zurich] Opera would release

[me]. Then they gave a non-committal answer – "if you must go, then go" and I asked for a "yes" or "no" answer as after all I am under contract to them now. Well, to cut a long story short, I signed for Valencia on Saturday – God only knows what kind of shit will fly loose tomorrow [when I'm back at Zurich Opera]. Valencia is May 3-21 – operas, one performance each, [of] *Lucia*, *Barbiere* (with [Sesto] Bruscantini), *Manon*, *Norma*, *Turandot*, *Cavalleria* & *Pagliacci*. So I have just 15 days to get myself together for all this mouthful.

As up to now, I haven't had the chance of getting to make a tape of *Barbiere* for you,[366] it doesn't seem that I will have much chance until after Valencia – and I need to keep the score [that] I wanted to let you have. So meanwhile I'm sending you the Callas records and photographs, so you don't waste too much time.

I could not even get round to see the Callas *Vespri* in Turin.[367] All the newspapers gave bad reviews, calling it "Callas's first miss". And friends who saw it said it wasn't good. The leading lady did all the kind of movements Callas made; except she's not Callas. In fact, she appeared like a caricature of Callas in the same opera at La Scala in 1957. Maybe for [the better] then that I did not make the effort to get to Turin and besides all the performances are sold-out so one would have to go through so much shit to have a ticket. [...]

Got your letters here yesterday (Monday). Am sad to learn of your mother's death – the only consolation – if she did suffer much, it is for the better.

Keep courage. [...]

Good thoughts

Gordon.

 57

Opernhaus, Zurich, Schweiz

Zurich
21 Aug[ust] [1973]

Hi May!

How're things with you? Excuse the scrawl – I'd figure you're amongst the few who's understand whatever the motives!

Am getting round to answering your tapes but right now so busy with *Ernani* that I can "puke" of the smell of Verdi. Still [the] music remains so wonderful in spite of all. [...] [Hammerstein's] *Carmen Jones* is in town with Leona Gordon[368] singing Micaela (coached her a couple of times) and will try to see the show tomorrow if not too drunk or otherwise.

Keep courage, write me at least until I get [a] tape to you finished.

Arrivederci.

Ciao.

Gordon.

366   Abrahamse was preparing the role of Rosina in Rossini's *Il barbiere di Siviglia* for Eoan's 10th Opera Season in 1974.
367   On 10 April 1973 the Teatro Regio in Turin was re-opened after extensive renovations. The opening event featured Verdi's opera *I vespri siciliani* directed by Maria Callas and Giuseppe Di Stefano. The leading role was sung by Raina Kabaivanska.
368   Leona Gordon (1928–1977), American soprano.

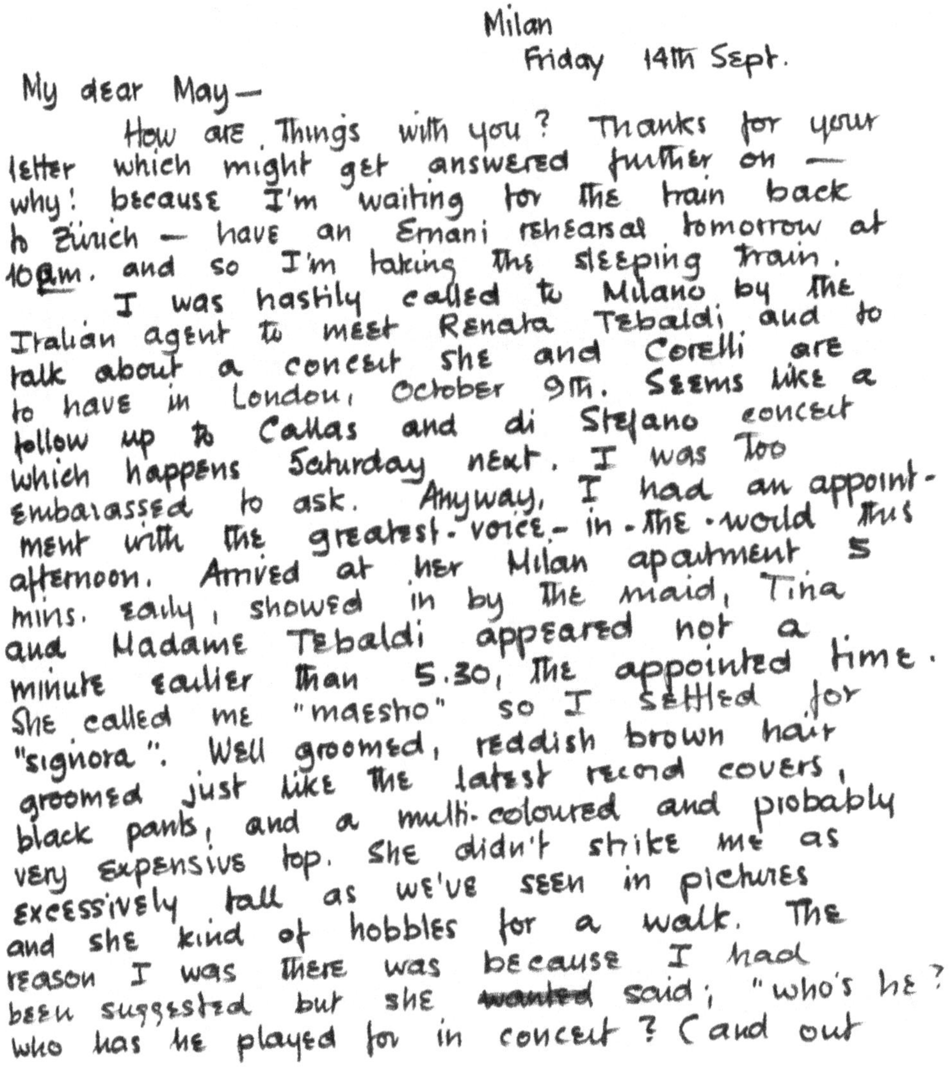

Milan
Friday 14th Sept.

My dear May—

How are things with you? Thanks for your letter which might get answered further on — why! because I'm waiting for the train back to Zurich — have an Ernani rehearsal tomorrow at 10 a.m. and so I'm taking the sleeping train.

I was hastily called to Milano by the Italian agent to meet Renata Tebaldi and to talk about a concert she and Corelli are to have in London, October 9th. Seems like a follow up to Callas and di Stefano concert which happens Saturday next. I was too embarassed to ask. Anyway, I had an appointment with the greatest-voice-in-the-world this afternoon. Arrived at her Milan apartment 5 mins. early, showed in by the maid, Tina and Madame Tebaldi appeared not a minute earlier than 5.30, the appointed time. She called me "maesho" so I settled for "signora". Well groomed, reddish brown hair groomed just like the latest record covers, black pants, and a multi-coloured and probably very expensive top. She didn't strike me as excessively tall as we've seen in pictures and she kind of hobbles for a walk. The reason I was there was because I had been suggested but she ~~wanted~~ said; "who's he? who has he played for in concert? (and out

Figure 4.7 The first page of Jephtas's letter of 14 September 1973, describing his visit to Renata Tebaldi's home.
Source: Jephtas-Abrahamse Correspondence, Eoan Group Archive.

Opernhaus, Zurich, Schweiz
[Letter begun in Milan but posted in Zurich.]

Milan
Friday, 14 September [1973]

My dear May –

How are things with you? Thanks for your letter which might get answered further on – why! because I'm waiting for the train back to Zurich – have an *Ernani* rehearsal tomorrow at 10 a.m. and so I'm taking the sleeping train.

I was hastily called to Milano by the Italian agent [Ansalone] to meet Renata Tebaldi and to talk about a concert she and [Franco] Corelli are to have in London, October 9th. Seems like a follow up to [the] [Maria] Callas and [Giuseppe] di Stefano concert which happens Saturday next.[369] I was too embarrassed to ask. Anyway, I had an appointment with the greatest-voice-in-the-world this afternoon. Arrived at her Milan apartment 5 mins. early, showed in by the maid, Tina and Madame Tebaldi appeared not a minute earlier than 5.30, the appointed time. She called me "maestro" so I settled for "signora". Well groomed, reddish brown hair groomed just like the latest record covers, black pants, and a multi-coloured and probably very expensive top. She didn't strike me as excessively tall as we've seen in pictures and she kind of hobbles for a walk. The reason I was there was because I had been suggested but she said: "who's he? who has he played for in concert?" (and out came the 3 or 4 names (little famous) I have on my list; May Abrahamse in South Africa, etc.)

Anyway, she went out and came back with an armful of disarrayed music while I played with the poodle who seemed extremely friendly as opposed to its owner who was very cool, in absolute self-control, and gave only (what seemed to me) calculating smiles when not talking.

She didn't know exactly [what] she would sing: for sure, *Bohème* & *Tosca* duets; about Corelli's repertoire she didn't know; and in the end she decided to stick closely to a programme they have already done in the States: "Se tu m'ami", etc. and talked about what key and tonality. Then she couldn't find one piece amongst the mass of music – so the maid was hailed and she had to go through all the suitcases. No it wasn't there, it was left behind in New York. Tebaldi: "Oh Dio! What am I going to do?" The maid suggested another piece: "No," came the answer, "I can't sing that in London". Then, bring me the tape recorder so we [can] find out what key "se tu m'ami" was in last time". So we spent half [an] hour hearing the beginnings of several pieces to check the keys.

That over, very demurely, she asks "can I hear something" – well, with nearly nothing in the written keys – I was lucky to make a pick and choose one that wasn't a tone up or down, and asked "will you sing?" – "No!" is the answer – "shall I sing?" – "Yes" she smiles. So I start "um-pah-pah" for 2 bars; and thought I can't [let] this woman listen to my out-of-tune voice, so [I] copped out; and continued my "um-paahs". After 10 bars she started to sing about 3 octave[s] lower (in a voice that any person might have); then got lost. So back to the beginning. Then we got to enjoy ourselves – I forgot to tell you, all this time I'm shitting with nerves, plus the gusset of my pants tore in the taxi; fortunately I was wearing underwear, so including having to concentrate, I had to think about keeping my legs as closed as much as

---

369 Callas and Di Stefano performed a series of "farewell concerts" in various cities throughout Europe in October and November 1973. Their London recital took place on Friday, 26 November 1973.

possible – well, we did this and that and I figure she was checking me out. With that over, with still not a word of "will you play for us" – nor "I don't think you'd do" she offered a drink – I chose "coke" – she nothing because as she told me – "if I drink, I get more thirsty, so I do without".

She gave me her music and also a folder; a last word, that I'll hear from her through the agent as to rehearsals and when Corelli would be in town. Good-bye, keep well.

I left somewhat perplexed not knowing whe[ther] she wanted me or not. Anyway, I had her music under my arm; and I figured even if I don't play the concerts, I did have the chance to talk with the famous soprano, and did play for her even if she sang down below the stave in a voice that was the least akin to the voice we know.

I talked with the agent after; and he figured if I had the music, that was it – but he would hear from Tebaldi and then I will know for sure.[370] Meanwhile go away and practise.

Now I really wanted to answer your letter, but first I wanted to share my afternoon's experience with you (hope you don't find it egoistic?)

Have been waiting every day for your concert tape.

Listen, I'm tired of writing and I better not lose the goddamn train to Zurich.

Write me all.

Love,

Gordon.

59

[Postcard written on his way to Vienna for the second Tebaldi-Corelli recital, posted in Vienna.]

Friday, [12] October [1973][371]

Hi there!

Am once again travelling – this time from Zurich to Vienna; and beginning to dislike the idea of always on the go.

Well, after the London Tebaldi/Corelli recital I am surprised to find myself still alive. I was all ready to pass out and die after the final duet. I'd like to write and tell everything but that'll have to wait until when the Vienna concert is over.

She was wonderful to me and I really tried my damndest to give her everything I could. It was even fun. Thought I'd be very nervous, but there was no time with so much to think about. The English press was not particularly delighted with me[372] – in a way I'm glad. It was *her* night.

I'd love to hear from you and if you can send newspaper cuttings. [I am] back in Milano on October 15.

Love.

---

370   Jephtas accompanied Tebaldi and Corelli in two recitals: in the Royal Albert Hall in London on Tuesday, 9 October 1973 and in the Grosser Saal des Musikvereins in Vienna on Sunday, 14 October 1973. The concert in Vienna was recorded and is the only commercial recording available of Jephtas. See *Renata Tebaldi and Franco Corelli in Vienna*, Vienna 1973, Myto Records Italy, ASIN: B00005090M.

371   Jephtas dated this postcard Friday 10 October. However, the most likely date was the 12th, since he played in London on Tuesday 9, probably travelled back to Zurich shortly afterwards, and was on his way to Vienna on Friday 12 to accompany Tebaldi and Corelli in their recital on Sunday 14 October 1973.

372   See letter dated 19 November 1973.

[Postcard from Vienna, Austria, sent just after the Tebaldi-Corelli recital.]

Mon[day], 15 Oct[ober] [1973]

Hi there!
    Great success for Tebaldi/Corelli.
    Much love.
    Gordon.

Via Plinio, 42, Milano, Italia

19 November [1973]

Hi May:
    Here are [the] threatened newspaper cuttings of Callas and I take the liberty to include what I have of my own activities – so happy reading. I can't translate all the German. Anyway I figure you'd just love to see Callas's dress.
    I quote [from] other of my reviews from London: – I wanted to talk about it on the tape; so here goes:

Times: .... the presence of a single none-too-effective accompanist![373]

Guardian: .... the pianist, at times so self-effacing that he became totally inaudible, was G[ordon] J[ephtas]. This discretion not only spoiled the duet from *Bohème*; but was the more tantalising in that when he could be heard, Mr. J[ephtas] sounded rather good. The accompaniment to [Rossini's] "La promessa" and the [Riccardo] Zandonai and [Arturo Buzzi-]Peccia songs was delicately but crisply played, while in the *Tosca* duet some splendidly loud chords crashed out.

Evening Standard: ... G[ordon] J[ephtas] contributed deft and slightly over-discreet accomp[animent].

Evening Echo: ... The accompaniments by G[ordon] Jephtas] were unfailingly tasteful and sensitive to the singers' needs. He almost made up for the lack of an orchestra in the 2 operatic duets.

(Vienna) Translation of German review: GJ the accompanist looks like a mixture of Jason King (a T.V. star) and an exotic Johann Strauss, is small & graceful. He accompanies

---

373 "There was not much fire on stage for the first hour of the evening. Perhaps it was the Royal Albert Hall itself, drably denuded of flowers and greenery. Perhaps it was the absence of an orchestra and the presence of a single none-too-effective accompanist. ... Perhaps it was the choice of composers. ... The effect was scrappy and unnourishing". Higgins (1973).

Tebaldi with affectionate devotion, Corelli with attentive objectivity. He has the tendency to take it easy at the more difficult passages but gets touchingly poetic at the interludes & postludes. It is evident that he is a good accompanist, called to something superior maybe.

So that's that. Have a good read. Tapes will come eventually.
Ciao,
Gordon. [...]

62

[Zurich, Switzerland]
[No return address stated, but postage stamps are from Switzerland.]

28 December [1973]

Hi there May –
How are things with you deep down south in the sun – what a great thought. Here it is pissingly cold and generally miserable and the joyous message of Xmas has not helped in the least. But still, one is still alive and that already is something – or maybe not.

With my opening preamble over, let me from the outset say that this is to be largely a bad news letter – so if you're not in the mood – stop here – and continue reading another day.

Here goes: – I want to put off our recital for a couple of years.[374] For one thing, I have lost my joy for music; so I need a while to find that joy once again; and for another thing, I've been *defeated*! At heart, I am [a] coward, and true enough to my sun sign (Fish), I dart away from danger rather than face it – but that is my nature, and can't be changed. My biggest error was to offer this venture to the Eoan Group – but we live to make errors! – I figure you understand why it had to [be] the Group – but it was a mistake nonetheless!

I have just come back from London and seeing Mr. Sydow – well to tell the truth, I just did not have the energy to put up any kind of fight – and even if I did win, we [would] then work under the most hostile of conditions which would only be harmful to our "art" ideals – and the Eoan Group certainly do not have that word in their aims, nor vocabulary.

So as things turned out, we exchanged not a single word about that infamous letter[375] nor any of the consequent happenings and results – and I liked the game and played along. So much for that. [...]

In closing, first of all forgive me and try and understand my system of madness and caprices and then don't worry if I go into a period of absolute hibernation – I might need it – who knows! South Africa doesn't love me too much right now – Everything I do and say is "not right" – at least those are the vibrations I feel – from the people who deal with my passport – through to the Eoan Group – through to the coloured people I've met in Zurich and sounded out – But who cares?

Write me, at least so that I might know whether you are irretrievably mad at me or not.
Ciao ... Gordon.

---

374 The next recital by Jephtas and Abrahamse was not until 1979, at the Nico Malan Theatre in Cape Town.
375 Jephtas had written to Sydow from Milan on 15 July 1973, proposing a recital with Abrahamse, to be organised and financed by the Eoan Group. It seems that Sydow never sent a reply.

Zurich
11 February [1974], Monday

Hi there May –

With equal promptness I am answering your so welcome letter of today. For one thing, in my drunken stupor, a pen is nowhere to be found – so you're getting an answer in pencil – (but that's no big deal!) – for another thing, my prompt reply[376] to your previous letter, I am appalled to find is still waiting to be mailed – so you'll probably get everything in one big heap! Well, that's just the erratic side of me! I'm sorry! […]

Glad to hear that Mr. Sydow is safely back – now I'm not going to make any comment about what you've "heard"[377] – believe it if you like – but better not to say anything – so no unnecessary compromises can arise. We will see what happens – if anything at all.

Big deal indeed, to conduct some shitty white orchestra.[378] You know, for me, to be frank, the word white is not operative, but what I'd like to know is how good these bastards are – do I sound high and mighty? I don't think so, because what matters is the music and not this "white must be good" mess. Let me not get on that subject!

Yes, for 2½ weeks I'm working on *Tabarro* & *Schicchi* – [Tito] Gobbi had his 1st rehearsal this evening – such an interesting man. I must count myself lucky indeed for getting the chance to work with the greats of the opera world – but believe me, I am paying the high prices – the solitudes, the tears, the desperation – (and how many people can understand that!). *Schicchi* & *Tabarro* go on March 2nd – I leave for Lisbon on Mar[ch] 1st, still not knowing [Donizetti's *La*] *Favorite* well enough – I'm still learning the Puccini!

I'm still trying to find my joy for music – as yet, I don't know – but as you say, music is so beautiful. I lunched with Maestro Santi today and he told [me] how Callas is wanting to kill herself & how di Stefano is stopping her by insisting she sings these concerts. I'm really so happy to work with a real conductor – I'm learning so much – he admires my piano playing – and I his fantastic comprehension for the theatre and vocal music.

Don't worry too much. I don't figure that our next recital will be too much past your 45th year[379] – and that's a promise. I think the delay of our recital has had a large play in my present depression. But I don't plan to write a whole discourse about that now! In fact, I'm already tired of writing – so I wait to hear your *Barber* tapes and want to help as much as I can. […]

Ciao.

Am in "Hotel Borges", Lisbon as from March 1st until April 20.

Much regards

---

376   This letter is presumably lost.
377   This might refer to Eoan's plans for Jephtas to return to South Africa and lead the group, or perhaps to Eoan's long wished-for tour abroad, which eventually came about in 1975 when it visited London and Aberdeen.
378   Jephtas refers here to the permit issued by the Department of Community Development on 15 October 1973 that gave him permission to conduct the Cape Town Symphony Orchestra. See the Eoan Group Archive: 37:300. It is clear from the permit that Jephtas would be restricted to conducting Eoan's productions, and would not be allowed to conduct the orchestra on any other occasion.
379   This recital finally took place on 3 March 1979, shortly before Abrahamse's 47th birthday.

Hotel Borges, Rua Garrett, 108, Lisboa – 2, Portugal

8 March [19]74

Hi there May –

I'm late with this reply – but with luck, it might catch you just before you go on stage.[380] My timing is all wrong, and what with travelling across Europe and what have you!

In answer to your immediate questions – *Barbiere* is a comic opera – therefore Rosina's love for the Count is no great melodramatic affair – but light-hearted and sincere as you rightly think. She *has fun, makes fun* – and wants the audience to have fun – not stupid fun; nor extreme exaggeration – she laughs much, always alive and high-spirited – study the Callas pictures – notices how she permits the character to cross her knees when sitting – something which is not permitted in the tragic operas for example. Also, because of the nature of the costumes, the period, etc. [...]

I listened to your tape – I'm not going to indulge into what I thought of the whole proceeding – and that is not the matter in question right [now] – so I'm going to jump right to your contribution. It is so nice to know that you are making such a fine effort to understand and pronounce the Italian well – that is, the business of the double-consonants or single consonants. Excellent. It is not always exactly right, but you [are] on a very good track. Watch the "r" – R when between 2 vowels, like "sarà" – is not rolled at all, but flipped only once, because if you roll it, it becomes "sarrà" – which makes 2 r's and therefore possibly another word or meaning. Always roll the "r" when there is a combination of vowel & consonant – e.g. *trema*, etc.

About the voice, it didn't seem to me that you need to find a lighter voice – it would be too white and colourless. The voice you used to start "Una voce poco fa" sounded exactly right – but you need to keep your singing high all the time – that is, the vocal position – and not sing the pattern of the coloratura – but every note in the same high place or position. The actual coloratura is fine, but you use all your energy to sing fast – it's not the speed that counts, but the articulation of the vowels – when you have all those scales, you need to think to repeat the same vowel for every one of the notes written above it – not only the 1st – and there is always time to sing all the notes, no matter what the tempo is.

Lots of luck, and let me know how things have gone. Can't be with you in body; but will be in spirit.

Hope this little can be of some help.

Good luck. Gordon

---

380 Abrahamse sang the role of Rosina in Eoan's production of Gioachino Rossini's *Il barbiere di Siviglia* in March 1974. Due to renovations at the Cape Town City Hall, Eoan could no longer use that venue and now had to use the Green and Sea Point Civic Centre, which was further away from the city centre.

Opernhaus, Zurich, Switzerland

Zurich
10 May [1974]

Hi there May –

So many thanks for all your mail – birthday wishes, letters and tapes which are avidly being read and answered whenever my arse gets itself in [g]ear.

Am on my way to Milano tomorrow (15 days late for a recital tour – probably lost the job!! – well, no matter?) – hence this is to be but a short note – doubled by the shameful fact that writing holds so little attraction for me.

Enclosed is a birthday surprise – first the Callas picture and autograph[381] (I had asked a Callas fan and friend and also friend of mine to get it when she sang in Munich earlier this year – hence the inscription on the back – he, of course, did not know that it was intended for you) – I need to apologize – it never occurs to me personally to ask for autographs and only now I realize that you might have liked that of Tebaldi, Sutherland, etc. But you know I'm not the kind of person who would ask, if mainly because I work with them, I could not appear as an open-mouthed, tongue hanging-out fan – do I explain myself?

The 100 francs is for something like 5 lessons with [Adelheid] Armhold – explanations will follow later – Callas and I think [sic] it might do some necessary good!!!

So until later – back in Zurich after May 25 [and staying there] until end of June.
Ciao.
Gordon.

66

Opernhaus, Zurich, Switzerland

Zurich/Milano
Sunday 11 May [1974]

Hi there May,

I have come to thoroughly disliking travelling, carrying and packing bags – yet I am thankful for this 4-hour [train] journey because it does get me to start some letters – usually long, long overdue answers.

I got your 4 tapes – (2 rehearsal ones, 1 *Barber* performance, and the Gems [concert] and your conversation) – I just loved the talking, which was so much better and more entertaining than most of the music before! Do it more often, though I realize that you dislike the mike as much as I the pen. You wouldn't believe it, I already have writer's cramp!!! Then there was an air-letter and another that I got the day before yesterday. Thanks – and so now I'll try and answer. I figure to start with the conversation and work backwards like a crab.

---

381   This autographed picture is apparently no longer extant.

Well, for once I have some good luck – the tape has not yet got stuck on me – am holding thumbs though.[382] Glad you like the explanation about singers/big halls and dynamics. I worry about my age[383] only because I am so ambitious about my music and want to do so many, many things which require time and more time and only too well realize how much longer the road still is. So the fact that I might run out of time bugs me – and I don't want to die too old. Wish I could feel like you.

Your explanation about the orchestra – thanks – one day we will know if what you think is so or not. How big is this orchestra[384] – how many string players? – they seem to have plenty of brass and wind. My idea from a letter from Manca a while back – and reading between the lines, was that certain members of the Municipal Orch[estra] were refusing to play under Manca's baton. But who knows what is the truth of the matter? [...]

Sorry to hear of your housing problems – hope you solve them soon! I have similar problems – need to decide where to live. These last 3 months I was keeping an apartment in Milan, another in Zurich and living in a hotel in Lisbon. Well, it's ridiculous, so I have to choose Zurich or Milan. I am in Milan so little these days and on the other hand I don't want to lose touch with the Italians – they are so closely related with my work. [...]

About [Eoan principal] singers gone away. You did tell me some of this before, but sorry I had forgotten. So now, for once I have the record clear. Well, I know only too well how well the Group handles their mail, never mind acknowledging! (Just because I have my writing-jacket on, this turns out to be the bumpiest train journey). What I find difficult to really understand is why they are now "enemies". Such nonsense. Well, one thing, if I come back I would want them all back, on their terms of course. I suppose that won't go down too well, so I might well find myself thrown out from the word go. Heaven knows. But you cannot make opera with 6 or 10 singers; and the others have had some experience and should be leading the wagon – that way some artistic growth can happen.

Glad you worked out some well-thought out movements for "Una voce poco fa". I dig the idea of the palms down pose for the cadenzas, because one couldn't really run around and tire yourself with no breath. Good. Wish I could have seen it. Sure, it can only have [done] you good – more about the vocalisms later. [...]

Having listened to what you say about your voice studies prompted the action to let you have 5 lessons with Armhold as a birthday gift. The fact that you sometimes need to stiffen your facial muscles in an attempt to keep the voice forward is a sign for caution and guidance. Of course, there is a way of singing in the mask without the face stiff. So hopefully Armhold can find the way for you. For every person it is a little different depending on the structure of the face, etc. It is also something that has to be demonstrated to be understood. Writing about it might only just confuse things, but I'm gonna make some comments, if they are clear to you use them, if not, discard them and when we get together next, we'll work at it also. Now what is [it] to sing forward? – it is to direct the air coming out (the sound) into the mask – you know the area behind the bottom of the nose, but out of the nose for Italian singing. And this air has to come from above rather than below. The mouth must be hollow and inside the mouth should be as open as possible. (Corelli for example, when he sings the vowel "o" and you're near

---

382 Jephtas here replies to the questions that Abrahamse had asked on a taped "letter", and towards the end he also comments on recordings that she had sent of a Eoan performance.
383 Jephtas was 31 when writing this letter.
384 The orchestra was called the Eoan Group Theatre Orchestra but consisted of ad hoc members of the Cape Town Symphony Orchestra.

[to that], has a tremendous huge open area where the air travels through - I got the impression he looks like an alligator when you see into his mouth.)

Back to us, that means that the tongue must be out of [the] way and not even thought about, and none of the face muscles tensed. Keeping the voice forward is not so much the physical action but mental too. You keep that air going to that same spot (mask) all the time. That's why Italian singers do not keep their lips shut too long when they sing the consonants for fear of losing the place where the previous vowel was sung. In fact, the biggest axiom in Italian singing is how to prevent closing your mouth when saying the consonants - also because the consonants, if said on the lip, lower the position of the voice. There's quite a distance between the lips and the nose. So Italian singers try to sing the consonants way up where the vowels were. Only in recitatives do they move down to the lips to make the speaking/singing clear to be understood. Take a phrase like "vivi ingrato a lei d'accanto"[385] and try to sing these *words* without ever closing your mouth except maybe for the double "c" - see what you come up with. Let me know what you make of this, maybe next time I can try by tape.

You asked once about portamentos.[386] Yes, they need work or rather more thought. First the portamento has to be made at the latest possible moment; it has a start and a finish and has to be sung on the vowel you were singing before the portamento, yet in the mask the sound must not travel up or down (except in specific cases when breaking the rule would provide another colour or vocal interest) but each sound of the portamento has to be in the same groove, which is then also where the next vowel will be sung. Does that make some sense? If not, ask again please.

I am always amazed when people say that a singer is finished. Gobbi in Zurich said a very interesting thing - no singer is finished because nobody loses their voice - it might be less and not as beautiful, but it's always there - : you might lose your nerve but the voice is never finished! (This was in answer to someone asking about Callas).

About your recit[ative]s - you're right about not having the knack. Recit singing is another art - and the first most important thing is to know absolutely exactly what you are singing about so that the word inflections and accentuations come out right. They are sung "on the lip" as the Italians say. If one is good, one does not alter the rhythm of the composer - but the speed is [at] your discretion - so you can make a whole phrase faster or slower depending on your meaning and expression. What you did get was to sing the last phrase of the recit which comes just before the aria or ensemble. Listen much to Callas - and remember not to sing faster than you are able to understand the words. Will talk more about this when I talk about the performance.

You ask about my future plans - the month of June I begin rehearsing *Otello* which opens in Zurich end of Sept[ember]. Verona have called me and there's a possibility to work there for July (holiday month in Zurich): but there are nationality problems - only Italians can be assistants in Italy. So the Arena di Verona is fighting the case, and if they really want me they will win. I'd like that because I want to break into the big Italian theatres - but you know how it is, one rarely wins. [I will be] in Zurich mid-August until [the] end [of] October with *Otello*, back in Dec[ember] and Jan[uary] for *Manon Lescaut*; then Lisbon Feb[ruary]-April for *Manon* (Massenet), *Samson and Delilah*, *Rigoletto* and also *Lescaut*; [then] back to Zurich for May and June for *Falstaff*. November is still being negotiated - probably Portugal - the theatre made

---

385 From Donizetti's *Roberto Devereux*.
386 Portamento: sliding from one note to the next.

a very good offer – 3000 dollars a month – they're interested in a long contract for '75/76 – well for that money. But that will be seen. I sound like a yo-yo and I am already tired of this life.

We're onto the Gems [concert] with half an hour on this train left – just crossing the border into Italy.

Listening to first chorus number – [Verdi's] *Lombardi*, is it? They sound undernourished and small in number for such heroic music. How many are they?

In case you wonder how I'm listening – I have earphones.

I don't know any names (maybe Gerald [Samaai]) – the "Recondita armonia" tenor has a good sound. Hate the pianist – but I guess I shouldn't knock him or her! [...]

Isis and Osiris – can't hear him too well, the aria needs more voice – should sing something else. There's the depleted chorus too – sounds like a handful singing at the Nyanga[387] Town Hall. This guy is bad news! [...]

We've arrived in Milano.

Ciao for now.

Milano, May 22 Wed[nesday]

This looks like it is to become a 100 page-never-to-arrive-epistle. [...]

So, what brings me to write to you today – two things. One, I'm sitting around here waiting for the phone to ring – a thing I hate, but absolutely hate. My agent called a couple of hours ago to see if I would go to Spain for *Elisir* and *Otello* (some kind of emergency) – now he's negotiating with the Spaniards and I'm not to leave the house until a yes or no has come through. It seems that I should think of changing my ambition in life to becoming the very highest paid assistant conductor in the business – – my latest fee in Lisbon was 100 dollars per day, now the agent is asking for more. Sounds a lot on paper, but believe me it is not, what with agent's commission, housing all over the place and for another thing, money and I have never been too close friends.

The other thing that prompts my writing is last night I went to Tebaldi's return to la Scala ... a solo recital with her American accompanist. It would have been nice if she had chosen me, but on the other hand I wanted also to see her and hear her from afar. Her very appearance [on stage] got at least a 20 minute applause, it seemed they were never going to let her begin, they were just so happy to see her – shouts of "Renata (first name terms between audience and public is reserved only for the greats – – it is Caballé, Scotto, but Maria (Callas) and Renata), welcome back... it is about time... you're the greatest".

Three nights previous[ly] I was at her try-out performance at the Piccolo Scala which is adjacent to the Scala and the size about one and a half of the Little Theatre in Cape Town. Well, a strange thing occurred – in that small place the beauty of the sound was completely lost, one could barely hear the bottom notes, and the critics started to wonder just how much of Tebaldi one would hear in the big Scala. Well at the big Scala last night the sound was again that wonderful liquid and velvety one for which she is so famous, one heard all the notes – which make me think that these great voices are made for the great theatres because from close range they are nothing. It reminds me of [Piero] Cappuccilli the baritone. Of course I had heard him at the Scala in a triumphant *Boccanegra*, and both times when I was playing the piano [for him] and he singing just a few feet away, all I heard was a raucous and catarrh

---

387 A (pejorative) reference to the black township of Nyanga outside Cape Town – inferring that standards in the coloured community were better than among blacks.

filled sound, but in the theatre it is a great voice. A phenomenon which has set me curious to learn more about. Back to Tebaldi of last night. You know, when one has a beautiful sound, one depends entirely on that and the details of expression get passed by – now, I'm not saying she does not express – she has unmatching charm and appeal to one who is watching, but if one were not looking at the source of that sound all the time, it could become a very boring affair – obviously why I prefer the Callas approach which is music, singing, expression and visual all at the same time. That must be a wonderful culmination to reach. [...]

Naturally everybody was there and coming out of the Scala there were again the millions waiting around to discuss and talk and wait for Tebaldi – a thing which in the last few years had not been happening because the performances had never provoked such interest. But what surprised me was the multitude of people who recognized me as the Vienna accompanist,[388] the respect they proffered me, etc. (something which makes me think would be difficult if not out of the question in South Africa). But I'm not trying to pat myself on the shoulder, what I want to say is that this display towards me, and before I could say boo or bah, hundreds of people around got to know who I was (also the many whom I had seen for years in the gallery and said hi to during the intervals) with the result that I felt obliged to move away from the scene I wanted to see (that is Tebaldi surrounded by all these fans, the shouting, the exhilaration) because it seemed how could I join the open mouthed and gaping fans when everyone around was making me feel too much of an artist, and worse yet, expecting something great of me one day. It is a good feeling in one way, yet though I don't find it so difficult to grasp, it [interferes in one] doing what one wants to do. So, the prices are always high. After her try-out at the Piccolo Scala, I went backstage to say hello to Tebaldi, and after the hugs and kisses and "maestro, how've you been" etc. everyone started to treat me like a celebrity, being shown across the stage, way made through the crowd – well what do you know – and I'm still in blue jeans – my agent keeps telling me "you know, I swear that one day I will see you all dressed up in suit and shirt and I won't believe it". Because here, on opening nights especially, the singers and all the staff involved get dressed up – I haven't yet understood exactly why or who they think they will meet; but of one thing I'm sure – that if the Queen of England did come (and that would be extremely improbable as she goes only to those operas that have live horses on stage, and then only to see how the animal will behave) I certainly would not be important enough to be presented – and who wants to shake her hand anyway. But enough of all this, the phone's ringing.

May 31st – [on the] train [from] Milan to Zurich.

What did I tell you – a never-to-arrive letter. Well, I did warn you!!! Well, here I am again. I didn't go to Spain – just as well, because I've not been too well – but more of that later. Now I mean to get on to the *Barber* [tape] which I have right here. So just a moment while I get the tape going again.

"Una voce poco fa" – applause – for you, I figure. All's well. Good – you're not going too fast – first scale good. I hear "la vince*rrr*ò" instead of "vincerò". First cadenza fine – you begin to surprise me. Allegro – good taste – "reggere" has two g's. The "ma" not to my taste – too fast – all scales on "ah" *no* good – because [you sing it] ½ way between throat and mask. Another unconvincing "ma" – and now it's too fast and no control. Good "cento trappole" & cadenza.

---

388 Jephtas here refers to his recital in Vienna of October 1973 with Tebaldi and Corelli.

Recit[ative] - "sì-sì" - understand very little - only final cadenzas - of Figaro[389] - nothing heard or understood - too fast - also you. Nice baritone sound. Bartolo[390] sounds okay ... You manipaulated the aria well - especially when not trying to outdo yourself with speed. Bartolo's okay as buffo - who is the Basilio?[391] "La calunnia" - not at all bad; [though] nothing special. [I] hear the "Rota" vocal additives which have been out of date for 30 years. Lots of loud orchestra. Hurts my ears with this earphone! Not so hot on high notes [in] this number. [...]

The duet: your voice [is] okay - like [the] 1st cadenza - word accentuation gone for a walk - but we have another race for time between you two & the maestro [Joseph Manca]. The baritone's kinda good.[392] ... Love the Callas cadenzas. Good high D. Bravi. [...]

Who is the Berta[393]? - she shouts good. [...] Thanks for letting me hear how things are progressing - apart from my heavy-handed criticisms of all it has been invaluable to hear the level of artistry. I return the tapes as I don't remember which you want back or not. Thanks, you're a honey. [...]

Callas is still on tour - sometimes singing alone, and there's talk of her being at Scala next season. Why doesn't she teach - well, she tried and it doesn't look like it's her thing. You know, artists more often can do things but cannot tell others how [to] or even why. As for her image - well, I don't know. For one thing, she just has to stand on stage and that speaks more volumes than any of the current famous sopranos who sing 3 acts and then one admires a trill, a note, an aria. I've heard a tape of one of her concerts and she isn't as bad as the newspapers say. But obviously, the public is expecting more from the very person who taught them to use their minds and ask for more.

My health's in a bad patch. Having trouble with my eyes. Rather bad eye-strain. It seems to [be my] concentration and my mania for working practically in the dark. Over the last week, I couldn't look at a score more than 3 or 4 minutes, and just when I needed so badly to study. The remedy is rest and vitamins - which I did. Now it's okay. I figure it's also psychological. [I] am sending [you] Sutherland's *Traviata* - after you've heard it a few times, I'd like to have it back for future reference. [I am] also [sending you] Suliotis's *Cavalleria* from last November down [in] South Italy and you'll hear how Art is not always beautiful and honey. The bell, organ and siciliana are my contributions - In *Traviata* the orch[estra] from after the Brindisi until the chorus before "è strano" is again yours truly. [Also the] harp and tenor back-stage.[394] [...]

We're hitting Zurich.

Ciao. All ze best [*sic*].

Love to all - I'm tired of writing (as you can see).

Yours,

Gordon.

---

389 Sung by Ronald Theys (died 2021), a tenor in the Eoan Group. See the programme booklet for Eoan's 1974 production of *Il barbiere di Siviglia*. Eoan Group Archive: 100:770 (also the source for the names in the following footnotes).
390 Sung by Martin Johnson.
391 Sung by Jacobus Erasmus.
392 Figaro, sung by Ronald Theys.
393 Sung by Josephine Liedemann.
394 These comments indicate that Jephtas worked as répétiteur and assistant conductor for both these productions, as well as playing the offstage bells and organ.

67

Opernhaus, Zurich, Switzerland

Zurich
Sunday, 27 October [1974]

Hi there May,
    Many thanks for the tape of the gems concert and the returned Cav[alleria] of Suliotis. Finally I am getting around to listening to the City Hall concert ... I find the tape very interesting and find that all the singers have something positive to offer. [Ronald] Theys has a very fine sound and sings well – that "Nemico della patria" [from Giordano's opera *Andrea Chénier*] is considered a throat killer. That you are the most professional has to be, with your experience etc., and I take for granted, but continue to be amazed that you always try for improvement and am so happy to note that you are paying extra attention to the Italian diction, the double consonants, etc. This [is] an area where the others fail, and go on instinct; but how can they be expected to know better without someone teaching and telling them what it is supposed to be. Listening to this tape makes me sad about one thing and that is that the Eoan Group could possibly reach a very high level artistically with the right and more knowledgeable teaching and instruction; but the level of teaching and know-how in South Africa is what it is. Maybe one day soon I will get my arse into gear and come out of my self [imposed] exile and come and do my share.
    "Casta Diva" is some really fine singing, the chromatic scale is not all it should be; and you still screw [up on] one breath – I notice you finally got the best place on the programme – the last before intermission – how did that come about – no, no, no don't tell me. [...]
    Nothing much else is happening here. Tonight is the 8th and last *Otello* for a while and I'm just home, getting my head calm to conduct the back stage band. I enclose ... a newspaper clipping of *Otello* so you can see the television monitor that we have back stage in order to be with the conductor. [...]
    All the best for now, I'm tire[d] of typing,
    Ciao,
    Gordon.

68

Opernhaus, Zurich, Switzerland

Zurich
14 January [1975]

Hi there May –
    This turns out to be my "coloured-folks-I-love-you-day!!" [...]
    I have re-read your last letter and it seems that I answered nearly everything on my previous tape except not saying much about the Youth Festival affair[395] – and now I find myself in the mood to speak my thoughts about the whole thing – and have you know my vibrations.

---

395 Eoan's imminent tour to the UK to participate in the 1975 International Festival of Youth Orchestras from 4 to 15 August in Aberdeen, and from 15 to 17 August in London.

First about the actual Youth Festival – it seems an organization [that is] interested in promoting the aims and fostering an increased interest in young people who have talent, flair and desire, into eventual professionalism. So they organize this festival in order to bring different kinds of people together; so they can know about other people, how they function; what they do – in other words, taking each group out of their box (which is their city or country, say) – and in this way stimulate their minds and aspirations. And art has much to do with contact with other people – if this were not true, I could have learnt what I know in South Africa – but I did not. So, the actual youth festival does not require a professional level of achievement – and in any case, such persons would already be involved in professional activity. So they have this Festival with courses, master classes and local performances usually culminating in a big public performance as with all schools, etc. [...]

Now these people have been interested in the Eoan Group for some time and for a varied number of reasons. In fact, they invited me to be their guest a few years ago when the Festival was in Lausanne, to view and see what they were doing.[396] [...]

They are going to invite the Eoan Group and are very well aware that the Group is not strictly a youth organization – more especially the vocal section – not too many people in the world under 23 sing grand opera – and we are not even 1 million coloureds (so I'm told – is that right?). It seems that they are interested to extend a guest invitation to those who are outside the age-group with the idea that also, and perhaps more, those few would after the experience go back and besides [being] leading forces – stimulate even a greater interest in the younger people who will be the performers of tomorrow. And as living [expenses], etc, during the course are paid by the Festival – this year in Aberdeen, Scotland – such an invitation is a big-hearted gesture – and must have taken much consideration against inviting more youth from whatever part of the world.

I am extremely in favour of the idea – the Eoan Group is not going to perform at La Scala or Covent Garden – which I guess might well be Manca's interpretation! – But [only] some members of the Group] are going to be invited – it would be impossible to ask all – and what is important, I think, morally and psychologically, is that some are coming – and maybe someday our great grandchildren will sing at La Scala. But a start has to be made and more interest needs to be provoked in Eoan activities – because it needs more young blood along with the experienced ones – talking just about the vocal section as it now stands; the elements are not enough, apart from whether [they are] good enough, to even plan *one* opera – so one must look ahead and think of tomorrow as it were.

And you know, the longer I am abroad, the more I realize that we as [coloured] people, we do have talent and are capable ... we people have it to be great. We are too busy being sorry for our unfair lot – and we are right – we *have* been humiliated – but the young have to learn to say "Screw you".

Mac, Barb[397] and I were talking about grants – their point was [that] coloureds don't accept them because of the always attached conditions. My point – nobody gives money away without conditions – and hell it is coloured people's tax-money too – (don't you pay taxes?) – so we feel humiliated, but shit we are cutting our own noses to spite our own faces. Mac made what was to me perhaps the most important thing, he said, "We coloured people

---

396   Presumably the 1972 Festival, when South Africa was represented by the (purely white) SABC Youth Orchestra conducted by Walter Mony, whose members included brass players drafted in from the South African Prison Warders' Band.
397   Friends from South Africa.

are too full of suspicions" – isn't that a big point. I have it too, but I do also say "Fuck you" to whoever bothers me.

Now reading between the lines of your observation of the Youth Festival business, I get a strong feeling that you are a conscientious objector – right or wrong?

Assuming right – I understand your reasons – the Group in its bluffing – the low standard – the disregard for getting better. Absolutely true. But this might well be the beginning of a change.

I need to ask you [to consider] one [thing] – to churn over what I have written, also that between the lines, and if you still remain an objector, to think about doing everything in your power to help, stimulate the younger ones – and if possible, keep your cool and in a big heart-ed effort voice only those opinions which can be of encouragement – throw the rest at me, by all means – I can handle it. [...]

Also another feeling I have – correct me if need be. I feel myself ready to conduct my first operas now and South Africa and the Group I need as my trial grounds (a selfish thing – but it would also help Eoan itself) and as (big secret!!) (only I know) I have not signed any contracts for next season – true, Vienna and Düsseldorf have asked for me, besides Zurich who would pay me the earth. Reason – because I plan to come home and rehearse and conduct my 1ˢᵗ opera – as it's my debut, it has to be my best opera – and that is *Traviata* – now you get a clearer view why I am more than eager in helping you now – and of course my Violetta can only be you *or nothing* – then will follow operas depending on what is available – I also want to have Joseph [Gabriels][398] etc. – but that's another story. So another point, if my reading between the lines is correct – the Eoan Group next year will have the very same administration – your conscientious objection now – however right you are – might just only hamper our artistic ideals, and the least one needs is an uncomfortable atmosphere – because artistic things cannot nurture under bad conditions.

So, like the Chinese say – although silence indicates approval – it is also the sign of a stronger personality.

Please chew over what I've said and whether my feelings are right or wrong.

To a great artist who always has so much of my admiration.

Ciao.

Gordon.

[Jephtas started writing this letter while in Lisbon, then continued it after travelling to Milan and thence to Zurich. No return address is given, but the letter was eventually posted in Italy.]

Saturday, 22 March [1975]

Hi there May,

How've you been? –

Now, 5 million thank-you's, first for your letter, and then the newspaper cuttings, programmes and 2 tapes of yesterday. I feel awful when I look at the postage costs – and I

---

398 It seems that Jephtas wanted to conduct a production of *La traviata* with the Eoan Group in Cape Town. In theory this would have been possible, since a permit for him to conduct the (white) Cape Town Municipal Orchestra had been granted some time previously (see letter of 11 February 1974). This initiative never bore fruit, but Jephtas did not relinquish this ambition, even mentioning it shortly before he died in New York. Hardine (1992).

can't understand why - from here when I mail things to you it costs only 1/3 of what you seem to be paying - maybe you should change Post Office? [...]

My birthday was a rather lonely affair[399] - besides, I worked most of the afternoon and evening - and for ever so many years I have always thought that the birthday should be the most happy day in an individual's life - I still have to experience that!!! [...]

Perhaps it's due to my not want[ing] to acknowledge the aging process we all are subjected to (like I've told you before, right?) Anyway, my pact with Corelli holds for a while - I won't admit to a month more than 23, then he can admit to 38 - (actually 52)[400] - the ratio is a bit cock-eyed - but Corelli is a star so he deserves to win, right? Wow, I sometimes wonder whether I am serious about this aging bit. All that was to say thank you for your birthday card and all my appreciation. [...]

To your cuttings - the programme first - I just love the picture of you and Arlecchino[401] from *Pagliacci* - you look exactly like La Callas in *Barber* - well, they say the greats have things in common. But tell me, what was that costume you were wearing? - that's how they [did it] 50 years ago - Rota needs some updating - hell? Your actual publicity picture - it's pretty; but I would have preferred an Afro - what do you think? On the next page the photos display that look-white-look and so I'm thrilled to see at least one black-is-beautiful-look. Maybe I'm making up things that do not exist. Am I? Well, I'm just beginning to get militant. God help me if I should land down home in this mood - [I'd] be in prison after day one. [...]

I've listened to the tapes many times. Well, I'm not going to criticize your colleagues - so let's deal with you. Slip-ups are perfectly forgivable and happen to the best. The important thing is not to let the public know - and you do that well - a great rule and advantage in performing. You know as well as I do what did not go well and those are the things to take care of in subsequent performances. I was indeed happy to note that you do not sing every phrase with your capital, that not all cadences have that finality and that your word colouring and pronunciation show miles of improvement. Keep the whip on yourself. [...]

Wednesday, 26 March

Well, I do procrastinate for sure!

It's leave-Lisbon-time and I've got to the airport too early in my anxiety to get out of this place - a whole 68 minutes before schedule. So what better than to try and finish this letter [...].

Now where have I got to - let's talk about Lisbon - an upside down season. 1st opera was *Manon Lescaut* - with Plácido Domingo billed as star - well, he cancelled by telegram on the day he was supposed to report for duty. Afterwards it leaked out that he was afraid to make his Portuguese debut in that opera - the tenor role is a bastard - and the public would expect more from such a publicised name. And then as he is one who sings nearly every night or other night he is tired. So the problem here was, that the only reason they were doing *Manon Lescaut* was because of him - they instead had cancelled the Massenet *Manon* with Freni many months before (and this was what enticed me here - so I already lost out before coming). So there the theatre sat with *Manon* and no Domingo. Of course, there was an

---

399 Jephtas had just turned 32.
400 *Recte*: 54.
401 Jephtas refers here to Gerald Samaai who sang the role of Alfredo in what turned out to be Eoan's last production of Verdi's *La traviata*. It seems that he could not remember Samaai's name at the time of writing and therefore referred to him by the role of Beppe/Arlecchino that Samaai sang in Eoan's 1972 performance of *Pagliacci*.

understudy who stepped in – but you know the business – to affront a public expecting a name needs courage, and understudies general[ly] are newcomers hoping for a break. Well, the public booed, and booed; so [for] the next performance he was replaced. The soprano was nothing too special, neither bad either – she was probably chosen to level the expenses – Domingo must be in the $15.000 a night bracket.

Next was *Rigoletto* and [Piero] Cappuccilli called in sick which he was; but as the soprano ([Ileana] Cotrubas)[402] and the tenor ([Alfredo] Kraus)[403] are excellent it got by fine with a baritone replacement.

Next was *Samson and Delilah* in French – well in the last few years I have been trying to pick up the language with not too much success – I fear [to] admit that I have no talent for remembering how to pronounce it – though I did study the music pretty much. Though I must have another go at it – Zurich asked me to prepare *Werther* for them in 1977 (again with Domingo) and in French – I'm thinking about it. *Samson & D* is a pain in the arse – I never quite figured out all the details of the plot – and my biblical memory is vague. Everybody comes to see the Temple crashing down which is the final 30 seconds of the opera – so it's a long wait, though true, she does have "Softly awakes my heart" and 2 other very pretty arias – and [Viorica] Cortez really was very good the way she manipulated singing now-in-the-nose-now-in-the-mask as the French language demands. The Italians, of course, simply forget about the nose-bit. I did my tit bits of conducting – most of Act I [of] *Rigoletto* is backstage orchestra – and [in] *Manon* I had my trumpet and flute, etc. – man, I'm learning.

Now I'm back to Zurich – in and out because of concerts in Italy in April – then May to prepare *Boccanegra* – now that is a wonderful opera – the pre-*Otello* genius of Verdi and I'm having a really [good] time studying it. Having given up my Milan apartment I will have to do most of my practising in Zurich and commute to Italy – Mabel and Joseph did offer – but hell, I'm so independent, and really more than that, I hate to cause disturbances – for one or two days [it's] fine, but a whole month would be an exaggeration.

I hate traveling – or better, I've had enough of the carrying suitcases; fighting with taxi drivers, putting up with those customs people who rummage through everything in such a way that the case no longer can close, because it was badly packed to start with, and then waiting around. I think I need a break – something like selling stamps or insurance. What do you think?

I need a cup of coffee – I decided to stop boozing yesterday – but I will start again tomorrow – my liver is very unhappy with me so I relented and thought to give it a little chance to catch up. [...]

Much love to all,
Gordon.

---

402 Ileana Cotrubas (*1939), Romanian soprano.
403 Alfredo Kraus (1927–1999), Spanish tenor.

70

[Opernhaus], [Zurich], [Switzerland]

13 June [1975], Friday

Hi there May,

Every now and then, or better, ever so often I have these days of utter desolation and solitude – and I am really so alone – not for the fact that I've never had the wish to make a liaison with another person – but for the fact that in these moments I never have the possibility of picking up the phone and dialing a number to a friendly ear who would merely be interested to listen to my artistic fears and musical doubts that have accumulated with time. To want to be a good musician and artist demands much sacrifice and heavy payments – literally in blood. So in such a moment of weakness – no, that is not the exact word, but I can't find an English equivalent – I turn to you to bombard you with my words and uncertainties because of all the people I know, you have been the closest to understand my artistic ideals without a great exchange of words, maybe largely out of intuition or sensibility, yet never ridiculing my ideas when not understood. And for this mutual respect I always endeavour to keep up a correspondence with you.

One is surrounded by people – and for someone like me, people smell the possibility of glory and hang-on, making inane and stupid comments to which one is constricted to answer with the perennial stage smile – but leaves no satisfaction. Well, we all play the game – so do I in order to climb the steps of the ladder – but there are the days when it is a real pain in the arse.

The artist is constantly surrounded by fears – the insecurity which surrounds the possibility of where he knows he wants to get to – whether he will have the strength or the courage is another story.

I'm writing you a whole lot of unconnected philosophical and nonsense thoughts – maybe if the word consequences do not make sense, maybe in between the lines you will understand what plagues me today.

In one way I have been very lucky in the sense that I have worked also with the very best and always commanded the maximum of respect for my own efforts – but this very advantage creates the disadvantage that one expects this maximum and that is not always possible.

Every while I get letters from other friends at home with cryptic comments like "do you still have to wait around for whatever comes your way" – and I spend weeks trying to understand what they mean to know – and then even more weeks to unfathom our coloured mentality – my own way of thinking has been so tainted by my Italian sojourn – that I don't even know where to start; and it seems to me that to write me compliments is not necessary – yet to deny my activities is equally as undesirable. I make what I do for myself; but all these people will readily bask in the glory if I get a 1st page spread in the *Cape Argus*; and then begin to pick the holes afterwards. Is that the provinciality of the South African society – or my imagination? – after all, a "spade" is supposed to be a "spade" (and in England, "spade" refers to a person who is not white and British).

I am so thrilled about the Eoan Group's overseas visit because I really want to work and pass on to all the artists what I have learnt – of course what has taken me 10 years to learn cannot be taught in 15 days – but it is better than nothing.[404] I do so hope not to be completely misunderstood by whoever is coming – my biggest competitor will no doubt be "the white man"[405] – but I mean to fight that in my way – for me [it] is important to impart that we coloureds have something to offer – once we have learnt what is required and forget our humiliation problem; be proud of what we are and make the very most of what we have going for us. Then we can get on to the job of perfecting our good things.

I talked with Benny [Benjamin Arendse] on the phone and was so appalled that he had simply not gone to see your *Traviata* – whatever his reasons, none of which I'm aware of – but art conquers all of that. Well, I remain baffled.

Hey, I hear you have television in S.A. soon[406] – how about some information.

I have written enough shit to you – churn it about; throw it away – whatever you prefer.

Cannot wait to hear something from you.

Much respect,

Yours,

Gordon.

71

Opernhaus, Zurich, Switzerland

3 July [1975], Thursday

Hi there May,

Well honey, here I am making another attempt at writing and answering your oh-so-welcome letter of last week. 20 million thanks for all the interesting news and things.

It is supposed to be summer (officially since June 21st) but alas it has been raining buckets full – or rather rivers full – and today is the first sunny day after 8 particularly lousy ones (you might well say, this is Europe after all – so it is judging from the weather!) [...] .

Friday, 11 July (mid-afternoon)

I must be the world's greatest procrastinator, second only to you probably. You've got to admit that I am making a good try of the championships. Talking about championships – just this week I saw Black Arthur Ashe beat white [Jimmy] Connors at the Wimbledon tennis.[407] I don't know tennis and rarely watch T.V. but for some reason that day I watched. Now that man is a great at his game – cool, calculated, dignified and a winner – never heard of him before – yet went to No. 1 on my list of people to be admired – and up for the "non-white-cause".

How am I feeling now? I get kinda ashamed when I let my depressions dominate when they come. I figure you understand – they come and go – so that's not the last of the story yet. To answer the question – yes, things are just dreaming away with innumerable possibilities.

About our coloured folk – well, I suppose one has to accept and resign to the fact that because of our "cut-our-noses-to-spite-our-faces" attitude we will never ever get anywhere

---

404 Jephtas travelled to England to work with the Eoan Group when they visited the UK in the summer of 1975.
405 He probably means Joseph Manca, who was known to be jealous of attention and praise given to others.
406 TV was only introduced to South Africa in 1976.
407 Arthur Ashe (1943–1993), African-American tennis player, who beat Jimmy Connors in the Wimbledon final in 1975.

as a people – such a thought bothers me frequently – yet who am I to want to change things – my name is not even Florence Nightingale nor Joan of Arc.

"Negative ideas destroy, positive [ideas] build" – true, right? To admit a truth, after all these years, I've never understood whether the Eoan motto is "live to serve (oneself)" or "live to serve (others)" – for my personal self the former is more just, but probably the second is the right answer.

True I will also give 12 masterclasses in conjunction with the London Opera Centre programme – but what it boils down to as things now stand – is that I will make musical preparations for the Opera Centre programme which centres on acting, dialogue, etc. My original idea was straight master-classes but in the end a compromise had to be made because of venue, administrative, etc problems and the desire to have the groupers experience as many varied things as possible. [...]

Lots of luck to all 42 of you for your final South African concerts up north, and your socializing with the British ambassador[408] and all – so "chic" all of you – [I] am grey with envy – eat as much as you can.

Yes, I know about a Eoan concert in Cardiff. Well, thank heavens, finally I will hear the singers in the flesh – and honest, I am looking forward to it. [...] [I]f possibly you have a choice, I would choose always "Casta Diva" for you in Britain:[409] Traviata's are many in England – and again you let yourself in [for] comparison from Miss Callas/Sutherland/Cotrubas down to Miss West and Jerico. *Norma* precedes only Callas, Sutherland and nobody would expect you to be better – so whatever result, and you will no doubt do your best, you will be judged on your terms. You might not agree, but calculation in every sense is perhaps the most important aspect in the music business. Now after all this, you might probably end up having no choice in the matter at all.

Saturday, 12 [July] (in the sun)

[...]

About Callas – 2 things happened just the time of her South African dates. First, di Stefano's 21-year-old daughter died of cancer in Milan which split the party – then Onassis was admitted to hospital and she immediately returned to Paris. He consequently died and as the Italian papers put it "the true widow of Onassis is La Callas". Consequently Callas is in refuge in Florida, U.S.A. and singing is probably the last thing she wants to do.

Well, you have 15 days to departure (and less when you get this) – have a good flight and study time in Aberdeen – it is summer, but make sure you have an umbrella – see you in London – and I don't expect to hear from you too much as you probably have much else to care to. I will be in Zurich mostly, except from those short journeys away. Have much fun – don't expect too much from Aberdeen, nor the Scottish, but have fun and good luck.

Ciao,

Gordon.

[...]

---

408 A reception at the South African Embassy in London, hosted by the Ambassador, was planned for the Group on 27 August 1975. Roos (2018): 168.
409 Abrahamse performed an aria during Eoan's concerts on their tour to the United Kingdom.

Figure 4.8 Gordon Jephtas and Ismail Sydow in London during the 1975 tour of the Eoan Group.
Source: Eoan Group Archive.

72

Opernhaus, Zurich 8001, Schweiz

Zurich
25 November [1975]

Hi there May,

So many, many thanks for your letters, press cuttings, etc. – all of which was so interesting to me.

Here I am to make an answer; and I really would like to write you a million-page letter to explain my feelings good and bad – but I don't have the courage because I don't think I can put my thoughts across even to you – probably the only person who understands how I function, etc.

I find myself in a very solitary world, in spite of all the present glorification[410] – but what is that anyway? I am *not* coming to [South Africa] in January as I so genuinely hoped and planned for. The fault is completely mine – I am cheeky, aggressive and direct about business, and what have you – so, I goofed and apparently ballsed up more than everything with the result that everything is off until '77. I feel I am letting you down badly, & I can only come to S.A. if I have the mental & positive assurance of having people of your artistic mentality *and* preparation around me.

As things stand, I am interested in "now" or "never", so I am not going to make any promises nor ask any promise from you. You follow your own nose to suit your needs and

---

410   Jephtas is probably referring to the good mood in the Group after they returned from their tour in the UK. This did not last long, however. Manca resigned from the Group in 1977 with no contingency plans in place. Overall relations must have soured, as no official farewell for him was held. Roos (2018): 169-173.

desires - and the rest - who knows. I AM SORRY. Our recitals mean so much to me, because they would be another beginning for EVERYBODY - but .... [sic] [...]

Forgive me, I am sorry, what can I do? - and if you don't hear from me for months - it is not because I don't care - I do - that's my problem - but probably because I need to clear my head about me and S.A. You are a great artist - and that you will always be - my greatest misfortune is not being able to make other great events with you *now*, but I keep on HOPING.

Ciao till who knows when.

Gordon.

73

Hotel Borges, Rua Garrett, 108, Lisboa - 2 , Portugal

22 January [1976]

Hi there!

I simply can't do without writing to you - so here I am, once again from Lisbon. Have been here since the beginning of the month - in fact, I arrived here with a very heavy New Year's Eve hangover; and consequently now trying to cure my liver and kidneys who have decided they do not like me at all.

But jokes aside - *Aida* opened 4 days ago with [Fiorenza] Cossotto - who ate up the floor-boards and made one think the opera should be called Amneris. Aida is the Mexican Gilda Cruz-Romo[411] of Metropolitan fame - okay. Tonight is [the] 2nd performance with [a] change of tenor - a young new one called [Nicola] Martinucci,[412] who, judging from the rehearsal, might very easily screw the high note in [the aria] "Celeste Aida". Later we have the Requiem and then *Ballo in maschera* with [Carlo] Bergonzi. Conductor [Gianandrea] Gavazzeni[413] cancelled much to my regret; but instead there are [Fernando] Previtali[414] and [Francesco] Molinari-Pradelli[415] - who really know the operas - every detail - nothing is left in the air. I have been sitting at the piano with my mouth hanging open, trying to seep in everything; and thanking my lucky stars.

I am not going to talk about me and Eoan - but I need a great favour from you.

Television has arrived in Cape Town - right. What I need to know is what Television sets cost - maybe you can get a brochure or simply inquire at the stores [...]

I am here until February 20th [...]

Ciao,

and thanks,

Gordon.

[P.S.] *Aida* is an awful bore of an opera - full of beautiful tunes one after the other, but nothing happens, and I have my hands full keeping 8 Egyptian trumpets in tune - not to talk about the 30 wind instruments a mile away from the stage. I go out of my mind, because we have to play one beat ahead in order to sound together with the orchestra [in the pit].[416]

---

411   Gilda Cruz-Romo (*1940), Mexican soprano.
412   Nicola Martinucci (*1941), Italian tenor.
413   Gianandrea Gavazzeni (1909-1996), Italian pianist and conductor.
414   Fernando Previtali (1907-1985), Italian conductor.
415   Francesco Molinari-Pradelli (1911-1996), Italian conductor.
416   *Aida* requires an onstage and an offstage "banda" in addition to the orchestra in the pit; Jephtas was obviously responsible for one or both of them.

74

Hotel Borges, Rua Garrett, 108, Lisboa – 2, Portugal

Lisbon
23 February [1976]

Hi there May, [...]

Thanks millions and more millions – I got all your mail in one jumbo lump – that is, 3 letters from Zurich got forwarded and your latest of Feb[ruary] 10ᵗʰ. [...]

I am thrilled to bits that you finally got around to doing the SABC concerts – it was about time. But you've done it, and congratulations. [...]

Here in Lisbon the winter is okay – the sun has been around often enough – at the worst it has been raining. I hear that in Milan and Zurich it is snowing like all hell has broken loose.

So Andrew Downie[417] is down there. I've read your views and personally I cannot agree more. I figure I should tell you the whole story from my point of view, so at least somebody will know what's happened. I would prefer to keep this between us for now. I have no intention of letting things continue this way – especially as it concerns me; and I must find a solution – and I mean to; for good or bad.

Some 3 years ago along with one of my famous negotiations to return to Eoan, came this proposal to do a musical comedy – me to conduct, Didi for dance – and director Andrew Downie. Andrew I knew from my Opera Centre days, also having worked with him in 2 productions and having coached his wife – Marion Studholme[418] – who sings much in S[outh] A[frica]. Well, I made a trip to London for the preliminary negotiations. Here I must intercede for a moment. Musical comedy is not my thing – I work in Italian opera which is something else – [in] Musical comedy, the emphasis is on the spoken word; dance routines, catchy tunes mostly with some kind of jazz beat, the scenic & stage decorations. But I consider myself [a] musician and can only work from the music as a basis. [...] Well, the whole thing fell through, and Mr. Sydow felt that my refusal [resulted in] the whole project going to shit. But I had to continue to say that musical comedy is not for me – but that fell on deaf ears; and understandably from their point of view, I was to blame. But what could I do? – (I kinda suggested [that] they get a black director from the States, but somehow the stars favoured Downie = exactly why I still don't know.) I could not start out by making artistic concessions within myself because it would from one thing snowball into more; and I could not place my own serious attitude to my work in jeopardy in order to make some people happy. This state of affairs contributed considerably to the refusal of our recitals; but we patched relationships and tried again. This time I handed the whole matter to London Associates because I was becoming too cheeky in handling and needed a smooth approach; and better if I kept my mouth shut. [...]

Well, so [after this] everybody goes home – I in Zurich – things look like we are going some place – finally – but the Eoan Group needs time to consider the finances. Half way through this period, I get an offer from the theatre in Catania (Italy) for 5 months work – what particularly attracted me was a new Bellini opera with Renata Scotto. So I get on the phone and ask for a decision from Eoan so I could arrange my life; and make my decisions. Next thing, the Eoan Group is annoyed that I wanted to speed up their decision – '76 was therefore out;

---

417   Andrew Downie (1922-2009), Scottish actor and singer who worked with the Eoan Group during their UK tour in 1975.
418   Marion Studholme (1927-2016), English soprano.

but '77 is being considered. Meanwhile the Andrew affair was getting preference from both London Associates (whom I thought were acting as *my* agents and [looking after] *my* interests). The British Council had conceded him a grant to go to SA and check it out; and see about this musical comedy (finally and irretrievably, everybody understanding, without me – and perfectly okay with me) – But I got the cools considering that Mr. White[419] gets preference. So that's where we stand, and it doesn't seem that I'm going to get anywhere.

I must add that Andrew will work on a shoe-string budget – it is his speciality and I do admire his work only because of that event [but] I can't work with him – it wouldn't get anyone anyplace.

I hope you do not get angry about all this which in the long run is so childish. I would just like somebody to know; *but preferably not say anything* – it would only make matters worse.

In the end I did not accept the Catania job [...]

So, you saw Jo[seph] Gabriels – yes, his mother died and we missed each other in Milano. Relationships there are somewhat cool too because I backed out of a gramophone record we were to cut together. Why, because artistically we did not go 100% with each other and again, like my usual stubborn self, I cannot bring myself to make compensations in that area. Jo and I are very close and I have been very worried and sad that his career had not got off its feet. Evidently, voice is not enough for making a career. Mutual friends in Milan are always on to me because they think that I am the one who should help and advise. But, I can't advise on how to make a career. So, I do hope that the talk of his singing with CAPAB holds true[420] – he needs a break – and with that voice deserves to sing more. [...]

Aida was not without tragedy – after the 2nd performance; 3 of the Egyptian trumpeters got killed in a motor accident. Then Cossotto came down with a heavy flu and a performance had to be cancelled one hour before [the start of the show] – they flew in a substitute but her plane could not land in Lisbon because of fog – the performance went on 2 days later without Cossotto – by this time the tenor had the flu too and packed up in Act III. Disaster – disaster.

The Requiem fared better – Cossotto got well and sang gloriously, soprano Raina Kabaivanska – good; more tenor trouble – Bergonzi cancelled because he got called to sing *Aida* at La Scala – the tenor that came, picked [up] the flu too – sang but packed up and got replaced at performance no 2. [The] conductor was [Fernando] Previtali.

Ballo has had better luck. Bergonzi arrived.

Maestro [Francesco] Molinari-Pradelli is today what Serafin was in the Callas period. It was a great privilege to work with him and my greatest triumph was to have a compliment from him – usually he is tight-lipped and rather unpleasant – but he said I was "formidable" – which means, I suppose, extraordinary – and after the 1st piano rehearsal Bergonzi led a round of applause for my playing. Well, I was very prepared and did play the shits out of the piano. Bergonzi is extremely professional, not so young, but that hardly matters when he sings. An exemplary school of singing – a maximum ease and constant use of the mask. Beautiful words – the gentleman of tenors they call him. And that he is. [The] soprano is Rita Malaspina,[421] who I know from Milano's singer studio days.[422] [...] Tomorrow back to Milano and the snow.

---

419 Jephtas means Downie's skin colour.
420 This also failed to come about. In an interview for Radio South Africa at the SABC that was recorded on 17 May 1988, Gabriels apparently expressed his disappointment with CAPAB, though his comments were censored by his interviewer and the interview was never broadcast. The interviewer, John Orr, left the following remarks on the worksheet accompanying the tape: "I've done some basic cleaning up [of the tape] so that it flows better, and have taken out a couple of rudenesses at the end about CAPAB". See SABC Sound Archives, catalogue number TM 7115/88.
421 Rita Orlandi-Malaspina (1937-2017), Italian soprano.
422 Jephtas means the time he accompanied for Llopart, the singing teacher in Milan.

Talking about Callas. I am always so impressed when working in these circles that there exists a most profound admiration for her work. Very, very often you hear phrases like "Here Callas did this". She really created a school of opera which the best professionals are still studying from. Went to lunch with Cossotto and she too began talking of the "great Callas" - they had sung together often enough - especially *Norma*. [...]

Am back in Zurich after Easter - for *Traviata* - that is mid-April and I must study *Werther* (Massenet) in French. [...]

For now, au revoir - don't despair - I am not - or at least trying not to.

Many thanks for all,

Ciao, and love to all.

Gordon.

75

Opernhaus, Zurich, Schweiz

Wed[nesday] 28 April [1976]

Hi there May,

I find myself home unusually early and in receipt of your writing and the newspaper cuttings. Thanks! [...]

About [Marita] Napier[423] - no, I don't know her - she's a friend of Joe & Mabel [Gabriels] - to tell the truth, I've never heard her sing - but her fame I know about - [Nello] Santi told me she's hopeless in Italian opera - and rightfully she sticks to German opera & making a big name - over here at any rate - in S.A. she will no doubt venture into the Italian, because all German opera stars would give their hind teeth to sing the Italian stuff. - She is smart - and our paths do not meet - nor do I have any interest to work with her. [...]

I really do care about that Eoan - I don't know why? If I knew what's good for me, I'd say "screw it" and continue my own business around here where I'm well enough established to make much money, be comfortable, etc. Well, my nature likes change and fighting - unfortunate me! [...]

My education idea has got off to a shit, shit start. Your teachers may be white (which is supposed to be a symbol of superiority) but seem hopelessly inadequate. What a mess. Let me think about it. What a horrible, horrible mess. Keep courage - I need you & the more experienced to keep some kind of light burning. Using Dagmar Foster books[424] - hopeless. Of course, I know them. No good for singers. [...]

You ask am I more happy with my more talented colleagues. Not true. The Eoan Group is talented. Here talent does not come into question - it's a different story - professionalism - like [Marita] Napier says "singing is not just a matter of voice". This is necessary for me - at home I am boss simply because I have been around more - here I work hard - know what I'm supposed to do, etc. Today was a wonderful day of *Traviata* rehearsals - Santi is fantastic - no detail is left undiscussed and rehearsed - and [Maria] Chiara,[425] not to mention [Piero]

---

423 Marita Napier (1939-2004), South African soprano.
424 Music theory books, translated into Afrikaans and published in 1968.
425 Maria Chiara (*1939), Italian soprano.

Cappuccilli and [Gianni] Raimondi[426] have been singing *Traviata* for at least 20 years. Opera is a wonderful Art – and the Eoan Group can get somewhere there too. Let's not pretend too hard – this is the highest world level – but Eoan can & must aspire & maybe in 20 years they can sing at La Scala – but that's not [in] my or your life unfortunately. We have to pioneer [it], though! [...]

Don't worry about Manca's tempo suggestion about *Rigoletto* – as far as I'm concerned it only demonstrates his lack of confidence. [...]

You will sing *Aida*, *Bohème* & *Butterfly* duets – it is INSANITY – I'd tell them to go to HELL. Maybe better not do anything until after your Sunday night date.

Let me not complain any more about the local inefficiency. Poor Eoan singers – you deserve better – you have so much to offer.

You say – "well, we live & learn" –

I say – "shit, *when* will we live & learn?"

What to wear – if you can fix something soft & [the] bluest [of] blue, *fine* – no gestures for [the] duet – [but] gestures for *Tosca* & *Vespri* by all means – *Tosca*, tragic gestures – *Vespri*, happy ones. Strangely enough, today in rehearsal [we] came into discussing gestures – Santi said, fast gestures like the Americans do, mean nothing – and all the singers, specially Chiara, agreed that fewer and slower gestures mean much, much more in theatre. Think about it.

It's raining here too – in fact snow – shit – Well, you can't have everything.

Tomorrow is *Traviata* dress rehearsal – [I] have an early call with [the] stage orch[estra] of Act I – May 1st is LABOUR DAY – 1st performance [is on] May 2.

Werther has been postponed until '78 – instead LUCIA – just as well for me and my French.

[I] really, really hope that I can get to work with Eoan because although the management & teaching is largely shit – all you singers are yearning for a decent music & singing education – and I am eager – more than ever.

Ciao for now ...

Gordon

P.S. [...] Is [Marita] Napier too heavy for Mimi?[427] – I wouldn't say so from what I know. Nobody ever said Mimi is a coloratura. [Mirella] Freni, the finest Mimi of our day has *voice* – all opera needs voice – Italian opera anyway...... and Napier is not Birgit Nilsson – does that make any sense?

Gordon.

---

426 Presumably the tenor Gianni, not Ruggero Raimondi (*1941), Italian bass-baritone.
427 The character in Puccini's *La bohème*.

Opernhaus, Zurich, Schweiz

Zurich
Tuesday, 18 October [1976]

Hi there May –

For weeks and days I'm thinking and wanting to get around to answering all your letters, but my tape-recorder is playing such shit with me; – so I'm hoping for it to recover or whatever.

I write about a more urgent matter. I need your ear, and advice and suggestions.

About our recital – when I was in Cape Town I talked with a friend, Kevin Kent,[428] [who] also is company manager for CAPAB – about handling this venture on a manager basis, etc. I know I probably should have asked Sydow but I cannot mess around or be messed around – more so if the initial capital is mine – and I prefer a strictly professional basis. Family, money and art don't go together, do they?[429]

I have now heard from Kevin after I finally decided what I wanted to do in terms of this recital – I plan to be in Cape Town from July through Sept. [1977] and wanted [the] Nico Malan [Theatre]'s date during the middle of Sept. The only free date left is July 29, [a] Friday, which has been provisionally booked. Is Friday a bad day for a public? – Is July 29 too soon in terms of you and I getting together?

Where else could one go? – what is your idea for the City Hall for a recital? – Have you ever been to the smaller hall at [the] Nico Malan where they stage plays – how would that be? In Cape Town someone suggested the Nico Malan foyer where they do have concerts. I rejected that – also it lowers the level too much my instincts say. What other places are there? Plumstead[430] sounds to hell and gone. Let me know what you think. I asked for a Saturday originally because of getting a public – [on] Thursday and Sunday one would have competition from [the] City Hall symphony concerts; and week-days are not so good in Cape Town – am I right supposing that? Let me know all as fast as you can.

Thanks. Till later –

Gordon.

---

428 Kevin Kent was appointed "New Music Organiser" at CAPAB in 1968.
429 In the light of his ambivalent feelings toward Ismail Sydow (with whom he lived during his youth when he was at the Eoan Group), it is significant that Jephtas still regards them as "family".
430 Presumably the "3 Arts Theatre" in the Cape Town suburb of Plumstead, which described itself as a multi-racial venue.

77

Opernhaus, Zurich 8001, Switzerland

Tuesday, 22 November [1976]

Hi there May,

Thanks for hearing from you. The only reason I've not written, or rather made myself heard, has been because none of my [tape] recorders are working and you know how I don't like to write so to try and beat my circumstances, I'm going to try and type my way through an answer.

Your last letter contained many tough things as regards Eoan and that is prompting me to get word to you. [...]

About your meeting – I'm very happy about two things and that is that you will have lights at the Joseph Stone place and the social club[431] ...

About you starting a drama class. I have millions of furies in my head and just wish I could talk instead of writing.

Now this new shit is all the wrong idea. Here I must step in and say my fill. I was the one who moved my arse about getting you and Ron[ald Theys] into that course with the idea of you helping *the singers* in stagecraft – drama is not your business – opera is. And that is exactly what I talked to Robert Mohr[432] about and why he suggested this particular course. Now why would you want to go and frustrate yourself by running a drama course? – there are others [who can do this] – [like] Peter Voges,[433] Bill Curry.[434] And if both you and Ronny went [to the course], why only you? That's a load of shit.

I suggest you go to Sydow and turn the whole thing down and tell him what my intentions were, and *if they permit you & Ron to do something with the singers – then fine*. Otherwise no [...]. Do you understand? – this shit is backfiring in a most undesirable [way] and I would not tolerate it for nothing. And if Sydow doesn't want to understand or whatever, then refer him back to me. He will not speak with me, but probably with Didi [Sydow's daughter]. – but anyway, then you can wash your hands of this situation. Unless of course, you want to start a drama school or whatever. I really feel shit the way this has turned out and why should you pay those prices?

From what I understand from you also those theory classes have turned into shit.

Most times I feel it is best to just give up on the Group the way the present circumstances are – and then on the other hand, so much could be done and is possible. I don't know. Maybe you and I are only dreaming, or what? [...]

Until later,
Thanks for all.
Yours,
Gordon.

---

431 At this time, the Group was launching several new initiatives at the Joseph Stone Auditorium in a bid to reinvent itself within the coloured community. The social club was part of that.
432 Robert Mohr (1925–1984), South African actor, head of the Drama Department at UCT.
433 Peter Voges (1937–2019), South African dancer, actor and theatre administrator.
434 Bill Curry (1931–2015), South African actor and director.

Opernhaus, Zurich, Switzerland

6 February 1977

My dear May,

How have you been? And what's happening down your way?

I'm okay – at least, I think so. Zurich Opera had a disastrous *Lucia* opening last night – the vocal and music company okay – but the scenery, stage-director and costume designer booed – and booed – and booed. Well, during the rehearsal we the music people hardly ever got to terms with the staging people – they had in mind a Polanski[435]/The Exorcist[436] type production – but the music of Donizetti is romantic – so the booing was not so much of a surprise – but the pressure of working under such unartistic conditions has been just too much for me to deal with, with the result that I am going to renounce the contract I signed here until 1979. It has been too hazardous – and I'm too old[437] for dealing with experiments and amateurism.

Amateurism, I wanted to deal with with [*sic*] Eoan but they turned me down so brutally – evidently they do not want my presence down there – so screw them.

Thank you for all your letters – tapes – cuttings – all of which have been so much appreciated. Your *Ernani* aria impressed me so much that it spurred me even more for our recital. Now, unfortunately, I've had this offer to work in S[outh] America from July-September[438] – and it is an offer I cannot turn down in the interests of my own career, so I must again delay our recital to a later date. Forgive me – but I am sure you understand. Maybe just as well, because I think it would be impossible for me to be in Cape Town preparing our recital and not be able to do some work with the Group – after I came out and gave of my time,[439] etc., they turn out so mean and hard. Shit man, I tried. They don't want me; – so that's that.

And now I learn that [David] Tidboald[440] will not have me near the CAPAB organization – so that's that too. Too bad for me.

So with all this carry [on], it would be just as well not to show my face in Cape Town for a while.

You know the greatest thing about the [1971] Durban recital was everybody was for us – now in Cape Town, too many things are anti-me which would just be unproductive artistically. What shit – but we will fight and win – at least for Art.

I ask you to understand that I cannot turn down this S[outh] American offer – to hold your faith and your courage – and deal with Eoan in whatever way is to your advantage – and your advantage only.

Am here till 1 July.

Much good wishes to all – and I believe so much in your work and art that I am just so heart-sore that we cannot do this recital now – but I believe, we will overcome.

Ciao

Gordon

---

435 Roman Polański (*1933), Polish-French film director.
436 A 1973 supernatural horror film directed by William Friedkin.
437 Jephtas was 33, turning 34 in March.
438 The details of this offer are unclear; however, two newspaper articles mention that Jephtas had worked in Venezuela. See Winston (1983) and Paulos (1986).
439 It is unclear what Jephtas means here. His last professional interaction with Eoan was in 1975 in London when he gave masterclasses to singers of the Group at the International Festival of Youth Orchestras.
440 David Tidboald (1926-2018), British-born South African conductor, the chief conductor of the Cape Performing Arts Board (CAPAB) in the 1970s.

[Transcription of a "letter" to May on cassette tape, Zurich, 20 February 1977][441]

[Side 1]
Today is Sunday 20 February and I thank you for your letters and for your tape. Which, all of which I'm gonna try and answer all in one go. How've you been out there? I'm doing just fine getting along in the rain, in the cold, in the shit that we're having right now, which I hate so very much; thank God there's no wind otherwise, it would be really the end. [...] You asked about my New York visit. Well I went to the United States this time, really to find work for 1979, 1980, and [Nello] Santi was going to be conducting at the Metropolitan at the same time and so my visit coincided with his, and we saw each other in New York City and I went to ... one performance at the Metropolitan, and he of course was very pleased to have me there and he told me to come by and see him in the dressing room blah blah blah blah blah because it was a big prestige deal to have his assistant from Zurich out there too. ... After this performance I went to the dressing room afterwards, it was *Tosca*,[442] Grace Bumbry[443] who was now a soprano, and Sherrill Milnes[444] and [Giuseppe] Giacomini, who I knew from Milano, so we all knew each pretty well ... when I was in the dressing room afterwards, the artistic director[445] of the Metropolitan came in and ... greeted me like he knew who I was: "Maestro" here and "Maestro" there and when he'd gone, Mrs. Santi turned to me and said: "Do you know who that is? He knows you" and I said: "I don't know; who is he?" and she mentioned some name which I didn't know [...] ... Afterwards, we all went to this cocktail party, in the Metropolitan. ... They asked me to come and speak with them, which was very nice, because I went to the United States to look for work, but not at the Metropolitan, because I didn't, I don't feel that I am ready to go to the Metropolitan right yet, my aim was San Francisco and Chicago, and Miami [...] Anyway, I went and saw the Metropolitan people and they were very nice ... When I first went to the States about 1971, I think, it was the same office and the same everything, so this time I went as a received person and the champagne was flowing, the red carpet was open, they were very friendly and we talked for an hour, and they are very interested in having me work for them and they think that I could be of great use to the Metropolitan and they want me to meet the chief conductor, [James] Levine,[446] which I couldn't do at the time because I was leaving [...] the fact that I was Santi's assistant in Zurich was an added thing ... But that was very, very nice at the same time I feel very sad because here the Metropolitan was talking to me in this way, and back home in Cape Town, they just didn't want to know my business. [...] [...]

It seems to me that to come to South Africa right now is not the right thing to do. I don't think I can be in Cape Town and not go to the Eoan Group and work with the singers and all that ... because I really care about the singers ... the Eoan Group have told me so bluntly that

---

441   We have here edited out minor repetitions, hesitations, "um"s and "er"s etc. without comment; larger omissions as usual are indicated by [...]
442   Santi conducted the singers mentioned here in six performances of *Tosca* at the Met from 18 December 1976 to 12 January 1977; it is not clear which of these Jephtas attended. See *Metopera Database*, http://69.18.170.204/archives/frame.htm, accessed August 2022.
443   Grace Bumbry (*1937), African-American mezzo-soprano, later soprano.
444   Sherrill Milnes (*1935), American baritone.
445   Perhaps Anthony Bliss, the general manager of the Met between 1975 and 1981. James Levine was the artistic director at the time, but was clearly not present on this occasion.
446   James Levine (1943-2021), American conductor and music director of the Metropolitan Opera from 1976 to 2016.

they don't want me at all ... it was no question of money because I offered them whatever price they could pay or nothing if they couldn't pay anything at all. But they've just turned the whole thing down so badly and I've been looking around here since I came back, in the meantime I've changed address again ... for the letter that they've sent me but I think I threw it away; I was just so angry or so upset or so sad at the time when I got this letter which was not even really written to me [...]

In the meantime, I have been unofficially approached by CAPAB to conduct an opera for them unofficially because David Tidboald is not too keen that I had been in Cape Town and be involved with CAPAB obviously, he has to protect his own skin ... but unofficially they've asked me to conduct *L'elisir d'amore* in April and May this year, which I unfortunately cannot do, but they did tell me that if I couldn't do that, there was the possibility of doing something else afterwards [...] ... I don't know how much power this Tidboald has to keep me out of there but we shall see. Anyway, I'm at the moment banking on coming out there to conduct an opera for them, and then doing our recital after [...] I have decided to wash my hands of the Eoan Group. You know, I have never been horny to make a career in Europe to become famous and all that stuff, all the things that I've done in the past, have been really as a stepping-stone, so that I could go back there and help my people. [...]

[there follows a long tirade against Ismail Sydow, the chairman of the Eoan Group, which closes with a complaint about Joseph Manca too]
[...]
You know, there are two things that I cannot tolerate. One thing is to be laughed at about my work and Sydow has done that time and time again [...] and the second thing I can't tolerate is to deal with people who don't know what they're doing – and this is exactly what is happening in Zurich Opera. In fact, just on Friday, I have finally cancelled my contracts here ... I talked at length with Santi on the phone, we saw each other in Zurich now that we were rehearsing *Nabucco* last week, we spent many hours talking together, and I told him how I felt you know my idea of amateurism is not the fact that you get paid or not paid, it's an attitude [...] Zurich Opera ... changed management[447] and a lot of people really don't know what they're doing [...] although the contracts that I have turned down [are worth] something like $40,000 [per annum], but money is not that important. ... In the meanwhile, I'm sure I will work out something. [...]

[Side 2 of the tape:]
Anyway, what I've decided: I'm gonna emigrate to the United States, I cannot deal with living in Europe anymore. I've had enough of seeing white people, I can't bear to see all these pale, pale people – I wanna vomit. And consequently, I am now dealing with moving to the United States and going to live there for the possibility of coming to work in Europe every now and then, and coming to South Africa every now and then, if this whole thing works out with CAPAB about conducting there and our recital[448] and so on for the beginning. I have a lot of possibilities in the United States – I talked with a whole lot of people, now I will have to see what will happen. [...] ... I cannot deal with living in Europe anymore and South Africa doesn't

---

447 It did not; the most recent change was the arrival of Claus Helmut Drese as Intendant in 1975. It is unclear what Jephtas means here.
448 Jephtas had been planning to accompany Abrahamse in a recital in South Africa; his rejection by Eoan at this time meant that these plans were shelved.

171

wanna know any of my stories, and the Americans are much, much more interested in what I do. So, I've decided that I'm gonna move out there. I dunno what will happen [...]. But that's how things stand at the moment ... Anyway, all the best and thank you very much for writing, and er, until another time, okay? You keep well, take care of your family and study the arias that you have, okay? Ciao, and thank you.

5. THE USA AND SOUTH AFRICA

5.1 "TO BE A COLOURED... IS AN ATTITUDE"

Ever since his very first visit to the USA in 1970 to attend a Boris Goldovsky opera workshop in Wheeling, West Virginia, Jephtas had longed to work in America. While he was there, he had remarked to a journalist of *The Intelligencer* newspaper: "Americans are more concerned about all aspects of art, instead of stressing only tradition as in Europe".[449] A number of subsequent opportunities did arise for him in the USA – at the New York City Opera (1970), Dallas Opera (1972) and the Chicago Lyric Opera (1973) – all of which he had been keen to pursue, though some obstacle always arose to prevent him. Either there were issues with work permits, or he was unavailable because he had been contractually engaged to work elsewhere. Finally, in 1977, fed up – he claimed – with "seeing white people",[450] he left Europe for North America. The opera scene there was hardly any less "white", though everyday life was much more multiracial.

Jephtas's first job in the USA was with the New York City Opera (NYCO), who appointed him their assistant conductor in 1977 (the same position that they had apparently offered him

Figure 5.1 May Abrahamse and Gordon Jephtas giving a recital in the Nico Malan Theatre (today Artscape) in Cape Town on 3 March 1979.
Source: Amanda Botha Private Collection.

---

449 Anon. (1970).
450 See his taped "letter" of 20 February 1977.

back in 1970, but which work-permit problems had thwarted). But Jephtas had only worked for two days at NYCO when he received a phone call from the Chicago Lyric Opera offering him a contract there instead. He accepted, resigning with immediate effect from NYCO, which was a regional opera company with local singers that Jephtas seems to have regarded as beneath his level of expertise. By contrast, the Chicago Lyric could afford international singers and was thus far more attractive to him. It was during this initial contract with the Chicago Lyric that Jephtas first coached the Italian tenor Luciano Pavarotti along with other top-notch singers such as Frederica von Stade and Luigi Alva.

Just over a year later, in January 1979, Jephtas accepted the post of artistic director to the Eoan Group and returned to South Africa. He was made responsible for planning, managing and co-ordinating the projects for all three sections of Eoan – dance, drama, and music. He wanted to revamp the image of the Group by shifting its main focus away from opera and by increasing the importance of the drama and dance sections. During his tenure, however, the only artistic project that came to fruition was a recital that he himself gave with May Abrahamse at the Nico Malan Theatre in Cape Town on 3 March 1979. He travelled back to the US shortly afterwards to resume his work at the Chicago Lyric, though he remained Eoan's artistic director, albeit working remotely. At some point in September or October 1979, Jephtas sent a blunt report to Eoan's executive committee articulating his perspective and his general concerns about the coloured community. His opinions were found deeply offensive, and the report was duly leaked to the *Cape Herald* newspaper, which made its contents public in an article entitled "'Coloured' Shock in Secret Eoan Report".[451] The original report seems to be no longer extant, but the reporter from the *Cape Herald* claimed that Jephtas had written of a need for coloured people to "stop imitating whites and instead to become self-reliant, developing a way of life peculiar to themselves". The article further quoted him as follows:

> We must begin to look at our own history, our own culture and our own neighbourhood. We must develop authentic coloured attitudes. We must have pride and see beauty in our colouredness. Being coloured is no longer a colour you see; it is an attitude.[452]

In the introductory chapter of this book, we noted how the first twelve years of Jephtas's correspondence with May Abrahamse suggest a negative, even resentful attitude towards his being coloured. From 1975 onwards, however, his letters intimate a reconciliation with who he was and with his own community. We cannot know to what extent his absence from South Africa had shifted his stance on coloured identity, but he was now in no mood to back down on his insistence that things had to change.

In response to the turmoil caused by the public discussion of his report, he gave a telephone interview to the Afrikaans newspaper *Rapport* that was published under the title: "You [i.e. coloured people] are just plain lazy!"[453] In it, Jephtas is adamant about wanting coloured people to depend on their own strengths to obtain what they want, and he asks: "How many of us truly reach the top and how far is the community willing to help themselves rather than waiting on others?"[454] He continued with a bluntness that was never going to be popular:

---

451 Salie (1979).
452 Jephtas, as cited in Salie (1979).
453 Original in Afrikaans: "Julle is sommer vrek lui!". Sidego (1979).
454 Original in Afrikaans: "Hoeveel van ons kom werklik bo uit en hoe ver is die gemeenskap bereid om homself te help eerder as om bakhand op ander te wag?". Sidego (1979).

The coloureds have for far too long been sitting back and waiting for people outside their country's borders to help improve their circumstances. Excuses about why they can't help themselves are always abundant. This is just plain laziness! ... The absence of certain opportunities is not enough reason to make no attempt at bettering yourself. Yes, you are not on radio or television, but how many of you have jumped out and tried to gain experience in some way or other? If you had to take over a broadcasting station in the country tomorrow, would you be able to do it? ... It's us who must accept that our hair is different, that our skin colour is different, and then move on and prove ourselves as human beings. ... Accept yourself the way you are. To be a coloured is no longer a colour. It is an attitude.[455]

Professor Richard van der Ross, the rector of the University of the Western Cape in Cape Town (at the time a designated "coloured" university), suggested that Jephtas's statements should be ignored, as "he has been out of the country for a while and is obviously out of touch".[456] According to the *Cape Herald*, the coloured poet and playwright Adam Small responded to Jephtas's report by saying that "culturally and in every other way 'colouredism' and 'colouredising' must be rejected. 'Colouredism is a kind of sick romanticism'".[457] But the uproar led to Jephtas prematurely ending his contract as artistic director of Eoan. In October 1979, he sent them a telegram from the US, stating simply that he was "not capable of dealing with people with no identity".[458]

After leaving South Africa in 1979, Jephtas remained in the USA. In 1980, he married an African-American woman in Manhattan who was twenty years his senior, one Nellie M. Barno.

Figure 5.2 The Nico Malan Theatre, which opened in Cape Town in 1971 as a whites-only building. It opened to all races in 1975 and was renamed Artscape in 2001. Source: Wikimedia Commons, Olga Ernst.

---

455 Original in Afrikaans: "Die Kleurlinge het gans te lank agteroor gesit en wag dat mense van selfs ver buite sy land-grense hom moet kom help om sy lot te verbeter. Verskonings oor waarom hulle nie self kan inspring nie, is altyd volop. Dis sommer vrek luiheid. ... Die afwesigheid van sekere geleenthede is nie genoeg rede om geen poging aan te wend om jou daarvoor te bekwaam nie. Ja, julle is nie op radio of oor televisie nie, maar hoeveel van julle het nou al uitgespring en op een of ander wyse die ondervinding probeer opdoen. Kan julle môre, as julle moet, 'n uit-saaistasie in die land oorneem? ... Dis net ons wat moet aanvaar dat ons hare anders is, dat ons velkleur anders is en dat ons daarvandaan net moet voortgaan en onsself as mense bewys. Aanvaar jouself soos jy is. ... Om Kleurling te wees is nie langer 'n kleur nie. Dit is 'n houding (attitude)". Sidego (1979).
456 Van der Ross, as cited by Salie (1979).
457 Small, as cited by Salie (1979).
458 Eoan Group Archive, 67:511. "Post Office Telegraphs". 1979.

As he admitted openly to Roland Jung, a friend from his Zurich days who visited him in New York in the early 1980s, he had married purely to get a green card to enable him to live and work permanently in America.[459] Although Jephtas seems to have continued living an openly gay life there, as he had in Zurich, we have no concrete information about his relationships with men, neither for his Swiss years nor for his American years. His letters to Abrahamse maintained the pretence of being heterosexual and even suggest that he and Nellie Barno lived together for a while in the early 1980s, presumably to maintain the fiction of marital cohabitation (he told Jung he was afraid of being found out), and perhaps also to split the cost of an apartment in New York. He moved several times in New York, eventually taking an apartment at the Ansonia Hotel, which was popular with musicians and artists, though "it wasn't cheap", as Jephtas's friend and colleague Barbara Mahajan has recalled.[460] Compared to his Zurich years, Jephtas's finances seem to have plummeted in the US. We have no proof of how much he earned – in a letter to Abrahamse of 11 July 1982, he mentions getting between USD 25 and 35 an hour for private coaching, though he adds "… sounds great, but it isn't". Jephtas also told Roland Jung a specific reason for his lack of funds: "the drugs are expensive". This is the first time that we have any confirmation of Jephtas taking drugs.

It appears that Jephtas worked mainly in New York City from 1980 to 1985. He never got a permanent, full-time, salaried position as a vocal coach or accompanist, but remained a freelance musician. His résumés and publicity materials mention that he had worked at the Metropolitan Opera House, but two of his American friends have contradicted this information. According to the soprano Leavata Johnson: "No, he did not work at the Met. He was supposed to get a job at the Met but it fell through … But he was at all the other places … California, Chicago, other big opera houses",[461] and this is confirmed by the mezzo-soprano Barbara Mahajan: "I don't know why [James] Levine didn't hire him. Of course, he coached quite a few people who were at the Met … I know he had the interview [but …] he wasn't chosen".[462]

During the 1981 season of the San Francisco Opera, Jephtas coached the American tenor Neil Shicoff and was also engaged as a prompt. Shicoff had apparently insisted on being coached by Jephtas, who wrote to Abrahamse on 22 October 1981 that Shicoff "threw such a [scene] with management to have a daily 2-hour private coaching with me, because 'he is the best there is' (said Shicoff), and this theatre engaged me as prompter & not as coach". Back in New York, he coached from his apartment, accepted private engagements when singers such as Grace Bumbry wanted him as their prompt, and accompanied singers at auditions and recitals. In 1985, two New York colleagues of Jephtas – Barbara Mahajan and the soprano Barbara Christopher – founded a small, non-profit opera company called Opera Amici. They appointed Jephtas their opera coach and conductor, though he never actually conducted.[463] Mahajan recalls this time as follows:

> Gordon named the company "Opera Amici". After we got our funding, we started putting on pro-ductions. First, we were doing it with just piano and then we started doing it with orchestra. Barbara Christopher met … Sibylle Werner – a German girl who was a conductor and had her own orchestra. So Barbara convinced her to start playing with us. Gordon didn't conduct … He played the piano for the piano productions. He would play and sing other parts at the same time. He was really good.[464]

459   Interview with Roland Jung, 17 July 2022.
460   Interview with Barbara Mahajan, 25 October 2022.
461   Interview with Leavata Johnson, 25 October 2022.
462   Interview with Barbara Mahajan, 25 October 2022.
463   E-mail from Barbara Mahajan, 7 October 2022.
464   Interview with Barbara Mahajan, 25 October 2022.

In early 1986, Jephtas returned to South Africa as the chorus master and senior vocal coach for the opera company run by the Performing Arts Council of the Transvaal (PACT) in Pretoria. In an interview for the Eoan History Project in 2009, the South African soprano Emma Renzi explained that she had personally recommended Jephtas for this position because he was "absolutely excellent" and had "a lot of experience".[465] We have no details about how he was actually appointed, though the political authorities will have had to provide some form of dispensation because it was against the law for a coloured man to work for a white opera company. He entered the country on 15 March 1986[466] and apparently began at PACT in April 1986, in time to prepare the chorus for a production of Verdi's *La traviata* starring Mimi Coertse as Violetta and the Puerto Rican tenor Antonio Barasorda as Alfredo, directed by Neels Hansen and conducted by the Italian Alessandro Siciliani.[467] Besides training the chorus, Jephtas acted as prompt for the production.[468] He also played for outside soirées and helped with the preparations for gala concerts. His duties as chorus master, as listed in his letter of appointment of 23 June 1986 (thus issued several weeks after he had begun work), included "to conduct and coach all concerts given by the Permanent Chorus" and "to control musically [sic] the experimental Opera productions".[469] Jephtas is indeed later listed in an internal PACT document as the "music director" of a "workshop" production of Puccini's *Gianni Schicchi*. However, he left the country on 1 August 1986,[470] just 5 weeks after having been officially appointed, so did not conduct the production. He was not happy in Pretoria. Four years later, in a letter to his friend Ronald Theys, Jephtas intimated that there had been friction with Mimi Coertse.[471] In August 1986, he was appointed as a vocal coach to the Utah Opera in Salt Lake City, a position facilitated by Glade Peterson, the General Director of the Utah Opera, who knew Jephtas from their days in Zurich (Peterson had been the principal Italian tenor at the Zurich Opera in the mid-1970s, where his roles had included Verdi's Ernani under Nello Santi in autumn 1973 - presumably with Jephtas as répétiteur).[472] An article about Jephtas published in *The Salt Lake Tribune* on 5 October 1986 claimed that he had "agreed to accept a job for four months as a vocal coach" at the "invitation of the South African government", and while this was probably a post-facto excuse for having embarked on such a brief return to South Africa (he would not have been issued a comprehensive letter of appointment in late June if his contract had only a month still to run), this article also offers more details about what had supposedly transpired there:

> "I was interested in going back perhaps for those reasons of guilt - people telling me that since I was successful I owed it to my country. Well, I thought I could handle the rampant paranoia that exists there, but after two days I found I could not".

---

465 Renzi (2009).
466 Gordon Jephtas's passport, p. 7. Eoan Group Archive.
467 The information given in this paragraph about Jephtas's employment with PACT and the productions in which he was involved is taken from assorted documents for this year from the PACT archives held by the UNISA Library in Pretoria (no shelfmarks).
468 Letter from Johan Maré of PACT to the Personnel Department of 3 July 1986, carbon copy in the PACT archives in the UNISA Library in Pretoria (no shelfmark).
469 Letter from Neels Hansen of PACT to Gordon Jephtas of 23 June 1986, carbon copy in the PACT archives in the UNISA Library in Pretoria (no shelfmark).
470 Gordon Jephtas's passport, p. 9. Eoan Group Archive.
471 Letter from Jephtas to Ronald Theys, 14 May 1990. Eoan Group Archive: uncatalogued.
472 See Fierz (1973).

Jephtas was given accommodations in a white hotel, but could not invite his coloured friends to stay with him. He also was troubled when he would see a black man working for the police, trying to make a living. "I knew he was the unhappiest of all people. How must it be for him each night when he goes back to his black neighborhood knowing someone might place a tire around his neck and set fire to it because he is working for the government?".

And then there was the ultimate insult. Jephtas was told by the people who hired him that negotiations were under way to make him an honorary *white* citizen of South Africa.

"They just basically assumed that I wanted to be white," said Jephtas, with a hint of anguish showing in his usually gentle face. "I have always been very proud to be a coloured man, proud of the things I have accomplished. But then to go back to my country and be 'made' white - it was very, very hard emotionally. Going back taught me that I won't be returning again. I cannot do what I want to in such a situation of negativity. You can't achieve artistically in a society that has so much paranoia".[473]

While this all rings true, it seems that there was also another side to the story of why Jephtas left Pretoria. Emma Renzi later recalled: "He was there [at PACT], and then there were problems ... with the drug; he picked that up in [whispers] New York; and eventually he just disappeared one night. He got himself into trouble or something. Back he went to New York".[474] The one story need not negate the possible truth of the other. But by accepting the job in Pretoria and living in a "white" hotel, Jephtas had already *de facto* accepted the status of an "honorary white" (an official category that was indeed utilised by the apartheid authorities when they wished to circumvent their own legislation) – in fact, his claim that negotiations for this were "under way" was probably a white lie, as they had presumably been part of his initial appointment process. By accusing the authorities of assuming that he "wanted to be white", Jephtas was simply shifting blame. His actions had already all but confirmed that it was what he wanted. Pretoria and its surrounding region had been under a State of Emergency since 20 July 1985, the rand had plummeted, the black townships were in turmoil, and racial violence was the norm across the country. By accepting a post with PACT in 1986, Jephtas had effectively declared allegiance to the white authorities, which in turn was bound to set him apart from the whole coloured community. To judge from his correspondence with Ronald Theys, however, the star singers at PACT still treated him in private as a "non-white". The strain on him must have been immense. Who could blame him for seeking refuge in substance abuse, or for simply packing his bags and leaving? It is notable that it is only after his 1986 departure from South Africa that he began signing his letters to Abrahamse proudly as "Boesman", an otherwise derogatory term for coloured people, and that he began insisting, in capital letters, that "BEING COLOURED" was better than "WHITE".[475]

The actual extent of Jephtas's drug problem remains unclear. It has been confirmed independently by both Emma Renzi and Roland Jung; the latter's recollection of Jephtas complaining about the cost of drugs suggests that he was using hard substances. However, Barbara Mahajan and Leavata Johnson, two American friends who remained close to him to the end, do not recall anything on his part except social drinking and a minor marijuana habit.[476] As so often with Jephtas, one story need not cancel out another, especially since it seems

---

473   Melich (1986).
474   Renzi (2009).
475   See his letters of 26 May 1987 and 8 February 1988, also the section "Editorial approach and terminology" above.
476   Interviews with Barbara Mahajan and Leavata Johnson, 25 October 2022.

that these reports date from different times during the 1980s; either way, we shall never know the full truth of it.

Jephtas travelled to Salt Lake City almost immediately after his return to the USA in August 1986. Besides vocal coaching there, he also assumed the duties of chorus master – perhaps ironically, one of the works for which he had to prepare the chorus and coach the singers in this season was *La traviata*, almost exactly a year after having done the same in Pretoria. It was also at about this time that he was photographed with Luciano Pavarotti (see Figure 5.7). In July 1987, the Utah Opera made him its very first "music director" for the next season, a title that seems to have been synonymous with the position of an assistant conductor.[477] His last letter from Utah to Abrahamse was sent in April 1988, though he is mentioned in the press there as having been involved in productions of *Gianni Schicchi* and *Pagliacci* in May 1988[478] and an operetta *Into the woods with Little Red Riding Hood* in August 1988;[479] he also accompanied the soprano Debbie Mitchell in a recital in September 1988.[480] We have no further record of him working in Utah, and there is also a gap in his correspondence with Abrahamse from Easter 1988 to August 1990.

In December 1986, the journalist Mark Paulos from *The Event* newspaper in Salt Lake City asked Jephtas why someone who had coached operatic stars such as Pavarotti and Scotto, and had worked in opera houses like Zurich, would choose to work with Utah Opera, whose chorus comprised amateur singers. Jephtas answered that he was in Salt Lake City because of the general director, Glade Peterson, and because Utah Opera provided him with the "chance to be innovative".[481]

Jephtas's presence at Utah Opera is notable for what it tells us about his career. He had worked at the Zurich Opera, then moved to New York City Opera, only to leave almost immediately for the Chicago Lyric, one of the major houses in the USA. This clearly upward trajectory was followed by a period of freelance work back in New York. Utah Opera, by contrast, had only been founded in 1978 and was on an even more modest scale than PACT in Pretoria, which at least had a professional chorus. Was Jephtas simply tired of the freelancing lifestyle in New York and wanted to be employed on a more permanent basis? Did he hanker again for the security and stability that he had enjoyed back in Zurich? Or did he hope to wean himself off drugs by leaving New York and moving to Salt Lake City, where even alcohol was strictly regulated? Either way, it seems that Jephtas moved back to New York in late 1988.

Emma Renzi later recalled how Jephtas had established himself as a vocal coach on the New York scene:

> Gordon was extremely gifted, absolutely top-class. [He was] like a sponge, it just went in, he had this absolute instinct for it. [He was] a good pianist. But he was [also] a good coach. And that is a very different thing from being a good pianist, or even a good accompanist. You have to know the languages, the style and be able to give everybody their cues. It is a completely different cup of tea to just playing the piano very well. Then he moved from Europe to New York. Lots of singers, well-known ones like Marilyn Horne, did go and coach with him. You know, if you [had] a role you haven't sung for a year or so, and you want to sing it in, you want a pianist who knows it. So, you go to the one who is recommended, and he was one of the best ones in New York. He was known for that.[482]

---

477   Anon. (1987).
478   Mathews (1988).
479   Anon. (1988a).
480   Anon. (1988b).
481   Paulos (1986).
482   Renzi (2009).

Both Barbara Mahajan and Leavata Johnson have similar recollections of Jephtas's gifts as a vocal coach: "he was outstanding ... he knew all of the operas; he knew the dialogue, so he was always able to sing the other parts for us ... and also his Italian was fluent; so he was really good at coaching the language as well".[483]

Jephtas's move from Europe to North America had a major impact on his career, his relationships, his personality, his health, and even his identity. The letters that he sent Abrahamse also underwent a major change. Instead of his long "epistles" from Europe, as he had called them,[484] his letters became much shorter and much less frequent. His pre-American letters are full of picturesque descriptions and dramatic tales, enthusiasm, zeal and passion. They range from descriptions of operas he has seen to vocal tips for Abrahamse, Eoan Group politics, his artistic ideals and aspirations, failures and successes. His self-doubts as a musician are expressed alongside behind-the-scenes gossip about operatic stars. But the main topics in his American letters are his financial distress, South African politics, reminiscences of better times together, and an insistence on his own professional stature. The most striking feature, however, is Jephtas's tone: his style largely lost its sophistication and instead became angry, frustrated, brash, even uncouth. He had always used pet names for Abrahamse, but these were now expanded by the use of "bitch".[485] It is hardly surprising that she seems to have been enraged by something that Jephtas either did or wrote in early 1988.[486] By this stage of their correspondence, it is clear that what had once been a deep friendship had dwindled away. The letters then cease until August 1990, when Jephtas was planning another return to South Africa in search of employment. He wrote again to Abrahamse, recalling their glory days, anticipating further joint performances in future – and asking for assistance with his return. Jephtas arrived in South Africa on 9 November 1990.[487] He kept "a low profile, in order to observe the musical scene in South Africa",[488] as a local journalist later wrote, and on 15 January 1991 he started a 3-month contract with the Eoan Group as a part-time research-and-development consultant, working just 3 hours per week.[489] His job was to write reports and to meet twice a week with Eoan's directors to present his research about the organisational structures that would be needed to launch a performing arts school (an initiative that never got beyond the drawing board in his lifetime).[490] He also did some vocal coaching for the Cape Performing Arts Board (CAPAB)[491] and gave one last concert with his friends from the Eoan Group in Cape Town on 10 March 1991.[492] Jephtas left South Africa on 20 April 1991, arriving back in New York City the following day.[493] As in 1979 and 1986, this final visit in 1990/1991 was also brief and unsuccessful – not least because he was sick and emaciated, and because everyone actually knew the truth that no one would admit, and that Jephtas had somehow imagined he might hide from the people back home: he was gay, and he was dying of Aids.

---

483 Interview with Barbara Mahajan, 25 October 2022.
484 See e.g. his letter of 16 September 1972 from Zurich.
485 See his letter of 12 November 1987 from Salt Lake City.
486 See his letter to her of 8 February 1988.
487 Gordon Jephtas's passport, p. 9. Eoan Group Archive.
488 Faiza Steyn: "Maestro" (newspaper article). Eoan Group Archive: 55:451.
489 Eoan Group Archive, 55:451. "Contract for the Employment of Mr. Gordon Jephtas Research and Development Consultant, 15 January 1991".
490 *Ibid.*
491 Roos (2018): 178.
492 Anon. (1992a).
493 Gordon Jephtas's passport, p. 10. Eoan Group Archive.

80

Lyric Opera, 20 N. Wacker Drive, Chicago, Illinois 60606, U.S.A.

Chicago, 24 October [1977]

My dear May,

Maria Callas is dead[494] – that was just about the saddest thing of the year. A great era of Italian opera singing has come to an end – at least we will always have her recordings. Some reports have indicated suicide because it is true that she did not really overcome any of the grief she suffered when Onassis died, so such a supposition is not entirely unfounded. But whatever, she is no more.

Thank you for [your] letter and all the newspaper cuttings – I was particularly vexed by the episode with the Eoan Group and the black singers.[495] Well, well, best to forget about them.

Let me get to your letter first; I have not read much about Callas because deep down I was really upset and reading obituaries would have made things only worse and here I was working right in the very theatre where she had made her American debut.[496] Anyway, I will send what I have. There was much coverage and the day she died they interrupted many T.V. programmes and did special coverage on her. [...]

What has been happening with me? Well, to tell you the truth, a whole lot of shit. 1977 up to now has been a decidedly bad year, led off by the Eoan Group finding some dumb reason for not wanting to engage me – they wrote and said that their committee had unanimously agreed [that] they could not – which I understood to mean would not employ me. Then I tried dealing with the CAPAB[497] lot and [Gregorio] Fiasconaro was the only one who has had anything nearly positive to say, but for the rest, either no response or negative answers. Well, all this was beginning to throw and rupture my self-confidence and I went and cancelled the South American contract and [the] Zurich contract. Then La Scala calls me for an interview [regarding] the next season and I go down to Milano only to find that my bad luck was more persistent than ever. Maestro [Edoardo] Müller,[498] [Claudio] Abbado's[499] assistant who was to see me and possibly engage me, went and had a motor accident the day before, was in hospital and so the whole appointment went for looping. Then I got engaged by the New York City Opera, finally; but on my arrival in New York my legal status had not been cleared and with the unions so powerful here and everything, I cannot tell you how very tired I am of all this hassle I have [had] to go through by not having the birth right to work in any country and the only place I have that right, denies me any possibility – but I will continue to fight in the hope that if I make enough of a pest of myself they will engage me just to get rid of me. Anyway, so

---

494 Callas died in Paris on 16 September 1977.

495 No information is available about this. In principle, Eoan allowed black South African singers to join; however, apartheid restrictions officially prohibited social mixing between people classified as "coloured" and "black", and racial tensions between these two groupings were also not unknown in the Eoan Group. Roos (2018): 43.

496 Callas's American debut had taken place in 1954 at the Chicago Lyric Opera when she sang the title role in Bellini's *Norma*.

497 The Cape Performing Arts Board was for whites only until the mid-1980s, so there was little chance that they would have engaged Jephtas.

498 Edoardo Müller (1938-2016), Italian conductor.

499 Claudio Abbado (1933-2014), Italian conductor.

I am just so pissed off with this whole situation I find myself in. Finally, I worked with the City Opera for two whole days, got a call from Chicago, signed immediately and here I am. All in all things have worked out for the best because I am much more used to the international level and the N.Y.C Opera has only local singers and the level of singing is not necessarily too good – I was privately appalled that the only decent singer over there is Beverly Sills – and I am not referring to voice – they all have that, but the art of singing is something else, right? [Here in Chicago] we have done *L'Elisir* with the famous [Luciano] Pavarotti,[500] next I worked on [Gluck's] *Orfeo* which opens tomorrow night and this evening is my first rehearsal of *Manon* with la [Maria] Chiara, and then *Barbiere* with [Tito] Gobbi directing and the new mezzo everybody is raving about, [Frederica] von Stade,[501] and [the tenor] Luigi Alva.[502]

About our recital – I am still determined to pull that thing off and in the very near future – first I have decided that it would be ridiculous for me to finance this thing – so I need your thoughts, feelings and ideas in a hurry. What do you think the possibilities [are] of finding a sponsor, and who would it be? Then, what about the Baxter Theatre[503] – would they sponsor? You could try talking to Roland Pead,[504] show him our previous programme and reviews and see who he can direct you to in the Baxter management and then I would be quite willing to open up a correspondence. What do you think?

Let me have your feelings – I am thinking tentatively of the first half of '78 – say roundabout May.

Thanks for writing and I will let you have some cuttings.

Keep well and much love to the family,

Yours,

Gordon.

c/o Lyric Opera
20 North Wacker Drive
Chicago
Ill. 60606
U.S.A. (until December 17)

 81

San Francisco Opera, War Memorial Opera House, San Francisco, California 94102, [U.S.A.]
[Letter written on both sides of an addendum to a rehearsal schedule and other scrap paper.]

[22 October 1981]

May – Oct 22 – just got your little letter today of Oct 11 – does it take that long? Am most thrilled about [Eoan's] 50th Anniversary [celebrations] – waiting to hear [Cecil] Tobin's suggestions first – hope we can figure something out. Of course, Joseph [Gabriels], me and whoever was there and is now still capable should appear on stage – get to work sweetheart.

---

500 Luciano Pavarotti (1935–2007), Italian tenor.
501 Frederica von Stade (*1945), American mezzo-soprano.
502 Luigi Alva (*1927), Peruvian tenor.
503 The Baxter Theatre is a theatre on the campus of the University of Cape Town.
504 Roland Pead (died 2009) was the front-of-house manager of the Baxter Theatre.

Figure 5.3 Gordon Jephtas and Montserrat Caballé in San Francisco in 1981.
Source: May Abrahamse Private Collection.

I don't have time to write now – your Montsy (Caballé, as she's called by her intimates) picture is still here – I'm still trying to figure out how to pack the plastic frame so that the SA custom guys don't fuck it up with their enormous paws – pazienza, we say in Italian. Meanwhile, I'm enjoying it too. I sure am real proud of myself. Like, I mean May – from Vasco[505] and the Eoan Group to San Francisco and Caballé, [Marilyn] Horne,[506] [Richard] Bonynge, [Joan] Sutherland, [Kurt] Adler,[507] [Pier Luigi] Pizzi[508] – and in a theatre where my colleagues this season – that is, the ones that are also working in this same season now – [are] Anja Silja[509] (wonderful German Callas type – good, in fact, superb for German and not Italian opera), [Teresa] Berganza,[510] [Plácido] Domingo, [Jean-Pierre] Ponnelle[511] (crazy, but very, very talented French designer and stage director – at present the highest paid in the business – $60.000 for his sets alone) [and] Margaret Price,[512] (an English – in fact, Welsh woman – whose career very, very often passed together [with mine] since my England days – she started out like a chirpy Mozart soprano like [Désirée] Talbot[513] – I sure do hate that bitch – and I am not the type for hating – you know that! – but she sure got my evil guts going – I don't want to physically harm her – God forbid – she'll have me in some S.A. jail for life – and that I can do without. However, I will not let a person like that or any other person get to mess with my talent – I will – believe me, I will trample. Like Callas used to say – "of course, I had to

505 Vasco, a suburb to the north of Cape Town, is where Jephtas grew up as a child. Jephtas and his family were forcibly removed by the Group Areas Act of 1950 when their neighbourhood was declared a white area.
506 Marilyn Horne (*1934), American mezzo-soprano.
507 Kurt Adler (1905–1988), Austrian-American conductor.
508 Pier Luigi Pizzi (*1930), Italian opera director and set-and-costume designer.
509 Anja Silja (*1940), German soprano.
510 Teresa Berganza (1933–2022), Spanish soprano.
511 Jean-Pierre Ponnelle (1932–1988), French opera director and set-and-costume designer.
512 Margaret Price (1941–2011), Welsh soprano.
513 Désirée Talbot (1926–2020), South African soprano and one of the founding members of the UCT Opera Company.

trample. So what did you want me to do? DROP DEAD?" And sweetheart, I'm not dropping dead for NOBODY. They [in Cape Town] are all such smart arses – who cares? – Let's get back to Margaret Price – then she became a famous Mozart singer – now she has progressed and developed into a magnificent late-Verdi singer – I heard her sing the "Salce, salce" [from Verdi's *Otello*] in Chicago – and in "Salce, salce" Tebaldi is my absolute idol – Callas thought so too – and after I heard this Price I said, shit, the bitch's good – we were supposed to have worked together in *Boccanegra* in Chicago one time – and then she & Carol Fox[514] had a fight on day one of rehearsals and Price walked out, never to be seen again in Chicago. Who else is working here – Nilsson (Birgit) has the reputation of having the loudest, most metallic voice in the world. I heard her in *Turandot* at La Scala[515] one time, and May, that sound was just "UNBELIEVABLE". I thought at [the] time, "Joyce Barker,[516] eat your heart out" – the only other *Turandot* I had seen till then was that rehearsal [you and I] had to practically lick [Gregorio] Fiasconaro's arse to get into[517] – remember? – I liked [Désirée] Talbot's Liù in spite of the English Italian – the black Leontyne Price is coming for *Trovatore*. Jimmy Levine, the music director of the Met, introduced her to me a few years ago in Chicago after a concert performance of *Forza* – I doubt if she will ever remember [me] – these people are besieged – and I mean besieged – every day of their lives – that, shit, how can you remember who's who – and STILL go out there and perform a whole opera – but I will hustle and make my case known to her – because NOTHING would give me greater pleasure than to walk out on to the NICO MALAN OPERA HOUSE with Leontyne Price in RECITAL.[518] Now sweetheart, you know, I am, AM, such a big schemer. I pay a lot of dues and suffer a lot – JUST LIKE YOU! – RIGHT? – but – so what?

Pavarotti is singing his first *Aida* here – so he'll be nervous and tense and up to shit as hell – We got on so very well in *Ballo* in Chicago last year – but since Eoan & Joseph Gabriels – and then Gianni Raimondi, [Giacomo] Aragall, [Giuseppe] Giacomini, [Ion] Buzea,[519] [Carlo] Cossutta[520] – so many – I have over the years [learnt] how to handle the big tenors – same with sopranos – starting with Abrahamse. Right.

I wasn't planning to write a whole long epistle!

Ciao!

– P.S. – One thing is clear to me, is that I will take that Abrahamse voice on a long brilliant trip – we are both not young anymore – and heaven knows what on earth we will be singing and playing[521] – but somehow, we *have* to. Don't you think so? – and with all the UPS & the DOWNS. – Just like [Richard] Bonynge did with the Sutherland voice – he adores that voice beyond comprehension – I feel much the same about the Abrahamse voice. You're probably the same age too. How old are you?[522]

Ciao – had performance [number] 5 of [Lehár's] *Merry Widow* tonight. The Sutherland is a grand PHENOMENON – Sometimes, most times, I feel like I'm just dreaming. Then on the other

---

514 Carol Fox (1926–1981), co-founder and general manager of the Chicago Lyric Opera.
515 See letter of 5 February 1967.
516 Joyce Barker (1931–1992), South African soprano.
517 During apartheid, coloureds were not allowed in classified "white" venues and had to obtain permission to be allowed to attend performances by white singers. Jephtas might be referring to a dress rehearsal of *Turandot* by the UCT Opera School, directed by Gregorio Fiasconaro, for which Fiasconaro had to grant them permission to attend.
518 Leontyne Price and Jephtas never performed together in South Africa.
519 Ion Buzea (*1934), Romanian tenor.
520 Carlo Cossutta (1932–2000), Italian tenor.
521 Their 1979 recital in the Nico Malan Theatre was the last they ever gave.
522 Abrahamse was 51 at this time.

hand I feel, and am very confident – just as they are – and very much their equal – they sense that too. The only singer I ever had an open fight with was Lionel Fourie.[523]

Ciao my great artist friend.

Gordon.

P.S. [...] The reason I wrote at all was because of this pink rehearsal addendum.[524] [Neil] Shicoff[525] is the leading U.S. tenor of the moment – I admire his work – we worked together in Chicago – *Bohème* – we got on real well – when he got here he threw such a bitch with management to have a daily 2-hour private coaching [session] with me – because "he is the best there is" said Shicoff – and this theatre engaged me as prompter & not coach – of course, I threw a bitch too – I mean, they have all these glorified coaches here too – but we reached an agreeable compromise and Shicoff gets a daily 2-hour coaching with me until orchestra rehearsal. A great triumph for me – just as Nico Malan was a great triumph for you – not mentioning [our] Durban [recital in] 1971.

Ciao

Gordon. [...]

[...] P.S. You always wanted me to bring Opera to SA – Eoan is not the way now[526] – I wish it were – but life ain't about having things the way we want – but I will do something for opera & music – I SWEAR.

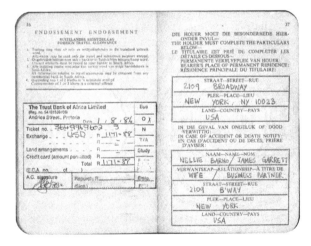

Figure 5.4 Jephtas's passport listing Nellie Barno as his wife.
Source: Eoan Group Archive.

Figure 5.5 Jephtas's green card.
Source: Eoan Group Archive.

---

523 Lionel Fourie (1926-1963), Eoan baritone.
524 The addendum is a rehearsal schedule on which Jephtas's name appears next to Shicoff's name.
525 Neil Shicoff (*1949), American tenor.
526 Eoan's opera productions came to a complete halt in 1975. Roos (2018): 162-166.

82

[New] York, [USA] [Address on envelope illegible, postal stamp "New York"]

Sunday, 11 July [1982]

My dear May,

How are you, sugar? I have been getting your letters – that is always such a pleasure.

For me, life has mostly been nothing but a pain in the arse. I have been mostly down in the dumps since I had no choice but to turn down San Francisco because it doesn't work out financially. Living in N.Y. I take care of the studio rent and expenses and the rent bill alone is $700 per month. This U.S. is a money-conscious and money guzzling country. Nothing else really matters – [not even] social standing, etc. Here you can do whatever you want provided you have the green pieces of paper or plastic credit cards in your pocket. To have the latter does not mean that you need to make lots of money – I now discover that the big credit thing is to be employed steadily by the same employer and not to change address. Familiar as you are with my life-style as a freelance musician, you see, I don't fit into that rhythm and so don't hold the major and important credit cards.

Freelancing as an accompanist (at auditions of which there are several during the winter months) or coaching from my studio at $35.00 to $25.00 per hour sounds great but it isn't. I learn that it would be great only if I had the [assurance] of 8 lessons per day, 6 days a week. But it's not like that – my clientele is as transient as I. Katia Ricciarelli[527] came and studied *Falstaff*, but that lasted only while she was singing here. Grace Bumbry employed me as prompter over at [the] City Opera for her *Medeas*. That was nice too – I made my rent in 3 weeks.

The services offered by U.S. living – the phone, the conveniences all carry a price and so often "you pay for everything" flashes through my mind. My woman[528] is American, we get along well when we are together but the bitch, like the Americans, bears no compassion and I can hardly run to her when the belts need tightening.

I don't do badly when I look around at others, but I do get thoroughly pissed off when I think of all the way that I have come and now I am engaged in the chase for the dollar to pay the never ending string of bills.

Now the summer is here and the Met and City Opera are closed and so much business is out until those start in September.

I am presently negotiating with the Met for a job next season. [James] Levine the director is away till mid-August. He and I have been talking since 1978. At this time a job at the Met would at least present that little security. The Met job is the only all year round job in the country – the whole country – so you can imagine how many people are after it. I'm high up on the list[529] – PRAY FOR ME.

All this preamble has been to prepare [you for] what help I need from you in this moment. A month or so ago my brother [Geofferey Jefthas][530] calls me up to announce that he had a

---

527 Katia Ricciarelli (*1946), Italian soprano.
528 Nellie M. Barno (1923-2015), Jephtas's wife since 1980.
529 According to his American friends and colleagues, Jephtas was never actually employed at the Met.
530 According to Geofferey Jefthas (2021), the original spelling of their family's last name has an "f". He is unsure why Gordon replaced "fth" with "pht". See Jefthas (2021).

LUCIANO PAVAROTTI and
GORDON JEPHTAS
SALT LAKE CITY '86

Figure 5.6 The Ansonia Hotel on Broadway in New York, where Jephtas lived for a while in the 1980s. Wikimedia Commons.

Figure 5.7 Jephtas and Luciano Pavarotti. Source: Jephtas-Abrahamse Correspondence, Eoan Group Archive.

cheque for the R 3000 my mother left. We made an agreement that he would let me have 1000. My brother by nature is slow, plus the [South Africans] are slow, so after a month [there is] still nothing and to me his original phone call was a godsend for at least temporarily.

Anyway, I still have a few lessons a week; but unfortunately last week I came down with pneumonia. New York City has 15 million people pass through it every day and this increases virus rates, etc. and pneumonia is one of the fatal diseases. I have been confined to the studio to bed for 2 weeks – again Nellie [his wife] can't help much, she is with her sister whose husband has just come out of hospital after a brain tumor operation and they are sharing that great anxiety.

I called Geoff, my brother, the moment I had the awful pains in my chest (and here again, doctor's fees and medication hold their price tolls) thinking to go into hospital. That finally made Geoff move his arse. Now here's where I need your *HELP*. Geoff's bank is in Wynberg; he lives in Mitchell's Plain and works beyond Bellville South which already creates a hassle just going to the bank.[531] This week I talked with him and he has been able to send me 400 – I don't have it yet – but it will help with this month's rent. I need the other 600 for next month, etc. He says the

---

531 Transport was presumably the obstacle for Geofferey, as the distance between Wynberg and Bellville South (his place of work) is about 32 km. Abrahamse lived in Crawford, which lies 7 km from Wynberg. This was probably one of the reasons why Jephtas approached her in this matter.

banking laws in SA are that he can send only 400 as a gift – Can you figure out by going to the banks and talking to all those whites you know – like Shell, etc. I told Geoff that I would ask you to find a way to get the rest to me. His phone is: 32-2057. PLEASE HELP ME GET THE MONEY.

I don't have a phone number for you – plus I cannot call S.A. from the studio phone – that's why I sent you a telegram – did you get that.[532]
Thanks –
Gordon.

83

[An envelope, postmarked in Salt Lake City, Utah on 3 July 1987, contains three items: copies of two newspaper articles and a photograph of Jephtas next to Luciano Pavarotti, on the back of which Jephtas wrote a brief message to Abrahamse in Italian. Since this is his only letter to her in a language other than English, we here give the original and our English translation.]

26 May [19]87

Ciao May,
Grazie per la letterina tua – molto, molto gradita.
Canta, canta, canta – per te, per me e per tutto che abbiamo cantato nelle nostre vite – io, in questa parte del mondo – tu, li in nostro paese.
Complimenti – e più complimenti per quello che tu stai facendo.
Ti ammiro moltissimo.
Il tuo accompagnatore umile ed umilissimo.
Boesman

P.S. E, apri bene la bocca dentro quando canti. Saluti.

Ciao May,
Thank you for your – very, very esteemed – little letter.
Sing, sing, sing – for you, for me & for everything that we have sung in our lives – me in this part of the world – you there in our country.
Congratulations – and more compliments for what you are doing.
I admire you very much.
Your humble, very humble accompanist.
Boesman[533]

PS: And, open your oral cavity wide when you sing. Greetings.

---

532 On 8 July 1982, Jephtas had sent Abrahamse a telegram stating simply "PLEASE CALL EMERGENCY GORDON".
533 "Boesman" is a derogatory term for a coloured person (see, e.g., the corresponding article in the online Dictionary of South African English (https://dsae.co.za/entry/boesman/e01015, accessed 31 July 2020). Jephtas's use of the term in his correspondence with Abrahamse, however, seems to convey a mixture of irony and pride in his identity, just a year after having apparently been appointed an "honorary white" in South Africa (see the introduction to this section).

84

Utah Opera, 50 West Second South, Salt Lake City, Utah 84101, [USA]
[This letter is written on the back of a newspaper article about Jephtas - here spelt "Jepthas"
- as chorus master at the Utah Opera]

Thursday, 12 November [19]87, Salt Lake City

Ciao May,
Just this morning I mailed one of my "you-stupid-black-bitch" notes[534] to you. And this afternoon arrives your 2-page epistle. Thank you. This pen is shit. Let me change.

[Changes from a black pen to pencil.] I am overwhelmed and overawed with the picture. Shit, May, you look radiant, fabulous, poised, calm, sure of yourself and *very sure* of your skills & your profession. The smile is magnificent, professional and oh so theatrical. And bitch, you are photogenic. And the hands (those big, ugly hands stately reposed and making a photographic statement - you are brilliant - [and] *you give the impression that you love your art*. My respects & admiration to you!!!!!!!!). I cannot say the same about your colleagues - nice people they might be, for sure. I don't know them so I should not criticize - a favorite S.A. pastime. What I do know is, I was always able to recognize a true artist by looking at it before I listened, and in 30 years (after learning the skill with Manca) I still have to be proved wrong. And they, your colleagues, don't have the ingredients for artistic greatness & achievements. You, yes - you have it. That face & smile you now have - and then your expertise on stage - movement-wise & vocally & experience. And you are 57 - you look like 31 - and probably sound like 29.
Well, *43* years into the music and singing business, you must have learnt & *retained* something, [or] else *you* wouldn't be where you are. Congratulations!
And when is the tape with your current vocal efficiency arriving - and I just need to hear the color of your voice. Some of those *Boereplaases*[535] you & I performed in public were just such vocal magic (your input), musical excellence (my input) and theatrical importance (both our inputs). Wonderful moments in the past.
We can still achieve more together AND FINALLY MAKE SOME MONEY AS WELL. I will never give up even if it took us 8 years to get from Durban to Cape Town.[536] Send me your Cape Town address.
Luv 'ya,
Gordon.

P.S. I *am* interested to hear your comments & response to the material I send you. SILENCE will help me nothing!

P.S.2. DON'T THROW IN TOILET UNTIL YOU HAVE READ & ABSORBED THE OTHER SIDE OF THIS PAGE. GRAZIE!! I am very interested in that house you plan to build. Don't forget now!!!!!!!!

---

534 This letter from Jephtas is no longer extant.
535 Jephtas here refers to "O Boereplaas", a popular Afrikaans song composed by Johannes Joubert to words by C.F. Visser.
536 Jephtas refers to the eight-year gap between the two recitals they had presented, the first in Durban in August 1971 and the second in Cape Town in March 1979.

[Jephtas added these further messages to Abrahamse on the reverse of his letter, around the article about him. See Figure 5.8]

AND, can you believe that in '79 I thought you should retire from the stage. I WAS WRONG – PS. I do write wonderful letters. Right? I talked with Ruth on the phone in one of my too-frequently-recurring-drunken-stupors. She's had a brain haemorrhage operation. She sounded perfectly coherent to me. Check it out please sugar.
Boesman

That Cape Town reviewer, Antoinette Silvestri in '79 called you "BEWITCHED BUT NOT BEWILDERED". I agree.

P.S.21: Sydow called you "Miss Supreme" the other day – Just like Diana Ross & the Supremes of the '60's. Bitch – you have it all. How about settling it for *money*!!!?????

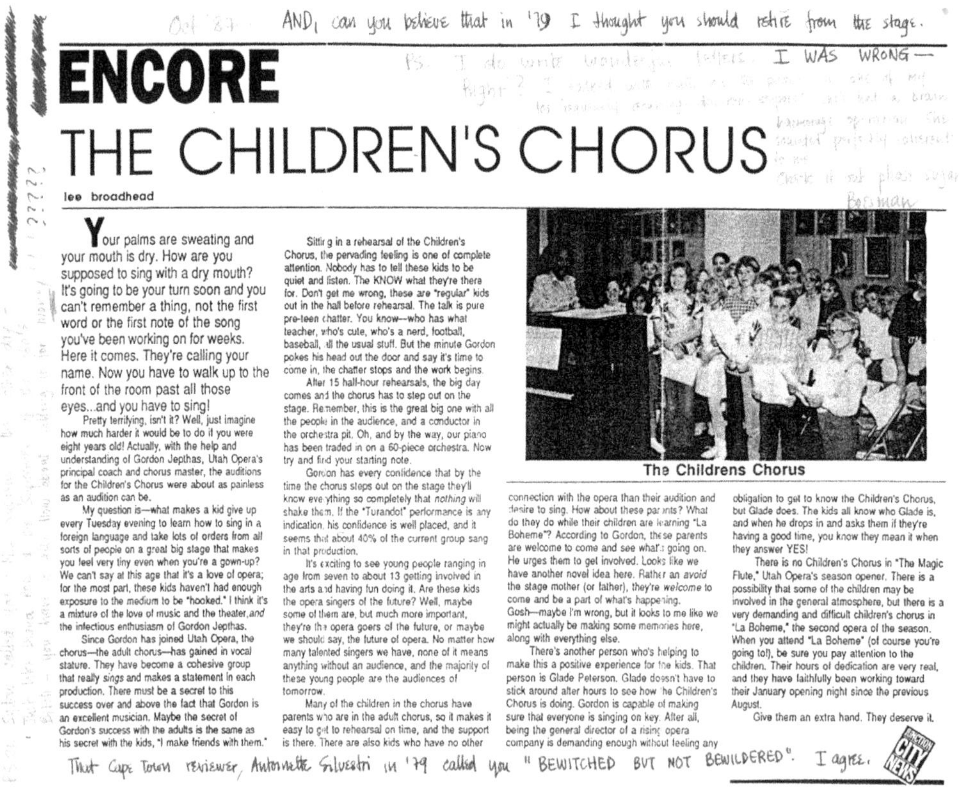

Oct '87 AND, can you believe that in '79 I thought you should retire from the stage. I WAS WRONG —

ENCORE

THE CHILDREN'S CHORUS

lee broadhead

Your palms are sweating and your mouth is dry. How are you supposed to sing with a dry mouth? It's going to be your turn soon and you can't remember a thing, not the first word or the first note of the song you've been working on for weeks. Here it comes. They're calling your name. Now you have to walk up to the front of the room past all those eyes...and you have to sing!

Pretty terrifying, isn't it? Well, just imagine how much harder it would be to do if you were eight years old! Actually, with the help and understanding of Gordon Jepthas, Utah Opera's principal coach and chorus master, the auditions for the Children's Chorus were about as painless as an audition can be.

My question is—what makes a kid give up every Tuesday evening to learn how to sing in a foreign language and take lots of orders from all sorts of people on a great big stage that makes you feel very tiny even when you're a gown-up? We can't say at this age that it's a love of opera; for the most part, these kids haven't had enough exposure to the medium to be "hooked." I think it's a mixture of the love of music and the theater, *and* the infectious enthusiasm of Gordon Jepthas.

Since Gordon has joined Utah Opera, the chorus—the adult chorus—has gained in vocal stature. They have become a cohesive group that really *sings* and makes a statement in each production. There must be a secret to this success over and above the fact that Gordon is an excellent musician. Maybe the secret of Gordon's success with the adults is the same as his secret with the kids, "I make friends with them."

Sitting in a rehearsal of the Children's Chorus, the pervading feeling is one of complete attention. Nobody has to tell these kids to be quiet and listen. The KNOW what they're there for. Don't get me wrong, these are "regular" kids out in the hall before rehearsal. The talk is pure pre-teen chatter. You know—who has what teacher, who's cute, who's a nerd, football, baseball, all the usual stuff. But the minute Gordon pokes his head out the door and say it's time to come in, the chatter stops and the work begins.

After 15 half-hour rehearsals, the big day comes and the chorus has to step out on the stage. Remember, this is the great big one with all the people in the audience, and a conductor in the orchestra pit. Oh, and by the way, our piano has been traded in on a 60-piece orchestra. Now try and find your starting note.

Gordon has every confidence that by the time the chorus steps out on the stage they'll know everything so completely that *nothing* will shake them. If the "Turandot" performance is any indication, his confidence is well placed, and it seems that about 40% of the current group sang in that production.

It's exciting to see young people ranging in age from seven to about 13 getting involved in the arts and having fun doing it. Are these kids the opera singers of the future? Well, maybe some of them are, but much more important, they're the opera goers of the future, or maybe we should say, the future of opera. No matter how many talented singers we have, none of it means anything without an audience, and the majority of these young people are the audiences of tomorrow.

Many of the children in the chorus have parents who are in the adult chorus, so it makes it easy to get to rehearsal on time, and the support is there. There are also kids who have no other connection with the opera than their audition and desire to sing. How about these parents? What do they do while their children are learning "La Boheme"? According to Gordon, these parents are welcome to come and see what's going on. He urges them to get involved. Looks like we have another novel idea here. Rather an *avoid* the stage mother (or father), they're *welcome* to come and be a part of what's happening. Gosh—maybe I'm wrong, but it looks to me like we might actually be making some memories here, along with everything else.

There's another person who's helping to make this a positive experience for the kids. That person is Glade Peterson. Glade doesn't have to stick around after hours to see how the Children's Chorus is doing. Gordon is capable of making sure that everyone is singing on key. After all, being the general director of a rising opera company is demanding enough without feeling any obligation to get to know the Children's Chorus, but Glade does. The kids all know who Glade is, and when he drops in and asks them if they're having a good time, you know they mean it when they answer YES!

There is no Children's Chorus in "The Magic Flute," Utah Opera's season opener. There is a possibility that some of the children may be involved in the general atmosphere, but there is a very demanding and difficult children's chorus in "La Boheme," the second opera of the season. When you attend "La Boheme" (of course you're going to!), be sure you pay attention to the children. Their hours of dedication are very real, and they have faithfully been working toward their January opening night since the previous August.

Give them an extra hand. They deserve it.

The Childrens Chorus

That Cape Town reviewer, Antoinette Silvestri in '79 called you "BEWITCHED BUT NOT BEWILDERED". I agree.

JUNCTION CITY NEWS

Figure 5.8 The reverse of Jephtas's letter of 12 November 1987.
Source: Jephtas-Abrahamse Correspondence, Eoan Group Archive. The date "Oct '87" presumably refers to the date of the article, as the letter on the reverse is dated 12 November.

85

Utah Opera Company, [50 West Second South], [Salt Lake City], [Utah 84101], [USA]
[This letter, 8 February 1988, and the subsequent letter, 3 April 1988, were found in the same enveloped, postmarked 10 August 1988. Both are written on the back of a copy of a newspaper article and are accompanied by a professional résumé of Jephtas.]

Monday, 8 February [19]88[537]
En route New York   Salt Lake City.

Ciao May sugarissima,

Now that you are so irretrievably mad at me, I cannot permit myself to give up on you. And, anyway, you *WILL* get over it. Believe me! I have more experience in [the] world, in international and in the global matters that affect LIFE.

Like you: People say "WHITE IS BETTER". And my firm conviction is "BEING COLOURED IS EVEN BETTER - if you know how to use it in your favour".

Sophie Tucker,[538] the colossal white red-hot mama entertainer used to say on her show, "I've been rich and I've been poor. And RICH is better."

And I have watched you (like a hawk) over the years get *kinda* mad at me - and now that I have finally got you "so" pissed off at me[539] I am as happy as a pig in shit. Now I will wait to see how you are going to handle the shit. That "goody-goody attitude" we South Africans cultivate and believe in, is *not* the REALITY of the world outside.

We confuse aggression with rudeness; insolence with good manners and shyness with exemplary behaviour!

We sure have our shirt back to front while we are trying to impress the western world that we are right. The western world simply laughs at us and further*more* only despise us as a nation, and takes our MONEY.

TURN OVER [the page] - IF YOU DARE.

Why does Marita Napier at the Met bill herself as the "German" soprano, and Elizabeth Connell[540] as the "English" soprano? They are both singing Lady Macbeth there now. It's impossible to escape one's origins.

2) Why is it that we cannot partake in the Olympics, why cannot South African Airways land anywhere in the United States. Where is the problem? You know better than I, but you and our other 49,999 million minds are scared to raise our voices. *And you* ARE A PROFESSIONAL SINGER.

---

537   It is possible that Abrahamse had put this letter in the envelope postmarked 10 August 1988.
538   Sophie Tucker (1887-1966), American singer and comedian known for her comical and risqué songs.
539   It seems that there had been a disagreement between Jephtas and Abrahamse, though the precise cause remains unclear.
540   Elizabeth Connell (1946-2012), South African mezzo-soprano.

3) Explain that to me. I will jump sky high should I finally get a reaction and a rebuttal from you. Yet I know that it will take you forever – just like it took you the best part of 25 years to discover that you can make money with your voice.

It's not you, it is *our CALVINIST mentality*.

Love you to pieces,

"JUST GUESS WHO".

86

Easter Sunday [3 April], [19]88, SLC [Salt Lake City].[541]

Ciao May,

I got myself 2 birthday cards on my 45th.

I think your card is real hot – thank you – real "bad" as Michael Jackson says.

The lion is such a graceful, lithe and strong creature. Well, he ain't the king of the jungle for nothing.

And so, your choice of card is just so appropriate. Grazie.

The other card came from Mardean [Peterson] (Glade [Peterson],[542] my boss's wife). We have known each other since Zurich. You, Mardean & Glade are the same generation. Glade was the leading Italian tenor in Zurich.

Ciao,

Gordon.

P.S. What do you know about Allan Boezak?[543] He's getting a lot of T.V. coverage here. 3 of us South Africans appear frequently on U.S. T.V. – Boezak, the pop singer [Jonathan] Butler[544] and me – I was on a 6.30 a.m. talk show this week. AND WE ARE ALL COLORED.

What does that say to you.

Boesman

---

541 It is possible that Abrahamse had put this letter in the envelope postmarked 10 August 1988.
542 Glade Peterson (1928-1990), American tenor. He and Jephtas had become acquainted when they both worked at the Zurich Opera House in the 1970s. Peterson founded the Utah Opera, where he engaged Jephtas as chorus master and vocal coach.
543 *Recte*: Allan Boesak (*1945), anti-apartheid activist.
544 Jonathan Butler (*1961), South African singer-songwriter and guitarist.

117, W. 79th Street
New York 10024
FAX: (212) - 724 · 9172

Friday, August 31, '90

Ciao May—

Remember me? I am touching base and re-introducing myself with the enclosed DEMO. And another cassette of a lady we both admired so, and learnt so much from. It is part 4 of a 4-tape series.

Gordon Jephtas

I have itchy feet again and more homesick than ever. So I am working on getting my arse back home. I am looking for a financial sponsor. Do you have any ideas or brainwaves?

One thing I am so thrilled about is that you are still singing. And, so happy that you did not follow my stupid and premature advice to you in '79. The only time to begin thinking about quitting would be when the audience no longer applauds you — and applause is something you always got and knew how to get. During our glorious years in the 60's (we were so young, so strong and so very enthusiastic !!) I used to be in absolute mouth-wide-open awe of that ability of yours — and, later I saw that only the BIG singers have that knack also.

Now I can hardly wait to walk out on stage with you, and sing our songs. ———

ii Short songs !!— nothing long and complicated ; and nothing breath, muscle and energy consuming.

Enjoy the tapes and if you reply, FAX me. Limit yourself to 1 page which does not have to be typed. White paper and black pen is good.
Fax takes only 30 seconds to transmit and that sure beats the 15 days in the regular mail.

Ciao sugar —

Your favorite piano-player.

P.S:
I asked Patrick to share my correspondence and tape to him — **PIANO-PLAYER**
to share it with you. _____ **MUSICIAN**
Did he ? _____ **EDUCATOR**
_____ **ENTERTAINER**
_____ **MAESTRO**

Gordon

>PS 2°: Share this stuff with your children + their husbands. Thanks

Figure 5.9 Letter dated 31 August 1990 with a drawing of Jephtas as a letterhead.
Source: Jephtas-Abrahamse Correspondence, Eoan Group Archive.

87

117, W.79th Street, New York, NY 11024, USA

[This letter was written on notepaper whose letterhead features Jephtas's face; the reverse of the sheet is a photocopy of a newspaper article. See Figure 5.9.]

Friday, 31 August [19]90[545]

Ciao May –

Remember me? I am touching base and re-introducing myself with the enclosed DEMO. And another cassette of a lady we both admired so,[546] and learnt so much from. It is part 4 of a 4-tape series.

I have itchy feet again and [am] more homesick than ever. So I am working on getting my arse back home. I am looking for a financial sponsor. Do you have any ideas or brainwaves?

One thing I am so thrilled about is that you are still singing. And, so happy that you did not follow my stupid and premature advice to you in '79. The only time to begin thinking about quitting would be when the audience no longer applauds you – and applause is something you always got and knew how to get. During our glorious years in the 60s (we were so young, so strong and so very enthusiastic!!) I used to be in absolute mouth-wide-open awe of that ability of yours – and, later I saw that *only* the BIG singers have that knack also.

Now I can *hardly wait* to walk out on stage with you, and sing our songs.

ii *Short* songs!! – nothing long and complicated; and nothing [that takes too much] breath, muscle and [is] energy consuming.

Enjoy the tapes and if you reply, FAX me. Limit yourself to 1 page which does not have to be typed. White paper and black pen is good.

Fax takes only 30 seconds to transmit and that sure beats the *15 days* in the regular mail.

Ciao sugar –

Your favourite piano-player.

Gordon

Thanks [...]

88

117, W[est]79th Street, New York, NY 11024, USA
Tuesday, 2 October [19]90

Ciao May –

I trust that you have now received my tapes to you of Sept. 13. Enjoy! Today I got a note from Patrick Cloete[547] to the effect that he left you to deal with some publicity work that he agreed to do for me in return for information for his needs.

---

545 This letter was accompanied by a two-sided page containing Jephtas's résumé and press reviews.
546 He is probably referring to Maria Callas.
547 It is unclear who this was, nor do we know more about his connection to Jephtas and Abrahamse.

I am *most uncomfortable* with such an arrangement. I *never* did ask Patrick to ask you. I did ask him to share my correspondence with you – but no more than that.

My first suggestion is that you put all publicity negotiations in the *DEEP FREEZE*, as we S. Africans put it – (Americans say, "move [it] to the back burner") – until such time as I can make a negotiation with you as regards the administrative costs and remuneration for your time. If I had wanted you to do this job I could have asked you myself in the 1st place and I did not need Patrick to do so – *and without my consent*. The whole thing, the way I see it, is *unfair* to you – I would never make such demands.

The whole thing came about when Patrick – a person whom I have met only once in my life, and in your house, and therefore I hardly consider to be someone I know, found me through Ronnie [Theys] and asked advice re coming to America. I, from my part did not want to volunteer *FREE* information, and I do not want to fall into another Sidwell Hartman[548] trap,[549] so I suggested that he do some publicity liaison in return. *I am always the nice guy and consequently always the FOOL!!* And my sole purpose was merely to see how serious & committed he would be.

And I never expected him to accomplish terribly much. And it now appears to me that he is *more air than substance!* – lots of talk and little achievement. But I never expected any much more – and the last thing I anticipated was that the man would roll the ball into your court.

I am so sorry and apologetic about that – *it was never my intention!!!*

So please sugarrissima, immediately put a *HOLD* on everything that concerns me until you & I make agreements.

Enjoy the day and the two more tapes I am enclosing now.

Again, my apologies,

Very sincerely,

Gordon.

P.S. What you can do for me is make a few phone calls for me and complete the added questionnaire re hotel information. I enclose $10.00 in cash so you can FAX the page to me. [This sentence was scratched out by Jephtas on 12 October, though the questionnaire was still mailed with the letter.] I do my final diploma EXAM in audio engineering and music technology within the next 2 weeks and then I need to get out. New York is going crazy and berserk with the crime and violence that *this society* is creating with the drugs, the guns and the GREED. How fast the world changes!! And I think I can handle home for a while – but it has to be Cape Town.

Thanx, sweetheart.

Yours truly –

Gordon

P.S.2. FORGET THIS FOR NOW. CANCELLED. [This sentence is scratched out.] Me, Oct 12 '90. See ya.

---

548 Sidwell Hartman (1957-2019), South African tenor and the first coloured South African to study at The Juilliard School.
549 The meaning here is unclear. They both took part in benefit concerts in South Africa in the 1980s to help finance Hartman's music studies, but something had gone awry between them, and they thereafter avoided each other.

P.S.3. Sunday, October 21 – changed my mind – please complete the enclosed questionnaire and FAX the information to me. Grazie. CANCELLED [This section is scratched out on 28 October.]

P.S.4. Sunday, October 28.
Changed my mind again. I think my brother will come thru w[ith the] information by telephone tomorrow. We'll see!!

Sun. Oct. 28
Shit, I sure know HOW to procrastinate – and I just could not bring my ass to stand on them long lines at the Post Office. SORRY. I AM WHAT I AM. BIG HUGS. TILL SOONISSIMO.

5.3 "I FEEL MYSELF SOUTH AFRICAN TO THE BONE". ILLNESS AND DEATH

On 4 July 1992, Gordon Jephtas passed away at the Goldwater Memorial Hospital in New York, one of the main hospitals in the city that catered for Aids victims. He was 49 years old. Two days later, the Cape Town newspaper *Die Burger* published an article that announced to the world the disease that had killed him: "Piano master from SA dies of Aids in America".[550] Its author, Aubrey Hardine, reported that he had traced Jephtas to his hospital several weeks before his death and had spoken with him on 15 May 1991 on account of rumours in South Africa that he had already died of Aids. Hardine had asked Jephtas bluntly whether or not he was suffering from Aids, upon which Jephtas answered in "slow Afrikaans" that "people [at home] should not kill me ahead of time; I will be back" and explained that he still wanted to go home to do *La traviata* one more time with his old friends at the Eoan Group.[551] Hardine's article then reported (incorrectly) that Jephtas had died on 5 July, that he had been at the Goldwater for six months, and that he had "specifically returned to America to die there". He went on to say that his "best friend" in the Eoan Group, the tenor Gerald Samaai, deeply regretted the loss of "this greatest of all piano masters".[552]

This article reflects the problematic nature of Jephtas's reception in his home country. Apart from its incorrect information – Jephtas had died on 4 July; "piano master" was an inadequate description of his profession; and Gerald Samaai was an acquaintance, hardly a "best friend"[553] – there is also a hint of *Schadenfreude* in the article. In Calvinist South Africa in 1992, announcing that Jephtas had died from Aids in the USA was tantamount to declaring him a moral degenerate. As discussed earlier in this book, Jephtas had scrupulously avoided coming out as gay among his South African friends and colleagues, ever maintaining a façade of heterosexuality, even though everyone knew the unspoken truth. Within two days of his death, however, *Die Burger* – a newspaper that for decades had been a mouthpiece of the white apartheid establishment – had essentially outed him to everyone. He may have escaped poverty and racial discrimination to work with the finest vocal artists of the age in one of the

---

550 Hardine (1992).
551 Original in Afrikaans: "In stadige Afrikaans het hy toe gesê: 'Mense moet my nie voor die tyd doodmaak nie. Ek kom terug...Ek wil nog vir oulaas *La traviata* met my ou maats in die Eoan-Groep opvoer.'". Hardine (1992).
552 *Ibid.*
553 The only other person from the Eoan Group who was close to Jephtas at this time and with whom he corresponded fairly regularly was the tenor Ronald Theys. Several letters to Theys, written in Afrikaaps in the course of 1990, have been made available to the Documentation Centre for Music (DOMUS), Stellenbosch University, by Jephtas's brother Geofferey.

world's great music centres, but in the end, the press of his own country managed to reduce him to just three things: coloured, gay, and dead.

In an interview with Geofferey Jefthas and his wife Maggie, they shared the following with us about Gordon's final visit to South Africa:

[Geofferey Jefthas]: When Gordon came here the last time [9 November 1990 – 20 April 1991], he said to me that he got this sickness. 'Cause then even my sister who stayed in Strandfontein didn't want him there. There was also black [circles] here under his eyes. But that time, we weren't aware [of] what Aids was…

[Maggie Jefthas]: …when people found out, there was still that stigma, severe stigma. That is one of the reasons he went back there [to America]. He would've stayed here [with us] … it's almost like they [the community] would stone him … he comes on and then people would run away. And that is why he left: for his own safety and for his own dignity.

[GJ]: The last time Gordon came back, I said [to him], "You don't go stay in the hotel, here is enough space". And then he tried to get a job here. He went to CAPAB and then they said to him, "You're over-qualified, we can't afford you". Gordon was staying here, then he said to me, "No, it's not that; they will never give this job to a coloured person". CAPAB was a white thing. He then tried to get a job as a music inspector [at coloured schools] but then he said, "No", because he won't pass the medical [test] because of his illness.

[MJ]: And that's why he went back.

[GJ]: Then he came home and said to me [that] he's going back to America, [and that] he bought himself a one-way ticket. He said to me, "I can handle myself better there than here because I can't get a job here, [and] I won't pass the medicals from the school's department; I'm rather going back" and so he bought himself a one-way ticket and he said, "bye-bye".[554]

Before Jephtas was hospitalised, his close friend Leavata Johnson took him under her care at her home in New York. When he died, she also handled Jephtas's affairs and arranged for his memorial service.[555] It has been thirty years since Jephtas's death, but even in her late 80s her memories of him remain vivid: "I could talk about him all day long – that's how wonderful he was to me". She also recalls the time when he became sick with Aids:

When he got ill, he lived with me. Gordon had Aids. Because back in that time, you know… everybody was just having a good time, I guess, and you met the wrong person or something, or they didn't tell you; I mean, Aids was such a big deal here in New York. I'm not gonna lie and say it didn't happen because that's what happened. I lost a lot of friends that died of Aids. … [After his death] his family wrote me a letter saying how they appreciated that I took care of Gordon and everything. I just adored Gordon, that's all.[556]

According to US statistics, roughly one fifth of those infected with HIV (comprising both men and women) contracted Aids through intravenous drug use, while three-fifths were

---

554 Interview with Geofferey & Maggie Jefthas, 21 June 2021.
555 Interview with Leavata Johnson, 25 October 2022.
556 Interview with Leavata Johnson, 25 October 2022.

men infected through homosexual contact.[557] Jephtas was gay and seems at some point to have engaged in substance abuse; these two risk factors were compounded by his place of abode, because in the late 1980s the infection rate in New York City was vastly higher than anywhere else in the USA, with Manhattan – where Jephtas lived – being the neighbourhood with the highest incidence rate of all.[558] The median rate for survival after diagnosis was some 17 months at the time.[559]

Years later, Abrahamse's daughters Trudy and Wendy recalled in interviews for the Eoan History Project that Jephtas had appeared emaciated during his last visit to Cape Town in 1990/1991 and that everybody in their community was aware that he was ill with Aids, but nobody had mentioned anything or had reached out to him. Instead, as Jephtas's sister-in-law recalled in the interview quoted above, he was ostracised by most people around him. This had been his third attempt at returning home to find employment and settle again in South Africa, after the debacle with Eoan in 1979 and his short-lived job in Pretoria in 1986. By late 1990, apartheid was not yet officially over, though its end was clearly imminent, with Nelson Mandela released from prison and the infamous race laws gradually being repealed. Jephtas's intense homesickness was probably fuelled by the prospect of a new South Africa, but will also surely have been a result of his terminal illness. Sophia Andrews, a mezzo-soprano in the Eoan Group, recalled Jephtas's last visit vividly, saying that "the last time he came down [to South Africa] was a sad time, because he was dying".[560]

Figure 5.10 A double page of the pamphlet for Gordon Jephtas's memorial service in 1992.
His surname is here given as "Jepthas".
Source: Eoan Group Archive.

557 U.S. Department of Health and Human Services (1991): 9.
558 U.S. Department of Health and Human Services (1991): 7; Jonsen and Stryker (1993): 247.
559 Jacobson et al. (1993).
560 Eoan History Project (2013): 106.

In contrast to *Die Burger*'s report of Jephtas's death, the American memorial service that was held on 14 November 1992 at the Church of the Intercession, an Episcopalian, neo-Gothic church on Broadway, offered a different picture of him. In the obituary written by Barbara Mahajan for the memorial pamphlet, "Maestro Gordon Jephtas" died "with great fanfare" on the evening of the US Independence Day, a night when "the city sky was ablaze with fireworks in coloured light ... – a befitting send-off for the man who had lived for the sound of music, a long way from the land of his birth".[561] The service included a musical tribute by friends and colleagues, including members of the Metropolitan Opera Chorus. The programme paid homage to Jephtas while the obituary mapped out Jephtas's humble beginnings and listed the many opera stars with whom he had worked. It also paid tribute to his commitment to his home country, saying that he had always wanted, in vain, to tour South Africa with his American colleagues and give master classes there. It went on to say how his friends knew that he often longed for home, and quoted Jephtas himself as having said: "I feel myself South African to the bone and God knows how much we as a nation are hated and despised. Yet, I am proud of what I have become and I'm very, very proud of what I am – a South African".[562]

It might seem strange that Jephtas remained so attached to his native land and so keen to be accepted there when the apartheid system had placed innumerable barriers before him. His sexuality remained against the law there; his hard-won international success was irrelevant to the white South African authorities; and his outspoken criticism had all but ruined his relations with his own, coloured community. But "home" for Jephtas seems to have been an emotional attachment all the more compelling for being so complex and unrequited – the more it rejected him, the more he wanted it.

Gordon Jephtas was cremated in New York and his ashes returned to South Africa. They are buried alongside his mother's ashes[563] at the Wynberg Methodist Church Cemetery in Cape Town. A few broken white tiles are today the only visible signifier of the grave site, which is otherwise overgrown with grass and weeds. There is no tombstone.

Figure 5.11 Gordon Jephtas's grave at the Methodist Church Cemetery in Wynberg.
Source: Hilde Roos.

---

561 Anon. (1992b).
562 *Ibid.*: 3.
563 Interview with Geofferey & Maggie Jefthas, 21 June 2021.

BIBLIOGRAPHY

Adhikari, M. 2005. *Not white enough, not black enough: Racial Identity in the South African Coloured Community*. Athens, Ohio: Ohio University Press.

Adhikari, M. 2009. "Predicaments of marginality: cultural creativity and political adaptation in southern Africa's coloured communities", in M. Adhikari (ed.). *Burdened by Race: Coloured Identities in southern Africa*. Cape Town: UCT Press, vii-xxxii.

Anon. (no date A). Interview with Joseph Gabriels, SABC Sound Archives, catalogue number TM 7115/88.

Anon. (no date B). *The Cape Tercentenary Foundation*. www.cape300foundation.org.za/archives-awards.htm, accessed 2 September 2022.

Anon. (no date C). *Eoan Group School of Performing Arts*, www.eoangroup.com/, accessed 26 October 2022.

Anon. 1964. "Showboat het waarlik iets vir almal", in *Die Burger*, 13 March.

Anon. 1970. "Is W. Va. related to cigarettes? South African Pianist Gives Impressions of Area, U.S.", in *The Intelligencer*, 17 August.

Anon. 1971. "Music Maestro Please", in *The Post*, 22 August. Eoan Group Archive.

Anon. 1987. "Utah Opera names music director", in *The Salt Lake Tribune*, 19 July.

Anon. 1988a. "Chamber music festival offers varied concerts", in *The Salt Lake Tribune*, 14 August.

Anon. 1988b. "Concerts by striking players begins this week's concerts", in *The Salt Lake Tribune*, 18 September.

Anon. 1992a: "Hulde aan 'n vriend", in *Die Burger*, 11 July.

Anon. 1992b. "Memorial Service Celebrating the Life of Gordon Jephtas", Eoan Group Archive.

Anon. 2013. "2013 kykNET Fiëstas honours best in Afrikaans theatre", www.bizcommunity.com/Gallery/196/483/2342.html, accessed 2 September 2022

Anon. 2022. "Italian diva and soprano Magda Olivero dies at 104', http://www.bbc.com/news/world-europe-29122477, accessed 18 October 2022.

Blanckenberg, E. 2009. *The Music Activities of the Cape Performing Arts Board (CAPAB)*. Unpublished master's thesis. Stellenbosch: Stellenbosch University [Online]. Available: http://hdl.handle.net/10019.1/2445, accessed 30 July 2020.

Brunner, Adolf, ed. Chris Walton. 1997. *Erinnerungen eines Schweizer Komponisten aus der Schule Philipp Jarnachs und Franz Schrekers*. Zurich: Hug.

Davids, Féroll-Jon. 2021. *Gordon Jephtas (1943-1992): A coloured life in opera*. Master thesis, Stellenbosch University.

Eoan History Project. 2013. *Eoan - Our Story*, eds. Wayne Muller & Hilde Roos. Johannesburg: Fourthwall Books.

Erasmus, Z. 2001. "Re-imagining coloured identities in post-apartheid South Africa", in Z. Erasmus (ed.). *Coloured by History, Shaped by Place: New Perspectives on Coloured Identities in Cape Town*. Cape Town: Kwela Books, 13-28.

Ericson, Raymond. 1971. "Joseph Gabriels of South Africa Makes Debut in Met 'Pagliacci'", in *The New York Times*, 7 February.

Fierz, Gerold. 1973. "'Ernani'. Premiere im Opernhaus Zürich", in *Neue Zürcher Zeitung*, 8 October, "Morgenausgabe" No. 465.

Friedling, L.J, and A. G. Morris. 2007. "Pulling teeth for Fashion: Dental modification in modern day Cape Town, South Africa", in *South African Dental Journal*, 62 (3): 106-113.

Graan, Mike van. 2015. "Open Stellenbosch: Beyond the rainbow, towards a change of climate", on www.litnet.co.za/open-stellenbosch-beyond-the-rainbow-towards-a-change-of-climate/, accessed 2 August 2022.

Hardine, Aubrey. 1992. "Klaviermeester van SA sterf aan vigs in Amerika", in *Die Burger*, 6 July.

Heyworth, Peter. 1967. "Covent Garden sees Modern 'Traviata'", in *The New York Times*, 20 April.

Higgins, J. 1973. "Appetizing return: Tebaldi/Corelli, Albert Hall", in *The Times*, 10 October.

Jacobson, L.P. et al. 1993. "Changes in survival after acquired immunodeficiency syndrome (AIDS): 1984-1991", in *American Journal of Epidemiology* 138 (11): 952-641 (December 1993).

Jonsen, A.R. and J. Stryker (eds.), for the National Research Council (US) Panel on Monitoring the Social Impact of the AIDS Epidemic. 1993. *The Social Impact Of AIDS In The United States*. Washington (DC): National Academies Press (US).

Kaplan, Robert M. 2004. "Treatment of homosexuality during apartheid", in *BMJ* 329 (18-25 December 2004): 1415-6.

Kieser, Barbara. (No date). "Die offene Drogenszene in Zurich", www.stadt-zuerich.ch/prd/de/index/stadtarchiv/bilder_u_texte/geschichte-vor-ort/Offene-Drogenszene.html, accessed August 2022.

Malan, J.P. 1984. "Manca, Joseph Salvatore", in *South African Music Encyclopedia*, Vol. III, 192-194.

Mathews, Anne. 1988. "Comedy, tragedy make for fine night at opera", in *The Salt Lake Tribune*, 14 May.

Melich, Nancy. 1986. "South African finds life away from home", in *The Salt Lake Tribune*, 5 October.

Moser, Eva. 2007. "'Nicht mitzuhassen, mitzulieben bin ich da'. Robert Oboussier, 1900-1957". Master thesis, University of Lucerne.

Paulos, Mark. 1986. "Out of...South Africa and Still Singing", in *The Event*, 3-16 December, 9.

Pistorius, Juliana M. & Hilde Roos. 2021. "Burgerskap onder konstruksie: Aida en Rigoletto by die Suid-Afrikaanse Republiekfeesvieringe, 1971", in *Litnet Akademies*, 18 (2): 102-131.

Renzi, Emma. 2009. Interview with Christine Lucia for the Eoan History Project, 30 August. Eoan Group Archive: uncatalogued.

Ringger, Rolf Urs. 1977. "Statik und Passionen", in *Neue Zürcher Zeitung* 43, Monday, 21 February.

Roos, Hilde. 2016. "Briewe aan 'n diva: die verswyging van gay-identiteit in Gordon Jephtas se briewe aan May Abrahamse", in *Litnet Akademies*, 13 (1): 31-55.

Roos, Hilde. 2018. *The La Traviata Affair: Opera in the Age of Apartheid*. Oakland, California: University of California Press.

Salie, A. 1979. "'Coloured' Shock in Secret Eoan Report". *Cape Herald*. Newspaper clipping with no date. Eoan Group Archive, 67:511.

Sidego, C. 1979. "Julle is Sommer Vrek Lui!", in *Rapport*, 11 November. Eoan Group Archive, 67:511.

Steyn, Faiza (no date). "Maestro", unidentified newspaper clipping. Eoan Group Archive, 55:451. We have been unable to identify either the newspaper or the date of this clipping; it is presumably from 1991 or 1992.

Talbot, Désirée. 1978. *For the Love of Singing, 50 Years of Opera at UCT*. Cape Town: Oxford University Press.

Tidboald, David. 2008. *People I made music with*. Cape Town: Umuzi.

U.S. Department of Health and Human Services, Centers for Disease Control. 1991. *HIV/AIDS Surveillance Report*, January.

Vosloo, Lisba. 2016. *May Abrahamse*. Documentary film, commissioned by kykNET.

Weich, Charlie (writing under the pseudonym "Emol"). 1956. "Kaapse Kleurlinge voer Italiaanse opera met groot welslae uit", in *Die Burger*, Monday, 12 March.

Winston, Mckinley. 1983. "Gordon Jephtas ... Maestro", unidentified newspaper clipping. Eoan Group Archive, 34:241.

Archives consulted

Eoan Group Archive, DOMUS, Stellenbosch University

PACT archive, University of South Africa Library, Pretoria

Stadtarchiv Zürich

N.B. The papers of Geofferey Jefthas have been digitised and in this form constitute part of the Eoan Group Archive.

INDEX

Ingram Content Group UK Ltd.
Milton Keynes UK
UKHW030641120423
420030UK00010B/1025